Toward the horizon

Toward the horizon

Lennart Edelberg and the Danish Hindukush research

Edited by Ulrik Høj Johnsen, Schuyler Jones,
Torkil Funder and Taj Khan Kalash

MOESGAARD MUSEUM

Contents

Introduction

By Ulrik Høj Johnsen

In March 1948, a group of men travelled slowly by car through the winding roads and narrow byways crossing the mountains of the Hindukush. Their destination for the day was the village of Gusalak, located in the deep valleys of the Afghan province of Nuristan. Two men in the group stood out from the others. Every step they took was a step into the unknown. These two men spent the coming months carrying out field research in the remote Afghan province of Nuristan, which borders on the then newly founded state of Pakistan. A long way from home, these two Danish scientists took part in the Third Danish Expedition to Central Asia under the leadership of Henning Haslund-Christensen. They were there to undertake initial field studies deep in the Hindukush mountains, where the notorious *Kafirs* ruled until the late 1890s, where they were converted into Islam by the Afghan ruler Abdur Rahman. One of the Danish men was Knud Paludan, a zoologist and medical doctor, then thirty-nine years of age; his partner was Lennart Edelberg, a thirty-two-year-old botanist.

That particular evening seems particularly important for Lennart. He was conscious of embarking on a great adventure. The car with the travelers and all their equipment was forced to halt in the late afternoon because an avalanche of large boulders had blocked the road. The boxes containing all the expedition equipment had to be carried by hand to Gusalak. Just as the problems seemed to increase, a group of Nuristani men approached and greeted the foreigners hospitably. They organized the necessary transport to the village. In his diary, the young botanist wrote the following:

> In a few minutes the sun had set, the stars sparkled over the valley, and the moon glowed brightly over the river and the terraced fields. I jumped up on a boulder by the road. From there I had a sweeping view of the valley. A feeling of being up to the task invaded me. I am not sure if I stretched my arms towards the moon and the stars, but inside me, a song of exhilaration broke out: an appreciation of the moonlight, the snow and of the cedars up there on the mountain ridge and of the commotion right below me – a hullabaloo for two white sahibs. Denmark – seemed so far, far away… [Translation by the author]

The first meeting with Nuristan, 1948. Photo: Lennart Edelberg.

To the young Lennart, Denmark seemed to fade further and further into the background, as he and Paludan moved deeper into the mountains. Lennart would be away from Denmark for two years, and it was obvious in the early spring of 1948 that Nuristan and the Nuristani people had made a tremendous impression on him. This meeting was to have a huge influence not only on the rest of Lennart's life; but indeed also on the lives of his wife, Margot, and their daughters. As he so vividly describes in his diary, this meeting demanded all his resources as a professional and as a human being. Nuristan became his second homeland.

Fragments of a life – a lively mosaic

Lennart Edelberg's life is too far-reaching to sum up in a single volume. His many interests, abilities, and activities were so diverse that it is a challenge to decide where and how to begin the story of Johan Lennart Fraas Edelberg. He was born in Copenhagen on May 19, 1915 and died in Ribe on November 11, 1981.

The more one tries to put him and his many accomplishments into a narrative framework, the more it feels as if, even from the afterlife, he is resisting against being subjected to any such explanatory devices. How, then, can we embark on a narrative intended to shed light on the man Lennart Edelberg? Lennart's close friend through many years, Schuyler Jones, offers an entry: In his chapter in this book, he describes Lennart as a *Renaissance man*. Throughout his life, he managed to combine wide-ranging interests and fields of activity through his curiosity, enthusiasm, open-mindedness and dedication. For a scholar formed in an academic world, where knowledge increasingly has been compartmentalized over the last decades, it is liberating for the author of this introduction to be introduced to Lennart's work and way of thinking. It is a way of thinking, where interests and perspectives that at first may seem divergent, indeed inspire each other; the efforts to preserve historical buildings in Ribe seem to have made him aware of the distinctive architecture and craftsmanship in Nuristan. Although the divisions between different academic disciplines were less pronounced in Lennart's lifetime, they were still there.

Lennart's writings about his ethnographic work remain free of the constraints of academic boundaries. Although he was not formally an ethnographer by education, he was one indeed in terms of experience in the field. His colossal importance for the Danish academic research tradition in Afghanistan and Nuristan in particular derives from that experience. His interests did not include theoretical figments of the imagination; rather, his work was always deeply rooted in the ethnographic material that he observed and collected. It was rooted in the people whom he met, in the architectural traditions he investigated, in the material culture he observed and collected, in transhumance, in the ecological adaptations observed, in systems devised to measure time – and, of course, in investigations of the fabled temple in Parun Valley.

This book seeks to offer insight into Lennart's ethnographic activities in Luristan, Iran (see Henrik Thrane's chapter), and especially in his work in the Afghan province of Nuristan. It is impossible to describe 'Lennart the ethnographer' without describing and understanding 'Lennart the man.' Many of the contributors to this book knew Lennart personally and worked with him in one way or another. Through accounts of their work with Lennart, one gets a clear sense of 'Lennart the man'; this perspective is crucial for an understanding of his interests, his work, and his accomplishments.

The early Danish research tradition in Asia

Leaving Carsten Niebuhr and the Danish Arabian Expedition (1761-67) aside, we note that the Danish lieutenant, Ole Olufsen's two expeditions to Central Asia in 1896-97 and 1898-99, marked the beginning of the Danish research tradition in Central Asia. In the monumental two-volume publication *Exploring Central Asia – Collecting Objects and Writing Cultures from the Steppes to the High Pamirs 1896-1899* (2002), Esther Fihl describes Olufsen's two Danish Pamir Expeditions to Central Asia as well as their clear scientific objectives.

Two decades later, in 1923, Dr. Carl Krebs led a group of five young Danes to establish a farm to test different crops and set up a fur trade station, Bulgun Tal, on the Zobel plains of Mongolia. Twenty-five-year-old Henning Haslund-Christensen (hereafter Haslund) was among them. The project did not last long, due to political turmoil at the time; nevertheless, Mongolia and the Mongolians never relinquished their hold on Haslund. He "learned the language of the Mongols, learned to sing their songs, and to listen to their stories," as Lennart writes of Haslund in *Den Store Danske*, a Danish encyclopedia.

Haslund left Bulgun Tal in 1925 and headed to China in search of a job opening. In 1928, the rest of the young Danes left Bulgun Tal and Mongolia as well – except for Krebs, who stayed there until 1936. Haslund, however, did find a job; he became a member of Svend Hedin's expedition from 1927-30 and then spent a few years in India, where his whereabouts and doings are relatively unknown.

In 1936-37 and 1938-39, we move onto clearer ground. Haslund organized and carried out two expeditions to Inner Mongolia, which are well documented. Those expeditions are known today as the First and Second Danish Expeditions to Central Asia. Christel Braae, a curator at the National Museum of Denmark, published in September 2017 the voluminous publication *Among Herders of Inner Mongolia – The Haslund-Christensen collection at the National Museum of Denmark*. Later, others followed.[1]

The 'Great' third expedition

Haslund no doubt wanted to return to Mongolia as soon as he could. Due to World War II, however, he was confined to Scandinavia. It was inconceivable to think about crossing borders in the name of research until after the world began to open up again after the dark years of war. On the horizon, people like Haslund and the men around him began to see the possibilities of exploring and researching "the wrinkled face of Asia," as Lennart would later poetically phrase it in the title of a book containing six radio speeches he had given (Edelberg 1961; Johnsen 2016, 8). The collection of speeches is a cornucopia of parallels between Asian and European culture and intellectual capacities.

While in Copenhagen during and right after WWII, Haslund wrote up material from his first two expeditions, but he also had time to plan his next expedition: the Third Danish Expedition to Central Asia. This would later become a national project in grand style. It would shed light on the blank spaces of the large-scale maps of Asia while placing Danish research and museums on the world map by means of a vast program of field projects and the collecting of objects for the National Museum of Denmark in Copenhagen. Haslund handpicked a large team of scientists for the third expedition. The expedition was organized so as to depart in several stages; the first consisted of the historian of religions, Halfdan Siiger (1911-1999), who also functioned as the expedition's secretary in the planning phase; the zoologist Knud Paludan, who was also a trained medical doctor, was attached in these capacities; and the young botanist, Lennart. Haslund and Lennart became acquainted by a coincidence; Lennart's cousin Erik was at a dinner with Haslund, when he was planning the expedition. As Haslund was searching for a botanist to join the team, Erik directed his attention to Lennart, and soon the expedition had a botanist. We know how this happened from a dedication that Lennart wrote in a book he gave to his cousin, where he thanks him for leading him on to the 'Afghan adventure' (See Torkil Funder's chapter).

The four expedition members left Copenhagen in October 1947 on M/S Malay as the vanguard to Central Asia. The expedition, which was based in Kabul, continued through 1950. After their base had been set up in Kabul, Siiger went to the Kalasha, a small ethnic non-Islamic group in the mountains bordering Afghanistan, and Lennart and Knud Paludan went to Nuristan, as described at the beginning of this introduction. They spent five months in Nuristan.

Later, more Danish scientists joined the expedition in Afghanistan, India, and Sikkim; the botanists Mogens Køie and his wife Aase Køie joined the Afghan mission with the cultural geographer Johannes Humlum and the zoologist Niels Haarløv in 1948. And in 1950, the conservator Hans Madsen, the paleontologist Erik Nielsen, K.M. Jensen, and the geologist Asger Bertelsen joined the expedition's mission in India and Sikkim together with the medical doctor Carl Krebs (who took up the leadership of the expedition in India and Kashmir) (Edelberg 1958, 273-274).

The interdisciplinary nature of the expedition was in many ways its hallmark, and this interdisciplinary character may well have been inspired by Haslund's association with the great Swedish explorer Sven Hedin. Haslund had worked for Hedin as caravan leader during three years in Mongolia with Hedin's Sino-Swedish Expedition in 1927-32. Hedin's expedition numbered hundreds of men and was known as "the wandering university" (Braae 2007, 77). Beyond that, the idea of a team with diverse expertise and a common goal would have appealed to Haslund, who had been trained as an officer in the Danish army.

The linguist Kaare Grønbech (1902-57) was the expedition's 'scientific leader'. Grønbech worked closely with a panel of scientists, among them Dr. Phil. Kaj Birket-Smith (1893-1977), who held the position as director of the Ethnography Department at the National Museum of Denmark from 1940-63. Grønbech had also participated in Haslund's Second Danish Expedition to Central Asia in Mongolia in 1938-39, together with the archaeologist Werner Jacobsen (1914-79) (Johnsen 2016, 8). Haslund's third expedition to Central Asia was, therefore, in many ways a continuation and expansion of his previous work. This meant that a substantial number of artefacts and considerable knowledge was brought back to Denmark in the 1930s.

Professionally, it was Kaj Birket-Smith who supported the expedition, together with Kaare Grønbech. Birket-Smith's paramount professional interest was the diffusion of culture: the temporal and spatial spread of cultural traits. This concerned major features of human life together with the history and development of humanity. His outlook was *global*, to use a word current in our own times. The way to this global view passed through the 'purest' forms of culture possible. For Birket-Smith, all peoples were seen as actors in a common story; by means of historical comparisons between cultures, patterns in the spread of cultural characteristics would be thrown into relief (Johnsen 2016, 9).

The mountain cultures of the Hindukush, the Nuristanis in Afghanistan, and the Kalasha in Northwest Pakistan, had caught Haslund's interest during the 1930s; at that time, he had heard of small ethnic groups that maintained ancient cultural traits, due to the remote areas they inhabited. For Birket-Smith, a focus on this group must have been extremely appealing; such a

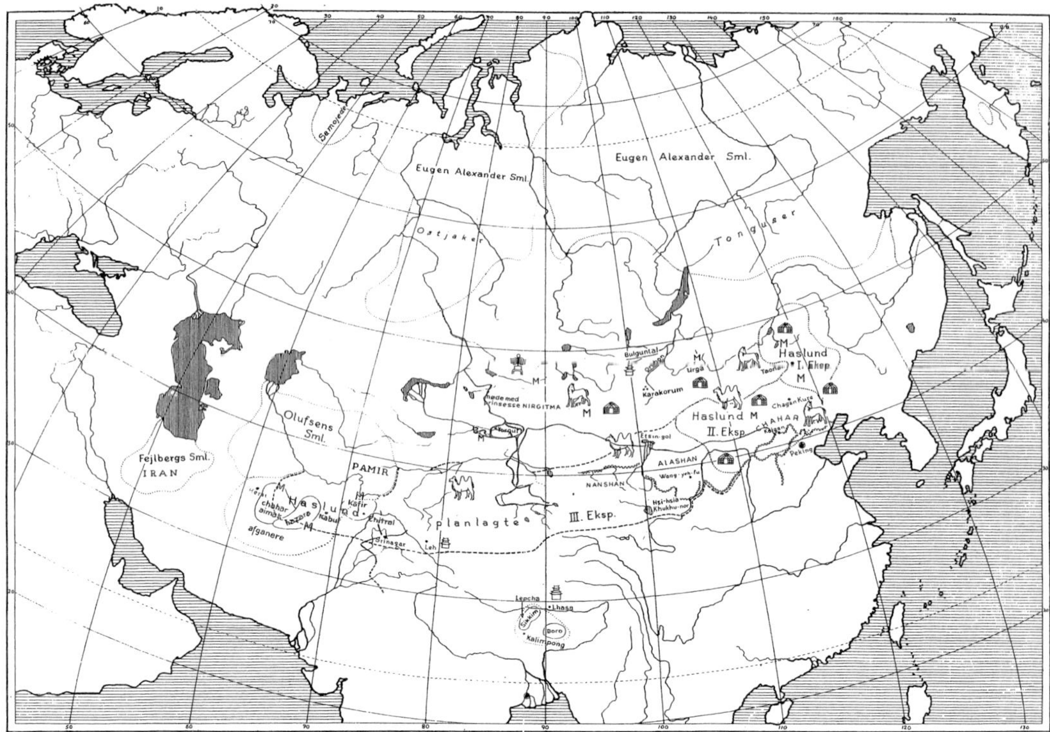

Map of Asia. Published in the article "Arselan" 1958.

group might provide an understanding of the spread of the Indo-European population and their cultural traits from 2000 BC somewhere in the Caucasus and down to India, where they founded the Hindu civilization. In the course of the migration down to India, as the Norwegian linguist, Georg Morgenstierne, had suggested, some members of this group remained in the mountains where their descendants maintained their culture, religion, and cosmology relatively unchanged for two millennia.

Another branch of the Indo-European group travelled westwards and ended up in Europe. By studying the ancient culture of the Kafirs of the Hindukush, it might – so the reasoning goes – be possible to study our own very distant past, which had been completely altered in Europe due to the continent's historical transformations. One should remember that ethnography, before it became a discipline on its own (in Copenhagen from 1945 and in Aarhus from 1963), was used as a supporting discipline for archaeological work. The idea was that certain contemporary cultures and their material culture could be used to explain archaeological material.[2]

The overall plan for the expedition was that different groups of scholars would work independently; one group beginning in Afghanistan, another in Sikkim, and a third in Mongolia. The different groups would later meet up in the Alashan mountains in Mongolia (today in China) and there conclude the scientific program of the expedition. "What a meeting that would be!" Lennart writes in the article "Arselan" published in *Naturen Verden* in September 1958.

This glorious meeting, however, never materialized. First, political turmoil in the entire region made it impossible, so Haslund decided that the HQ of the expedition should be in Kabul. Second, Haslund died on the night of September 12, 1948 at the expedition's base in Kabul, due to high blood pressure.

From botanist to ethnographer

Lennart worked as a recently qualified botanist at *Statens Ukrudtsforsøg* (National Weed Killing Tests) from 1946-47, where weed killing experiments were conducted in and for the agricultural sector. Some of his letters to Margot from the expedition reveal that he never seemed to like that work. In fact, the seeds of his later activities in environmental protection may very well have been sown during this period. After receiving a thrilling call from his cousin Erik, it was clear to him that the possibility of joining the expedition was a unique opportunity to move his professional focus in a radically different direction from killing weeds. Margot supported Lennart and his aspirations – as she continued to do throughout their life together. Margot stayed behind in Denmark with their first-born daughter Vibeke and the newly born Susanne.

Joining Haslund, Siiger, and Paludan, Lennart departed Denmark as a botanist. But another field of research was about to be added to his resume: that of ethnographer. Haslund, as the leader of the expedition, had given Lennart 'ethnographic tasks.' Since he and Paludan were travelling to Nuristan, Lennart was also directed to collect artefacts. Haslund himself had the overall responsibility for carrying out the ethnographic investigations. However, from the late autumn of 1947 and into the spring of 1948, Haslund was busy in Kabul organizing the next group of scholars arriving in Afghanistan, among them Johannes Humlum and Aase and Aage Køie. In addition, Haslund died in September 1948. He was buried in Kabul the following day in the Christian cemetery near the grave of one of his old friends, the Buddhist scholar Marc Aurel Stein.

Dr. Carl Krebs visiting the grave of Haslund in Kabul. Photo by Schuyler Jones, 1969.

Lennart spent a total of nine months in Nuristan during 1948 and 1949. During that time, he collected several hundred objects for the National Museum in Copenhagen as well as relevant information about them. In a report to Haslund dated June 26, 1948, Lennart emphasizes that: "in the ethnographic field, I am only a layman; experts, therefore, will most probably have further information about the objects" [author's translation]. However, when it came to the understanding and the interpretation of these objects, Lennart himself was truly second-to-none in Denmark,

Interestingly enough, Lennart published his botanical findings, as he was obliged to do; but it was his ethnographic interests in Nuristan that prevailed for the rest of his life. The findings of the overall expedition are too profound to list here, but Lennart himself points to the fact that the "National Museum has come into possession of a particularly comprehensive collection from the Kafirs" (Edelberg 1958, 277). This, of course, should be understood in the context of the material collected during the Henning Haslund-Christensen Memorial Expedition, or simply the Scientific Mission to Afghanistan 1953-54.

The Scientific Mission to Afghanistan 1953-54

Haslund's unexpected death in September 1948 left many of the ethnographic tasks planned for the third Danish expedition unfinished. When Lennart returned to Denmark in 1949, he began to write up the many artefacts in the National Museum in Copenhagen, which he had collected in Nuristan. While doing so, new questions must have occurred to Lennart, as he was examining the objects and one result was that he began to form a plan with Hans Madsen, who was working as conservator at the National Museum – a rather ambitious plan for a follow-up expedition to Afghanistan. Originally, the expedition was to include at least seven members – a conservator, a zoologist, a film photographer, a musicologist and no less than three members with ethnographic tasks: Lennart, Ferdinand and Siiger. In the end, though, the expedition was smaller than originally planned.

The members of this new Danish scientific expedition to Afghanistan set out from Copenhagen on April 20, 1953. The expedition consisted of four members: Lennart (this time primarily as ethnographer and only secondarily as botanist), Klaus Ferdinand as ethnographer, and Peter Rasmussen as film photographer. The fourth member of the expedition, the anthropologist Prince Peter of Greece and Denmark, was also the formal leader of the expedition, although he was in India where he had resided for many years.

The expedition was planned to extend until May 1954; it was to last for a year – just as it had for the Third Danish Expedition to Central Asia. Birket-Smith at the National Museum of Denmark was the man in scien-

Expedition members in the autumn of 1953.

tific charge. Together with Kaare Grønbech, they constituted the expedition committee in Copenhagen. During meetings with expedition members, they had worked out a list of research topics to be investigated in the field. The plans for Nuristan included mapping the region, investigations into climatic conditions, detailed descriptions of Nuristani houses, agriculture, handicrafts, music instruments, sound recordings, textiles and dress, data on local calendar systems, and so on. As the expedition was also to concern research

on nomads in central Afghanistan, which primarily was Ferdinand's task, questions regarding the various tribes and tent types, different burial traditions, agricultural practices, and a range of other cultural features were also on the list. There were many questions to be answered. The aims of the expedition were high, reflecting Lennart's plans for a larger expedition. Ideally, it would have included Hans Madsen, who had taken part in the Third Danish Expedition to Central Asia in his capacity as conservator, and Lennart's good friend from Ribe, Thomas Alvad, to focus on music traditions.

Unfortunately, the 'leadership' in Copenhagen – Birket-Smith and Grønbech who constituted the expedition's committee – were unable to find the necessary funding to realize the proposed plan in its entirety. In the correspondence between Lennart, Klaus, and Prince Peter (who stayed in India most of the time) and colleagues at home, one senses an increasing irritation on the part of expedition members towards the committee in Copenhagen.

The trio reached Kabul in the spring of 1953, where they set up their HQ and contacted Lennart's old acquaintances from the 1948-49 expedition. Access to Nuristan was not obtained as smoothly or quickly as they had hoped. The expedition had to apply to the Ministry of Defense through the Press Department in Kabul. In the application dated August 11 1953, Lennart stated: "The mission wants to finish the ethnographic investigations of Nuristan as a study of the Nuristani daily-life, music and poems, and throw light over the study of the Arians as a whole." As such, the expedition was interested not only in contemporary Nuristani society but also in traces of the old pre-Muslim culture that might provide insights into ancient cultural traits. Although their first application was turned down by the Afghan Ministry of National Defense, the expedition finally got permission in September and entered Nuristan toward the end of that month. They were able to stay there for seven weeks.

In a report dated November 11, 1953 that was sent to the expedition leader, Prince Peter in Kalimpong, Lennart writes that besides the motion picture film sequences (which were later edited to make the film *Kafiristan – the Land of Heathens*), Klaus had been studying the social structure of the Nuristanis. In the 1950s, social structure was the theoretical name-of-the-game in anthropology. This was due to the influence of A.R. Radcliffe-Brown's functional structuralism at the British school based in Oxford. Lennart, who was not familiar with – and quite possibly not interested in – social structure

In the mountains, autumn 1953. On the left, Ahmad Ali Motamedi, later director of the Afghan National Museum, Klaus Ferdinand and Lennart Edelberg. Photo: Peter Rasmussen.

as a theoretical concept, focused his research on practical matters such as dairy production, transhumance, recordings of traditional Nuristani music, calendar systems, songs and hymns, and the work of the *bari* craftsmen in making Nuristani buildings.

The group returned to Kabul at the beginning of November 1953. Peter Rasmussen, the photographer, left Afghanistan in December; meanwhile, Klaus and Lennart spent some time with the nomads in southern and central Afghanistan. Later in the spring, Lennart returned to Nuristan once again. This time, he visited the Waigal and Parun Valleys, while Klaus focused on the study of nomads in Eastern Afghanistan.

Margot Edelberg with Nuristani women. Nuristan 1964. Photo: Lennart Edelberg.

Lennart returned to Denmark in July 1954, but Klaus remained in Afghanistan where he continued his research despite the fact that the expedition committee in Copenhagen had on several occasions declared the expedition to have been 'terminated.' Although he received his last salary cheque from Copenhagen in May 1954, Klaus did not have a job waiting for him in Denmark. Therefore, he remained in Afghanistan, hoping that his financial situation would improve. Eventually it did, due to additional funding from Copenhagen. His wife, Marianne, joined him in August 1954. She stayed until May 1955, when they both returned home, travelling overland through Iran and Turkey to Lebanon and from there back to Denmark.

Scientific missions in 1964 and 1970

Ten years would pass before Lennart visited the valleys of Nuristan and their inhabitants again. He had started work as a teacher at the Cathedral School in Ribe in 1950, and this work took most of his time and energy. The

Edelberg family had also grown during these years. Nevertheless, Lennart still found time and energy to continue his ethnographic research. During the 1950s and at the beginning of 1960, he published several articles relating to Nuristan (see Per E. Børdahl's chapter). In 1964, he made another fieldtrip to Afghanistan – this time with Margot and Susanne. They spent the months of July and August in Nuristan visiting the valleys of Waigal, Parun, and Bashgal. Later on, they went to Luristan in Iran (see Henrik Thrane's chapter) In Nuristan as well as Luristan, Lennart collected artefacts that were later deposited in the ethnographic study collection in Aarhus. From 1958, these were in the capable hands of Klaus Ferdinand.

In both the 1964 and 1970 fieldtrips, Lennart brought some of his family members with him, and Margot played an important role in this additional ethnographic work. She helped not only with the study of the social life of women, with whom she could stay at times, when a male presence was prohibited, but also with the study of Nuristani music. Margot was a schoolteacher in Ribe, where she taught music classes as well as other subjects.

Lennart and Klaus

During the Scientific Mission to Afghanistan 1953-54, a strong friendship was formed between Lennart and Klaus. Klaus was born in 1926 in Herlufsholm and was twelve years junior to Lennart. In 1947, he graduated from Copenhagen University in geography and archaeology; in 1952, he obtained the title of Mag. Scient. in ethnology.[4] As one of the very few students of ethnology in the 1940s and beginning of the 1950s, Klaus already had a good deal of experience in conducting extensive fieldwork in Denmark and Sweden; moreover, he had participated in the National Museum's West Greenland Expedition in 1950.

They seem to have been an excellent team in the field. Lennart was an experienced fieldworker, who knew his way around the far corners of the world, and Klaus was a freshly trained ethnologist from the university. More importantly, they had good chemistry between them. Although their careers developed in different directions, their friendship would remain intact thereafter. Klaus never returned to Nuristan after their seven-week visit in the autumn of 1953. Nevertheless, he and Lennart kept in close contact over the years, resulting among other things in the First International Hindukush Cultural Conference in 1970 and the first ethnographic exhibition in the newly opened Prehistoric Museum at Moesgaard, also in 1970. Young Ahmad Ali Motamedi was with Lennart and Klaus in Nuristan in 1953. He later became Director of the Kabul Museum and was a good friend of both of them for many years.

The Nuristan research tradition

Lennart's fieldwork in Nuristan in the period from 1948 to 1970, gave him a prominent position in the international circle of 'Hindukushologists.' In the early 1960's, Lennart met his colleague and subsequent friend, the anthropologist Schuyler Jones, who was also working in Nuristan. Their collaboration culminated in the publication of the monograph *Nuristan* in 1979.

This was the first proper monograph on Nuristan ever made. As Jones describes in his chapter in this present volume, Lennart's approach was always inclusive, collaborative, and open towards colleagues – nationally as well as internationally. The Danish scientific establishments were never competitive, as was the case in many other places. Furthermore, Lennart was first a teacher and secondly an ethnographer. He need not worry about publishing a certain number of articles in specific academic journals. In that sense, he was a 'free bird,' who was not constrained to adjust to the conformity of academia. What is so remarkable is that the number of his publications and his ethnographic insights and research in general were second-to-none – especially when it came to Nuristani architecture and house construction.

Lennart's personality seems to have opened many doors for him throughout his life. As is evident from Jones' description of Lennart, he infused his surroundings with trust, kindness, and cooperation. It was, therefore, probably no coincidence that Lennart became the prime force behind the idea to make an international Nuristan research center in Aarhus, where Ferdinand was building up both ethnography as an academic discipline and Aarhus University's ethnographic study collection. Some of the material collected during the Third Danish Expedition to Central Asia was placed in the study collection; this was a part of the 'payment' for the financial support of the city of Aarhus to the expedition in the 1940s. Furthermore, as the plans to move the museum from its location at 'Huset' in Mølleparken in the centre of Aarhus to Moesgaard Manor, plans were made to open a semi-permanent ethnographic exhibition in this new Moesgaard Museum (see Flemming Bau's chapter). Ferdinand, Lennart, and Siiger, who at that time had taken up his post as professor of the History of Religions at Aarhus University, made plans for a permanent exhibition on the mountain cultures of the Hindukush. This would include both the material collected in Nuristan by Lennart and Ferdinand as well as that collected by Halfdan Siiger among the Kalasha in NW Pakistan just across the border from Nuristan. As he describes in his contribution to this book, the exhibition designer, Flemming Bau, worked closely with Lennart in preparing the exhibition. In the late 1960's a large part

Lennart and Georg Morgenstierne. At the First International Hindukush Cultural Conference, Moesgaard 1970.

of the collections made in the 1940s by Lennart and Siiger were transferred to Moesgaard on permanent loan.[5]

The exhibition opened with the rest of the Moesgaard Prehistoric Museum in 1970. Another important event happened in November 1970: the First International Hindukush Cultural Conference. For five consecutive days, the lecture hall at Moesgaard Museum housed, with a few exceptions, all the leading 'Hindukushologists' from a number of different countries. Lennart and Klaus both acted as hosts, but there is no doubt that the driving force at the conference was Lennart.

The whole idea was to join forces, to discuss different questions and problems regarding the cultures of the Hindukush; to inspire and inform one another. In that sense, the conference seems to have been a huge success. Professor Wolfgang Lentz, the German scholar who had participated in the Deutsche Hindukusch-Expedition to Nuristan in 1935, pledged to donate his material consisting of diaries, hundreds of photographs, maps, etc. to the study collection in Aarhus. These documents were examined by Schuyler Jones in Marburg in the 1980s, and he assisted Professor Lentz in organizing the donation. The second half of this material was organized by Svend Castenfeldt. This set moved to Aarhus in 1986 – just a couple of months before Lentz's death. Both Halfdan Siiger and Lennart also agreed to let their books and papers join what would become the Hindukush Research Archive, which became part of the Ethnographic study collections, which is part of the Ethnographic Study collections. The artefacts and these archives were transferred to Moesgaard Museum in 1999, where there were experts who could handle and conserve the material in a proper way.

As a research archivist and ethnographer, Svend Castenfeldt has tirelessly spent more than twenty-five years organizing this vast material. Although Castenfeldt formally retired in the mid-2000s, he continued well into the 2010s to improve the organization and infrastructure of the archive. He has also always been extremely generous with his time in assisting scholars who are interested in the contents of the archive. The tremendous work done by Castenfeldt means that the research papers and other documents of Lennart, Siiger, and Lentz are very accessible to researchers, thereby adding a huge value to the archive's resources.

Research and results

Throughout many years, Nuristan and the Nuristanis were a part of not only Lennart's life but also of Margot's. The Edelberg home in Holmevej, Ribe, was full of photos, objects, books, and documents relating to Nuristan and Afghanistan. Nuristan was often a theme in Lennart's Geography classes at the Cathedral School, where he had augmented the ethnographic collection of the school with different artefacts from various valleys in Nuristan. As mentioned above, Lennart published numerous articles over the years as listed in the monograph *Nuristan* with Schuyler Jones.

After years of work, fruitful discussions, and collaborations, Jones and Lennart submitted the manuscript for *Nuristan* to the Akademische Druck-u. Verlagsanstalt in Graz in January 1978. There was another manuscript, however, lying on Lennart's desk in his office in Holmevej: *Nuristani Buildings*. This focused on the extraordinary buildings in Nuristan, and the craftsmanship of the bari. As a social group, the bari are the traditional carvers, smiths, weavers, potters, and builders of Nuristan. The bari do not have any rights to own land or livestock.

Before 1900, they were bought and sold. Although their skills were recognized, even admired, their talents did not earn them any social rewards. They remained, socially speaking, at the bottom of society in Nuristan. The bari, however, remained a core interest for Lennart from his very first visit in 1948 onwards. Lennart became sworn brothers with a bari named Abdullah. This man was the grandfather of Kakail Nuristani, who is one of the contributors to this book.

During all his subsequent visits, Lennart measured and photographed many buildings and carefully recorded structural details of the buildings, including the symbolic nature of their carved decorations. It was originally Lennart's close friend from Ribe, the architect H.H. Engqvist, who encouraged him to investigate and publish information about the architecture and buildings of Nuristan. *Statens Humanistiske Forskningsråd* (SHF) made some funds available for the publication. In an application to SHF on March 3, 1981, Lennart wrote that due to a major reconstruction at the Cathedral School starting in 1978 and continuing in the following years, he would not have the necessary time and peace to finish the publication.

Lennart sent his application to SHF requesting funds that would enable him to take a one-year leave of absence from his job in Ribe Katedralskole. He sent another application to the Ministry of Education to request a leave

Nuristani house. Photo: Lennart Edelberg.

of absence from August 1, 1981 to July 31, 1982. In the application, Lennart
wrote:

The Nuristani collections from the Haslund-Christensen expeditions which are
owned by the National Museum are deposited in the Moesgaard Museum, as well as
Moesgaard Museum's own collections from Nuristan, Afghanistan, and Luristan, Iran.
Part of the materials from Afghanistan are on permanent display in the museum's
ethnographic exhibition. The before mentioned material should be scientifically treated.
The material includes almost all types of everyday life objects as well as a number of
objects from the pre-Islamic period in Nuristan, in total at least 1300 artefacts. [author's
translation]

As appears from the application to SHF, Lennart's intended not only to finish
his book on Nuristani buildings but also to work more thoroughly with the
collections from Nuristan and the Kalasha. Several of the artefacts from these
collections had been on display in the Moesgaard Museum since 1970. The
findings of his continued studies into household items and furniture could be
incorporated in *Nuristani Buildings*. He had furthermore arranged with the
Danish ethnographer Henny Harald Hansen that they should work together
on the textiles in the collections. The study collection in Aarhus also included
many hundreds of photographs from both Nuristan, Kalashadesh (the land of
the Kalasha in Pakistan) and Afghanistan in general, and Lennart wanted to
catalogue all the photos during his research year. Besides these major tasks,
there were several minor tasks as well – such as preparing the sound recordings from 1953 for Thomas Alvad to publish, cataloguing the many hours
of film recordings, which were not used in the film *Kafiristan – the land of
Heathens* and the publication of articles, etc.

From the application it is obvious that it was urgent for Lennart to begin
the work right away. Although there were not many years before his planned
retirement, he wanted the work done "while I still have a reasonable recol-
lection," as he states in the application in March 1981. Lennart's 'sabbatical
year' – as Henny Harald Hansen humorously called it – started on an unfortunate note. During the summer, Lennart had dislocated his shoulder in an
accident. In spite of his injury, he started his work in August. His diary reveals
that the textiles in the Nuristan and Kalasha collections were among his first
tasks. During the autumn, he spent longer periods at Moesgaard, where he
lodged in a guest room in the old manor house. Lennart and Halfdan Siiger,
his old expedition comrade from 1948-49, embarked on a close collaboration
on their field collections from the middle of November onwards. But before
that, he planned to complete his work on *Nuristani Buildings*. Lennart kept a

research log book from early August 1981. Unfortunately, he quite abruptly stopped writing in it at the very end of August. During the very last days of August, Lennart suffered what must have been a series of strokes that left his right arm less useful. Despite this Lennart transcribed more or less all his notes and letters up to November on a typewriter. Unfortunately, this task was not as comprehensive as it would have been if he had had full mobility in his right arm.

Lennart never regained his strength, and on November 11, 1981, he passed away. His sudden death left not only his family and many friends in shock and sorrow; it also left a lot of work unfinished. A group of Lennart's friends and colleagues made a plan to rework and publish Lennart's manuscript on Nuristani buildings. This group consisted of Klaus Ferdinand, Torkil Funder, and Birthe Stubsgaard. Although the publication did not have the magnitude that Lennart had intended, it was nevertheless published in 1984. To this day, *Nuristani Buildings* remains the only publication on the rich house-building traditions of Nuristan.

The context (of the book)

The majority of chapters in this book are the proceedings of a seminar, which was held at Moesgaard Museum / Aarhus University on April 31 and May 1, 2016. The seminar was organized by Ulrik Høj Johnsen, at the time both curator of the Ethnographic Collections at Moesgaard Museum and a PhD student at Aarhus University (2016-20). Johnsen's PhD project focused on the value of museum collections. At the time of the seminar, he was working with the collections of artefacts, photos, films, and sound recordings from the mountain cultures of the Hindukush. Because he was working with the Hindukush collections – and therefore also focusing on the history of Danish research in Afghanistan and more specifically in Nuristan – Johnsen organized the seminar so as to shed light on Lennart, who was the driving force in the Danish Nuristan research tradition.

More than fifty persons – scholars and students from Denmark and abroad, family and friends of Lennart – attended the seminar. Fifteen presentations were given over the course of two days. All the presenters at the seminar were invited to contribute to this book – and fortunately most accepted. In addition, two chapters have been written by authors who were not able to be present at the seminar.

Participants in the seminar April / May 2016. Photo: Jens Vellev.

Unfortunately, the political situation in the region made fieldwork in Afghanistan and Chitral impossible. As a result, in September 2016, Johnsen was forced to change his intended regional focus and thereby the related collections. His initial plan to collect and publish different perspectives on the Danish Nuristan research and to celebrate the contributions of Lennart Edelberg, however, was and continues to be of paramount importance. First, such a book would be the first of its kind. Moreover, it would in a certain sense describe and to some extent conclude the research tradition so far. Hopefully, this book will provide an important steppingstone to future research in Nuristan, the Hindukush region, and Afghanistan in general. Second, the book pays tribute to Lennart, the driving force behind the Danish Nuristan research tradition. He would have turned 100 in 2015.

The chapters

This book is divided into three sections. The first section, comprised of six chapters, focuses on the Danish Nuristan research tradition and Lennart's decisive role in shaping it. The two chapters in the second section offer insights on Nuristan and Lennart's work from the perspective of the Kalasha in Chitral, North West Pakistan. The final five chapters of the third section focuses attention on Lennart as a person.

Chapter 1 offers a rarely heard voice – one from contemporary Nuristan. Kakail Nuristani, the grandson of Lennart's sworn brother, Abdullah, offers an account of recent developments in Nuristan. Basically, this covers the time since it became impossible for foreign scholars to travel to Nuristan in the late 1970s. Kakail was invited to the seminar, but, unfortunately, he was not able obtain a Danish visa due to the extremely strict visa rules of the Danish government. To participate, his recorded presentation was displayed for the seminar audience on a large screen. His chapter is a reworked version of his presentation. Many thanks to another contributor to this book, Birgitte Glavind Sperber, for taking the time to transcribe Kakail's presentation for this book. In his chapter, Kakail describes developments – or their lack – in Nuristan, where it has been close to impossible to travel since the 1970s. When Lennart was there in 1970, the province was still relatively quiet and safe. Everything changed dramatically after the Soviet invasion in 1979. It was at this time that the first Afghan mujahedeen resistance showed its teeth. Since then, as Kakail vividly explains, the situation in Nuristan has deteriorated dramatically for the local population. Local people are struggling to survive in a time of civil war and religious fanaticism as well as the lack of a basic infrastructure and, for many, due to sheer poverty. Very importantly, he points to the value and importance of Lennart's work. The publication *Nuristan* by Lennart and Schuyler Jones remains, as Kakail describes, the most important presentation of and documentation on Nuristan. Today most of the traditional Nuristani culture that Lennart saw and described, has vanished. This deterioration did not result from the Kafirs' conversion to Islam in 1896; rather, it took place quite recently, after 2005, when Salafism washed over the Nuristani valleys as a response to the American military presence in Nuristan. The singing and the dancing traditions that Lennart and Klaus documented in 1953-54 were kept alive up until 2005.

The music recordings that Lennart and Klaus made in Nuristan during the Haslund-Christensen Memorial Expedition 1953-54 are the focus of **chapter 2,** written by the music ethnologist Christer Irgens-Møller. The work of collecting music recordings was heavily inspired by Haslund. He, personally, had collected well over two hundred recordings among the Mongols in the 1930s.[6] The music recordings of the 1953-54 expedition in Nuristan comprises 209 pieces of music with a total playing time of twelve hours. Lennart's friend from Ribe, the musician Thomas Alvad, catalogued the material; unfortunately, Lennart did not live to see it published. That was achieved, however, by Irgens-Møller. He was contacted by Klaus in the late 1990s, and the two formed a plan to publish the material. The book, *Music in Nuristan,* was published in 2009. It includes a thorough presentation of the music recordings, their significance, and the instruments collected. In this book, Irgens-Møller provides a summary of the central insights presented in *Nuristani Music.* Some of the music described can be found and enjoyed on the Afghanistan website of Moesgaard Museum as well.

In **chapter 3,** Peter Bakker, Kristoffer Friis Bøegh, and Yonatan Ungermann Goldshtein offer an account of "The languages of Edelberg's Nuristan and environs". A paramount interest of the expeditions in 1947-52 and 1953-54 was to take a close look at the links between the 'Old Kafiristan' (from before 1890s) and Nuristan and the Nuristanis whom Lennart encountered in the middle of the twentieth century. The overall question of the links to an Indo-European point of origin was of particular interest; the work of the Norwegian linguist Georg Morgenstierne among the Kalasha (Kafirs) in NW Pakistan, bordering on Nuristan, was central to this exploration. The three linguists, Bakker, Boeegh, and Goldshtein place the Nuristani languages in the context of this work.

In **chapter 4,** the ethnographer and research archivist, Svend Castenfeldt, recounts the captivating story about a magnificent, but lost, temple in Nuristan. The temple, a symbol of pagan *Kafir* past *par excellence,* was destroyed in the 1890s by the troops of the invading Afghan Emir. Castenfeldt vividly unfolds how foreigners, who found their way to the secluded valleys of Nuristan, were intrigued by the temple, which was central to the Kafir winter solstice. Lennart was one of these foreigners, who throughout the years pursued the quest to unveil the secrets of the temple. As described in the chapter, the quest proved extremely difficult partly because of personal antagonisms and shadows from World War II. In the mid-1980s, however, the puzzle finally was put together by the chapter's author. Castenfeldt had carefully organized the Lennart Edelberg Research Archive in Moesgaard Museum, and cataloguing the vast material, he had recovered some of the central pieces in the puzzle. By way of resolute perseverance Castenfeldt recovered the missing pieces in Marburg, Germany, and completed the puzzle with the Kafiristan Group in Aarhus. Although Lennart never himself saw the complete picture, it could never have been completed, had it not been for him.

Chapter 5 is written by Flemming Bau, who as exhibition designer, worked with Lennart in creating the exhibition *Nuristan and the Kalash Area,* which was on display from 1970 when the Prehistoric Museum at Moesgaard had just opened. The presentation of the mountain cultures of the Hindukush, was – as we shall later see in Torkil Funder's contribution – an integral part of Lennart's curriculum in the Cathedral School in Ribe; but the Moesgaard exhibition certainly qualifies as a highlight in this respect. Through the exhibition a larger museum audience was offered scholarly insights into the lives and material cultures of the Nuristanis and the Kalasha. The third main aim of his efforts to provide information was that of publishing, which Per E. Børdahl records in the last chapter of this book. Bau's chapter, however, offers insights into the museum context in the late 1960s and early 1970s as well as Lennart's skills as a communicator in the exhibition galleries.

The first section concludes with a contribution in **chapter 6** by the visual anthropologist Christian Vium, who presents a photo essay based on the extensive photo collections of Lennart from his different expeditions and travels to Nuristan – from 1948 to 1970. The nineteen carefully selected photos are accompanied by a poem, written by Vium, bringing visual impressions – through the lens of Lennart's camera – from Nuristan and some of its inhabitants. It shows not only Lennart as a phenomenal photographer but indeed also something central about his particular way of looking at the world.

The second section of the book offers insights on Nuristan and Lennart's work from the perspective of the Kalasha in Chitral, North West Pakistan and in the scholarly work on them. The Kalasha still maintain the ancient polytheistic and animistic religion of the Kafirs, who inhabited the area today known as Nuristan – The Land of Light. In **chapter 7**, the Kalasha scholar, Taj Khan Kalash, draws an outline of the Kafir history, which includes the Kalasha Kafirs. He also traces the word *Kafir,* which literally translates into 'heathen' in popular and academic writing and thinking. Kalash builds upon the material collected by Lennart's expedition companion from the Third Danish Expedition to Central Asia, Halfdan Siiger. He stresses the paramount importance of their joint efforts in describing the mountain cultures of the Hindukush – not least for contemporary scholars such as himself.

Chapter 8 is written by upper-secondary-school teacher Birgitte Glavind Sperber, who offers a perspective on "Nuristan in Kalasha myth, history and life." Like Lennart, Sperber was a teacher at the Cathedral School in Ribe; since the early 1980s, she spent a considerable amount of time among the Kalasha in NW Pakistan. Through her observations, conversations, and knowledge about the Kalasha, she investigates through 'thick descriptions' the mythological relations between the Kalasha and the Nuristanis as told in the Kalasha myth. She argues that myth and history is closely interwoven in the Hindukush mountains.

The third and last section of this book focuses attention on Lennart as a human being. The Danish research tradition in Nuristan was heavily – if not solely – influenced by Lennart. To comprehend the research tradition, we need to understand who Lennart was as well as what his motivations and inspirations were. The chapters in this section, therefore, are written by friends and colleagues of Lennart. These are people who saw him in the field, published with him, and shared his research interests.

In **chapter 9**, Lennart's closest collaborator in his research in Nuristan and friend, the anthropologist Schuyler Jones, describes Lennart as a true 'Renaissance man'; not only was he an unfailing inspiration for his friends and colleagues, but indeed, also a thinker who moved beyond the limiting borders of much academic work. Lennart was, as Jones writes, a 'scientist, teacher, investigator and explorer,' who was able to make connections based on his particular approach to life. Such a capacity is as rare today as it was back in the 1960s and 1970s. Jones, furthermore, provides a close-up perspective into their joint work – including the making of the publication *Nuristan* from 1979. As Kakail Nuristani explains, this publication is nothing less than a tower of light in the scholarly work on Nuristan.

The architect Erik Hansen provides **chapter 10**. Hansen participated in the seminar in the spring of 2016. At the time, his friend Claus Christensen presented his paper, as Hansen himself did not have the strength to make the presentation. Hansen's chapter is based upon this presentation and has been reworked in close collaboration with Christensen. Hansen passed away on December 31, 2016 at the age of eighty-nine. Among other projects in Afghanistan, Hansen was working on the restoration of a thirteenth-century Ghurid Portal in Herat. Through Hansen's contacts in Afghanistan, Lennart came in touch with Afghan technicians who made the drawings that were published in *Nuristani Buildings* in 1984. This publication, which was published three years after Lennart's death in 1981, is considered the most authoritative publication on this unique architecture of Nuristan.

In the **chapter 11**, Lennart's friend, archaeologist Henrik Thrane, shares recollections of his friendship with Lennart and the Edelberg family. Thrane also takes us to the Central Zagros mountains in Western Iran, where the Lur tribe lives. Along with the archaeological expedition in Luristan in 1964, Lennart carried out fieldwork among the Lurs with Thrane. This work resulted in a Lur collection of objects and photographs, which are today in the Ethnographic Collections of Moesgaard Museum. Importantly, Thrane offers a rare glimpse into how Lennart conducted his fieldwork.

The following piece, **chapter 12**, is written by Torkil Funder. Like Lennart, Funder was an upper-secondary-school teacher at the Cathedral School in Ribe and became Lennart's close friend from 1965 onwards. The chapter consists of thirteen short stories. Together they form a mosaic that offers unique insight into 'Lennart, the human being.' Each of the stories has a photograph – or group of photographs – at their centre. As the creator of the mosaic, Funder takes us from Lennart as a young student of biology, to his days as a vigorous teacher in the classrooms, and to his time as an interested observer and fieldworker, who is learning by doing. The mosaic captures something that was essentially Lennart: his incessant open-ended interest in the world and his equally incessant need to initiate his fellow beings in 'the profound patterns of life' as he had seen them.

Per E. Børdahl, married to Lennart Edelberg's eldest daughter, Vibeke, provides the concluding **chapters 13 and 14** on Lennart's bibliography. In chapter 13, Børdahl carefully presents Lennart's main publications and places them in a relevant context. In chapter 14, he presents Lennart's near-complete bibliography. Some 30 reader's letters from his last 20 years of life are not included; their themes are summarized in the first section of the bibliography.

Notes

1. In 1944, the Danish geographer Carl Gunnar Feilberg (1894-1972) published his thesis on the black tents of the nomad tribes of North Africa, and South and Central Asia under the title "*La Tente Noire: Contribution Ethnographique á l'Histoire Culturelle des Nomades*". The study of nomadic populations was later taken up by Klaus Ferdinand, who studied nomadic and semi-nomadic groups in Afghanistan such as the Chahar Aimaq and Hazara nomads.

2. This tendency was abandoned in anthropology as anthropologists generally objected to their contemporary informants being regarded as modern survivals or living representatives of Stone- or Bronze-age peoples. Interestingly, if one goes through the permanent archaeological exhibition on the Stone Age at Moesgaard Museum, one will find prominent anthropologists explaining cultural phenomena in the Stone Age through contemporary material from Siberian ethnic groups.

3. Arselan is the name of a fabulous Mongolian animal, and it is how the Mongolians pronounced Haslund's name. The article was co-written with Klaus Ferdinand to commemorate the death of Haslund on the tenth anniversary of his passing.

4. His first two major papers were: "Mongolian and Tibetan Nomadic Cultures with special reference to the breeding of domestic animals" (1948) and "Cattle-breeding among the Primitive Tribes of India" (1952).

5. Since 2014, Moesgaard Museum and the National Museum of Denmark have been engaged in discussions to deal with all old loans. As a result, these collections were formally transferred to Moesgaard Museum in June 2017.

6. Digitalized versions of the 213 recordings made by Haslund in Inner Mongolia are available on the website EUROPEANA.EU.

List of references

Birket-Smith, Kaj (1941-42) *Kulturens Veje – Naturfolk og Kulturfolk* Jespersen & Pio: København.

Braae, Christel (2007) "Mongoliet er vort Maal: en beretning om 1. og 2. Danske Ekspedition til Centralasien." In: *Nationalmuseets Arbejdsmark 1807-2007*: pp. 71-86. Nationalmuseet: København.

Braae, Christel (2017) *Among herders of Inner Mongolia – The Haslund-Christensen collection at the National Museum of Denmark*. Aarhus University Press: Aarhus.

Edelberg, Lennart i samarbejde med Klaus Ferdinand (1958) "Arselan – Et udblik over dansk forskning i Centralasien." In: *Naturens Verden*, 41 (September): pp. 257-289.

Edelberg, Lennart (1961) *Furer i Asiens ældgamle ansigt*. København: Gyldendal.

Edelberg, Lennart & Schuyler Jones (1979) *Nuristan*. Akademische Druck- u. Verlagsanstalt: Graz.

Ferdinand, Klaus (2005) *Afghan Nomads: Caravans, conflicts, and trade in Afghanistan and British India, 1800-1980*. Carlsberg Foundation, Rhodos International Science and Art Publishers: Copenhagen.

Fihl, Esther (2002) *Exploring Central Asia. Collecting Objects and Writing Cultures from the Steppes to the High Pamirs*, vol. I–II. Thames and Hudson: Copenhagen, London, New York.

Jettmar, Karl and Lennart Edelberg (eds.) (1974) *Cultures of the Hindukush. Selected Papers from the Hindu-Kush Cultural Conference Held at Moesgård 1970*. Beiträge zur Südasienforschung, Südasien- Institut, Universität Heidelberg, 1. Franz Steiner Verlag: Wiesbaden.

Johnsen, Ulrik Høj, Armin Geertz, Peter B. Andersen and Svend Castenfeldt (eds.) (2016) *In the Footsteps of Halfdan Siiger: Danish Research in Central Asia*. Moesgaard Museum: Højberg.

1. Nuristan today

By Kakail Nuristani

My grandfather, Wakhil Abdullah Nuristani, was the person who hosted Lennart Edelberg when he came to Nuristan on an expedition in 1964. From then on, he was Lennart's companion in his research. Unfortunately, the information I have on that expedition and my grandfather's involvement and my grandfather's companionship with Lennart is very limited. It comes from what my mother as a young teenager and my father, Khalilullah Nuristani, as a young man have told me.

My grandfather passed away in the seventies – a long time before I was born. From what my father told me, my grandfather always spoke highly of Lennart and his family. And my grandfather often talked about him, as he came to Nuristan several times. He would tell the people of Nuristan about his expeditions and their importance. For him it was of the utmost importance for the outside world to know about Nuristan, its culture, and its people.

Through the efforts of Lennart, my grandfather was invited to meet the King of Denmark and the Crown Princess, Margrethe, who inaugurated the Nuristan exhibition at the then newly opened Moesgaard Museum. My grandfather was also given a medal of honor by the king of Denmark.

That is how our relations with Denmark began, and this legacy was then handed over to my father. Unfortunately, after my father died all contact with Danish expedition members who had come to Nuristan to conduct research as well as with the country of Denmark itself was lost. Fortunately, contact with Denmark was re-established in 2012. Through an article that was published in The New York Times, Ulrik Johnsen reached out to me and we developed a dialogue. Ulrik was working for the Moesgaard Museum in Aarhus, and he informed me that an ethnographic exhibition had been there for thirty years on the culture and the people of Nuristan. Since then, Ulrik and I have been in discussion regarding ways to conserve the unique culture and heritage of the people of Nuristan. A couple of years ago, Ulrik informed me about the seminar that he planned to conduct about Lennart and his work in Nuristan as well as on the people of Nuristan. Now today, his hard work bears fruit.

It was planned that I should attend the seminar and provide a presentation on Nuristan as it stands today from the Nuristani's perspective. Unfortunately, I was not able to get my visa in time, and that is why I have recorded a video to be shown at the seminar. Thanks to modern technology, I am still able to address those attending the seminar and let them know a little bit of what Nuristan is like today and what changes have transpired.

I am proud of my culture, both the Islamic culture today and the *Kafiri* before that, and there are a lot of things that I want to preserve. You can think of me as a person who holds Nuristan very dear and very close, because that is how we were brought up. That was how my father was brought up, and that was how my grandfather had his children brought up. I am not going to give details about the culture, the heritage, and the languages of Nuristan. Lennart and Schuyler Jones have done an absolutely wonderful job of presenting that in the book *Nuristan*, which was published in the seventies. I do have a copy here with me. After intense use, it appears to be in very bad condition.

I was actually raised with that book. Since my early childhood, I have seen every single page and every single picture a thousand times or maybe more. This copy of the book also took a long journey with my sister to Canada. She kept it there for ten or fifteen years, until I got it back just recently.

Lennart and Schuyler Jones have done such a wonderful and fantastic job in detailing every single aspect of the Nuristani people, their culture, and their social norms, their geography, their architecture, and ways of life. It is done so thoroughly that I have never been able to go through everything from A to Z. But I have read most parts of the book, and it is very, very accurate. I actually learned more about my culture by reading this book than I have by interacting with people. Seen retrospectively, I believe it makes sense to divide the history of Nuristan into three phases and look at the culture, the heritage, the people, their mindset, and their social norms.

The first phase is the pre-Islamic era – before the time when the Kafirs were forcefully converted to Islam by the Afghan king Amir Abdurrahman Khan. That was an era when all the present cultures of Nuristan were at full strength. Back then, what we had was the true culture of the Kafir people: the true heritage, the true system of social law, and everything.

The period following the 1890s marks beginning of the second phase that the Nuristani people experienced. This is when Lennart and a lot of other expeditions came to Nuristan to observe the culture, the language,

Abdullah outside his house in Nuristan in1970. Photo: Lennart Edelberg.

and the people and they were able to draw a picture through research on this neglected and peaceful historic part of the country. This phase was basically from 1890s up till 2005.

I am making a very broad assessment here, because Nuristan itself remained relatively isolated until 2005; it was not easy to get into that mountainous area. Furthermore, it seemed to be forsaken as not so important as far as local and regional politics were concerned.

This is the reason why I consider this long period of years as a time when the true Nuristani culture started slowly to diminish. Part of that true culture had vanished with the introduction of Islam but the part that still remained – like the music, the culture, the people, the feasts, the individuals who were anxious to achieve status, and all the other things that were not in one way or the other in direct conflict with Islamic teachings – were still there. They were still there to be observed when Lennart visited the valleys.

The Nuristani people have always been a free willed, free minded, liberal people. These same qualities are to be found among people in other communities in Afghanistan. In Nuristan, however, you will find these characteristics to be very strong; women, for instance, have a very prominent role in decision making in the daily life of the family, as women have always enjoyed a special status among groups and families inside Nuristan. This is true to the extent that the social attributes and the social aspect of Nuristan's strength, when it came to families, was more matriarchal than patriarchal. Furthermore, women in Nuristan – especially the mother, the sister, and the wife – would always have a very equal role to play and would be listened to. Women were given due respect in the society. And, as mentioned, the singing and the music – the culture that defines the people of Nuristan – was there up until 2005. This marks the beginning of the third phase.

Changing times

There is a reason why I say 2005 and not 1996, which is when the Taliban first came to Afghanistan and took over the entire country. This is because basically the radical form – the extremist form of Islam – was repelled by the Nuristanis or always at least kept at a bay until 2005. That was the time when the American forces after coming into Afghanistan went into Nuristan and started building a base in Nuristan, and that is when the people took that event as an interference or transgression. So, 2005 was the time when things started going downwards – really downwards for the people of Nuristan as far as preserving or conserving their true identity or true culture is concerned.

Before the American forces started building their first bases inside Nuristan in 2005, we did not have insurgencies, we did not have terrorism and we did not have anything of that sort in Nuristan. But as soon as American forces came into Nuristan, the entire ordeal of armed forces coming into the territory that had been guarded by the Nuristanis for thousands of years, had a very negative impact on the minds of the people. So, what happened was basically a cataclysmic effect that all the tribespeople and anybody else inside Nuristan wanted to oppose. They started adopting and believing in a radical form of Islam as a means to fight off the international forces that had set up bases inside Nuristan.

And that was actually the beginning of the decline of Nuristani culture that we held so dear even after the introduction of Islam. It was there, it was very pronounced, it was very powerful. People used to enjoy celebrations; music and dancing was considered to be part of our culture; mingling freely between men and women was part of our culture; playing ice hockey was part of our culture; being open and hospitable was part of our culture. Sadly, after the influx of international forces, that culture began to slowly disappear.

Now most Nuristani people consider music to be bad. The people of Nuristan have abandoned singing and dancing and anything that gives the joy of living and is not just about surviving out there. Now, that part of the country is as isolated or perhaps more isolated – more difficult to get into and harder to get out of than it probably was in the 1880s or the nineties or any time during the twentieth century.

The Danish expeditions into Nuristan – and Lennart's in particular – were vital in documenting and describing our ancient culture. Thereby, they inspired other scholars to work in the not easily accessible mountains of the Hindukush. The expedition inspired the interests of other researchers and other scholars who came to Nuristan in the following years and talked about the Nuristani people. They revealed them to the world to give them credibility and to let the world know that such people also exist.

People like David Katz, Schuyler Jones, and Max Klimburg added publications to the works of Lennart, which is the most comprehensive work on Nuristan that I have come across. There have been other researchers on the Nuristanis and our languages. Although Nuristan is a very small area, it is distinct in the features and qualities that it presents to the world. We speak five different major languages. And in that small area there are fifteen to twenty different languages along with different dialects spoken. So, after the Danish expeditions, a lot of people took an interest in Nuristan.

Unfortunately, all that interest on a scholarly level could not translate into direct developments for the Nuristani people. Most of them are illiterate and do not have schools. Nor do they have proper medical clinics. Even today, we do not have hospitals or schools or roads – so life is still difficult for people in Nuristan. All of them are in survival mode. Probably if the people who were there up until the 1970s returned, they would recognize all the roads and houses. They would probably find the same stones that they left behind.

The one thing that really impresses me about the people of Nuristan is their resilience in the face of the changes that have come to Nuristan during the past many years. I previously divided Nuristani history into three eras; three periods of major change in Nuristan since the conversion of the people to Islam, the era before the 1890s. Not a lot was happening inside Nuristan, but people were still preserving their culture. People were living their lives and they knew how to. There was scarcely any interference from the outside world.

Today the government holds strong in Parun and Mormun, but those are about the only two places where the government holds strong. The other parts of Nuristan are basically under the control of local authorities and local people, which is not to say that insurgencies can really occur in parts of Nuristan, contrary to the way the media portrays it.

What has happened in the past several years is due to the indifference of the central government as far as the people of Nuristan are concerned. Basically, the government has been leaving them to live on their own. Even if the government did not do it officially, they have it in their hearts and in their minds that, if the people of Nuristan are to survive, they have to do things their way. So, at a time when Nuristan needs the central government the most, there is not a lot of expectation that the central government will come and build up Nuristan. The people of Nuristan have been resilient. They have opposed insurgencies in parts of Nuristan where there is no government, and they have not allowed either the Taliban or other forms of insurgencies to take hold and to take root.

We have never heard in the past fifteen or sixteen years of a revolt that was based in Nuristan, but they have often been triggered in other parts of Afghanistan. There have been no insurgence operations in Nuristan such as those in Kunar, in Laghman, in Jalalabad or, for that matter, in Kabul. This is evidence that the people of Nuristan, although they are not pro-insurgency, they are not expecting a lot from the government either. So, it has put them in a situation where they have to take matters into their own personal hands and survive. This, in turn, provides a very complicated and intricate situation.

The fact of the matter remains that from my personal experience – and I have been to Nuristan quite a few times in the last several years – I can say

I have never faced any fear or any danger when traveling into and out of Nuristan. The central government and the international community felt that it was the one part of Afghanistan where people feel alienated. For the past fourteen years, we have spent close to 130 billion dollars of foreign aid for construction, reconstruction, and reintegration work in Afghanistan. Sadly, we do not have one single meter of paved road inside Nuristan – let alone buildings or high-rises or anything like that.

So, that is why Nuristan is a complicated place to get into and a difficult place to work – even for local Afghans. This is not to say that the people of Nuristan have completely renounced any form of development, or that they are opposed to change. No! Truly, the people of Nuristan want governmental investment. They extend a helping hand wherever the government needs one, and they stand by the government and shout slogans. They cannot be enemies, as was claimed in one report.

So, the current situation in Nuristan is that of grievances basically toward the government. This is because the government – the central government of Afghanistan – has showed what may be termed a weak administration or management, and when the central government is weak its network only extends as far as the main cities. Nuristan, with its rugged terrain, is in the same situation as around 70 per cent of the provinces of Afghanistan. All of which are facing hard times.

Despite all this, the people of Nuristan are still hopeful. They stand with the government. They stand with the international community and people who come in. No harm is done to them and they are welcoming them as hospitably as they were in the fifties or the sixties or the seventies or even before that. And because of such great indifference on the part of the central government towards the Nuristan people they are left to survive as best they can. The people live in very difficult conditions. They have no money circulation, no industries inside Nuristan, no schools, no entrepreneurs, no businesses. Moreover, when the situation is so tense, it becomes really difficult for the local community to think of anything other than survival. So that is one of the reasons that the proud culture the people of Nuristan used to enjoy and took pride in just a few years ago is diminishing at an alarming rate. I remember, only a few decades ago, that we used to sit down together when I was a young boy. My aunt would gather all the children in her house, and she would start telling stories about Saifan Maluk and Saif Maluk – which is the exact story of Homer's *Iliad* or *Odyssey* in other words. And she would remember the story and she would tell the story with such clarity that people could imagine all those events. Now – one or two decades later – I cannot find a single person who knows that story and who could sit down and tell me about the trials and tribulations of Safar Maluk who set out on a journey and came back after twenty or twenty five years; and I have not been able to find anybody who knows that particular story except for my aunt who passed away a couple of years ago. So, as far as the culture and wellbeing of the people of Nuristan is concerned, the most important aspect is diminishing very fast and a lot of other cultures are finding their way into the public culture in Nuristan – even into the language itself. Many people in Nuristan now prefer Dari and Pashtu to their local language. Many children are brought up with their parents speaking to them in Dari and Pashtu. Parents believe that, to succeed in life, their child needs to know the other languages of Afghanistan rather than Nuristani; moreover, they are planning for him to leave Nuristan when he finishes his primary education in Nuristan to go somewhere else.

Such pressures are affecting the traditional culture, the language, and the people to a great extent. And it is proving very difficult to preserve such things – even though there are people who are trying to preserve their culture. There are lots of people inside Nuristan who want to preserve their traditional culture. They do not want to belong to other ethnicities. We speak a certain language and we want to continue with that language. We want to be Nuristani, we want to be known as Nuristanis, although even within the Nuristani branch we have got a lot of different languages. We have five or six major languages and those languages are mutually unintelligible. In the valleys, one may only be a twenty minutes' walk away, and one will have to communicate with the people from the next village in a third language, which most probably would be Dari or Pashtu. Otherwise you could not understand each other. The culture would be different; the feasting manners would be different; the feasting culture would be different; the marriage ceremonies would be different; the dowry rules would be different, and so on. So, it is a part of the world that has, unfortunately, not been paid any attention for many years except by the expeditions that have come. The only thing that I can see in retrospect is from the scholars. These are the individuals who took the initiative to come over to that forgotten and forsaken part of the world and then to tell people who we are and how we have been and what we do. Apart from that, no government has ever been interested in developing that area. We lack education. We lack infrastructure. We lack everything. This is one of the major reasons – and probably if you ask me, the only reason – why a part of our society has even thought of joining the insurgencies since they offers them better incentives than the government. So the situation is dire, but one that in no way is really hopeless. If proper measures are taken within a very short span of time, we could move in different directions. We could make inroads into the current dire situation and change it for the benefit of the people. We could set up education. We could do something about the preservation of the culture, the language, the legacy of the Nuristani people, and we could stop this ancient and very proud culture from completely vanishing, completely disappearing.

An important way to deal with the problems that the Nuristanis and our culture is facing, is to re-establish connections which have been lost for many years – like the connections with scholars such as Lennart and Schuyler Jones. We could re-establish Nuristan as a nation and as a place, which is full of so many amazing things, the nature of the people, and the strength of resilience that they have. It is commendable that the people of Nuristan and the Kafirs of the past have expressed the wish in so many thousand years to preserve and serve their culture and language.

I am saying this now because as a Nuristani I can very easily see how resilient these people are and how sincere they are towards change. Sadly, circumstances have not been favourable in that conditions have not been conducive for the Nuristani people to develop into the society that they could have made. Finally, I would like to say that the research that Lennart and Schuyler Jones undertook in Nuristan in the early sixties and the seventies became a monument in the book that I have that was written by them. Lennart and Schuyler Jones's book is easily the highest and most comprehensive authority on Nuristan and the way of life inside Nuristan. I have always wanted to meet and sit down with all the individuals, every single person who has shown immense courage in the past when times were better to come to Nuristan and stay with the people of Nuristan and learn their culture and show their culture to the peoples of the world outside. I admire them all for the work that they have done. I thank them on behalf of my people and on behalf of all Nuristan for the work that they have done.

I salute them for their effort. But for now, there is still a lot of work to be done. if we want to save the culture that is vanishing – that is being destroyed right now. And that is not possible without sincere people such as you – such as all those people who have given due importance in one way or another to this region.

Lennart recording a singer from Waigal.

2. Choir music and polyphony in Nuristan

By Christer Irgens-Møller

Lennart Edelberg was a botanist and geographer by training. In addition to these topics, he carried out meticulous investigations in meteorology, calendar systems, and pagan mythology. Architecture and building construction became his main research interests. Music documentation was thus a small corner of his immense field of investigation. However, the mission to Nuristan was in honor of Henning Haslund-Christensen, for whom the recording of music became a new and indispensable endeavour in the aim to investigate all aspects of unexplored cultures. Thus, it was also essential that Lennart and Klaus Ferdinand were supplied with a technical wonder of those days: a brand new reel-to-reel chargeable tape recorder with a maximum recording duration of five minutes. Recordings were augmented with extensive photo documentation and even motion picture film footage, which was in the hands of photographer Peter Rasmussen. Thus, field recordings of music were obtained thanks to these technological advances.

Accordingly, the music documentation obtained in Nuristan was conducted meticulously like all his work in general. Lennart had a natural talent for listening and a good ear for picking up melodies. He noted down a selection of song texts for later elaboration by the Norwegian linguist Georg Morgenstierne.

Lennart's field notes contain typology and drawings of the instruments; he includes information and indigenous names of the parts as well as local varieties of names of the instruments. Morgenstierne also assisted with these matters. The tuning of the stringed instruments and the individual notes of the flutes were recorded with great care. Furthermore, Lennart also gathered information on the indigenous names of the different voice parts in the choral music.

These working methods proved to be crucial for my investigation of the collection, even though more song texts would have been desirable. In addition, more information about the musical context would have been useful, let alone data about the musicians and singers who were recorded.

The limitation of five minutes per tape presents other challenges. On the 1953 recordings, Klaus and Lennart often made comments on tape during the recording sessions, drowning out the music itself. In some longer sessions, they have paused the tape recorder, which in some cases results in audio bites that break into the periods of the music. They may have done this due to the limited duration of the individual tapes and anxiety about having enough tape in general. Perhaps like a photographer's approach as to give an audible impression in musical 'snap-shots'. This practice is disruptive when one attempts a musical analysis – particularly when a recording has been terminated in the middle of a song or actually breaks into the progress of a flute line.

On the 1964 and 1970 expeditions, recording was in the hands of Lennart's wife, Margot Edelberg. This time, they brought along a newer tape recorder that made longer recordings possible; in spite of this advantage, these sessions lack ethnographic information and are merely supplied with raw data such as date and location. Despite these drawbacks, Margot Edelberg's recordings include extraordinary situations such as a Waigali female choir and a recording of children singing in a school – situations which are entirely absent in the 1953 recordings.

These factors aside, the mere existence of these later recordings proves that the musical traditions of Nuristan persisted – in spite of a renewed influx of Muslim missionaries during the sixties.[1]

The collection

Lennart's documentation consists of 220 recordings in all; the majority stemming from 1953-54. The tours of 1964 and 1970 are comparably less well documented.

Geographically, the coverage comprises the valleys of Waigal, Parun, Ashkun and Bashgal. The Ashkun valley is documented in two villages, Wama and Kurder, and in 1953 only.

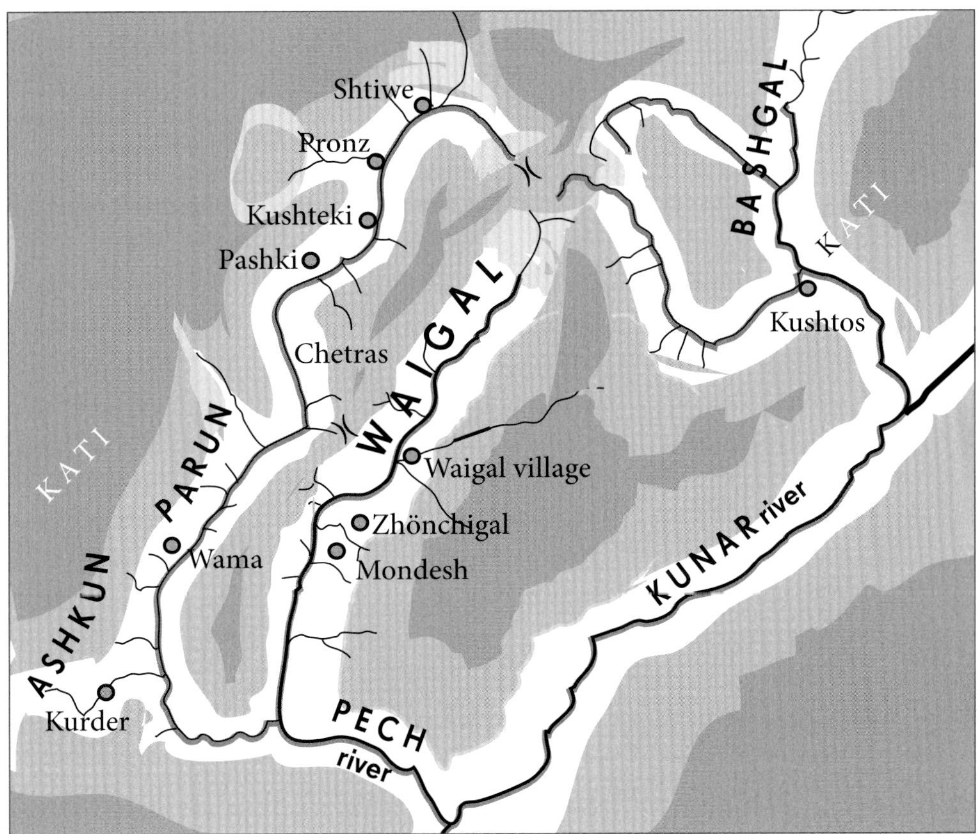

Map of Nuristan by the author.

The Bashgal Valley is solely represented by the village of Kushtos. Its neighbouring village, Kamdesh in the Bashgal Valley, has been documented by Austrian ethnologists[2] and confirms that the music of this village is clearly related to the style of Kushtos. Apparently, there was a pronounced hostility between the two villages, which ultimately led to a war in 1996 during which Kushtos was burned to the ground and devastated.[3]

In the present account, focus is on the choir music of the Waigal and Parun Valleys as well as Kushtos in the Bashgal Valley. Common features are described, accompanied by a number of examples displayed as graphics and as note examples.[4]

In the following, common characteristics for the entire documentation are condensed, and diversities are established.

Common characteristics

Above all, choral singing and dance music are common features. The number
of recordings alone proves that singing (and dancing) were a recurring part
of gatherings in the community. Although song texts with a religious content
had been abandoned because of the Islamic conversion, the musical traditions persisted, broadly.

The extensive number of recordings of choral music proves that singing
was a recurring event and served as a vehicle for confirming the social ties
of the community. Dances were performed to singing assemblies, and flutes
and drums were played for dances reviving war and homecoming events. The
Waigali term *nâd* translates as a song, a musical piece *and* a dance, proving
the unity of these activities.

Generally, vocal music is predominant in the three valleys. The polyphonic songs of Waigal are abundantly represented and comprise a marked
characteristic. In Parun, call-response songs appear, along with choir songs
in smaller groups, as call-response songs. Songs in unison (included in the
term monophonic) also occur. In Kushtos in the Nechingal Valley songs in
unison prevail. Particular melodic qualities make the Kushtos singing easily
recognizable.

Rhythm accompanying songs along with clapping is a common feature,
underlining the frequency of dance gatherings. It is notable that drum, percussion, and clapping accompaniments are employed everywhere; notable also
is the frequent participation of flutes – in Waigal and Parun in duos and in
Kushtos as solo flute. Flutes are end-blown like the Arabian *ney*. The Waigali
and Paruni flutes have two holes, and the Kushtos solo flute has five holes.

Diversities

In the music of Waigal valley, the individual parts are frequently organized in
pairs: two lead vocals on top of the choirs, two drums and two flute players
for the dances, the harp (*wadzh*) and fiddle (*saringi*) as an obbligato pair of
instruments.

All vocal and instrumental pairs supplement each other with intertwined
melodic and / or rhythmic patterns, often in a complementarity. The wadzh
and saringi mutually support these rhythmic-melodic patterns. For the flute
pairs, the leading melodic motif is supplemented by a varied motif, or supplied
with a complementary line.

Two flute players, and drummers on dâd and timki. Photo: Klaus Ferdinand.

In Waigali choral music the prevailing rhythm is based on a division of three. The individual phrase takes up three bars and the subdivision of a single bar is in three beats, underlined by the drum and clapping.

In the dance music, drum patterns appear in binary rhythm (2 or 4), performed by the *dâb,* a large frame drum, with a subdivision in three delivered by the small drum, the *timki.*[5]

It is remarkable that on a majority of the recordings of duos of *wadzh* and *saringi,* the main division is in (a fast) 7. Still, this rhythm can be perceived as a division of three. The predilection for the 7 division is related to its frequent use in the music of Afghanistan as a whole.

In Parun, in the vocal music, complementarity appears in duos or smaller groups. It may be a rhythmic chant performed by two groups or even just as a duo, where the pause of the leading line is filled by a short motif so the result is an unbroken melodic flow. This appears in several recordings from Pronz, 1953.

Wadzh and saringi players in Waigal village6. Photo: Peter Rasmussen.

In Kushtos, choral singing is performed in unison. The accompaniment is performed on one frame drum – the *bambuk*. Clapping is often employed along with intonation on a single note from the assembly. Pieces with drum and five-hole flute are also represented.

The Waigali polyphonic song

Lennart describes the songs as:

> …songs or verses sung to music, frequently in the form of a prayer or a hymn to pre-Muslim deities. Today [1953] such songs are known only to a few of the older men. Many popular songs now are concerned with the deeds of a hero/ancestor, or with a particular event in the life of such a figure. Some others are love songs, and in addition, there are songs sung by shepherds when herding their animals or churning milk.[7]

Lennart considers songs to be part of the oral traditions.

Songs for gatherings and dancing were sung chorally, and by everybody present, most often accompanied by a drum – *dâd*. Often, a *wadzh* (harp) and also presumably a *saringi* (fiddle) was played as accompaniment. Polyphony is predominant, led by one or two singers, with the assembly chanting rhythmically. It is still practiced in Waigal as shown in a video from 2009.[8]

The Waigali polyphonic song figures in 63 out of 106 musical recordings from Waigal valley. Apart from a few variants, which are accounted for below, the lead singers' lines are identical. Additionally, this type of song is documented with women singing (2 recordings), and a learning situation with children (3 recordings). As such it is the quintessential song and may be designated the *standard* choir song. Basically it is organized as a *call-response* song.

Musically described, the song is built up the same way in every case. The lead singer sings the characteristic melodic phrase, which is mirrored immediately by a second singer – the *support* singer – who, in turn repeats this initial phrase. In the pause, the lead singer begins a new phrase, starting out a second above the support singer's tonic and in the continuation of his phrase overlaps the support singer.

Graphically, the two voices can be displayed:

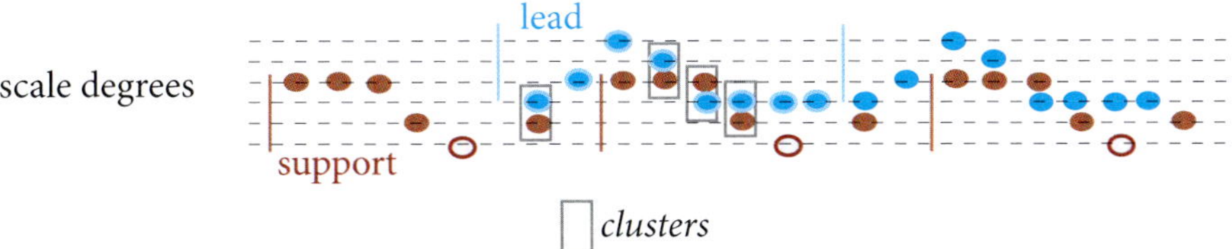

Graphic model of the melodic outline of the two lead voices. Note that the lines are scale degrees.

After a number of repeats (5-6) the choir joins in, following the rhythm and phrasing of the support singer's phrase, and simultaneously the drummer joins with a two-beat figure.

The choir often sings rhythmically on a single note, some following the basic note of the lead singer, some following the first note of the support singer. This results in a chant with a number of second clashes within the sound of the choir and between the individual singers' lines (clusters). Some singers even chant as if they speak their lines.

Polyphonic song, Kamale kimile, recorded in Mondesh 1953. Music example 1.

The beat is based on three divisions of a bar. Within the bar, the single beat is subdivided in three, clarified and supported by the drumbeat falling on beats three and one of this subdivision. The choir often adds a clap on the third beat of the subdivision, thus filling out the pauses of their phrase.

The text which is derived from the field notes follows:

1 *Kamalek* (the king) – spoke quietly with me and my father.

2 *Kolum Sunera* ("valley of the world") with you, myself, my father – spoke Persian.

1 All the world – earthquake, father fight.

2 Kalash (= king?) came to see *mija* ("When a *pache* gives his daughter to a man, their son again becomes a mija").[9]

Men singing; in the background a drum player.

As mentioned, about two thirds of the songs are this *standard* song. The remaining polyphonic songs are musically based on the same formal pattern; however, they are varied in respect to the two main melodic phrases of the lead and support singer.

'Oh Poethre'

Another kind of polyphony is discussed in the following song, *O Poethre*. Again, the harmonic concept is characterized by clusters, but here, the choir chant is a fixed note thus resulting in a more 'clean' harmonic output.

"O Poethre" – polyphonic song from Zhönchigal 1964. Music example 2.

Abdul Wahid's transcribes the following vocals as 'oe' / 'ou' = *fr* [y] as in Yves, 'ae' = [ə], ee [i] as in fill, oo [u] as in full, sh [j] as in you.

This song was accompanied by a *wadzh* and sung by three or four men who are familiar with the words as follows:

OH POETHRE OH MEER AZAR OH

1   Oh my son, Oh Meer Azar oh, coming successfully after the fight, after taking his revenge.

2   Quickly, he is playing / dancing like horse playing in pasture, like thunder, he acts quickly.

4   You came from the pasture of Laegal, You came from the pasture of Asheedle.

Verses 3, 5, 8 = verse 1; verses 7 and 9 = verse 2. The text is a tribute to a war hero who has returned from a raid. In verse 2, his riding, strength, and speed are praised. In verse 4, his return path is specified.[10]

The song is introduced by a small rocking two-note pattern by the *wadzh* that continues as accompaniment for the song. The lead singer follows a melody that is spun around a fixed chanting note from the choir.

Parun

The documentation of vocal choir music from Parun is limited in comparison with that of Waigal.[11]

The selected song is extraordinary in several respects. It was recorded in a night camp in the Chetras area between Pashki and Wama. The participants were the porters. In this session, the men also sang the greeting song "Daliwakum" known from a prior recording made in Pronz.

The song in question lacks both text and title. It has been performed in a longer session and the recording was paused several times. Moreover, there are interruptions in the music such as spoken comments by Ferdinand and use of the tuning reed. (Employment of the tuning reed was a prompt to be able to check whether the tape speed was correct in playback.)

The song is polyphonic in a setting of four parts: two choirs, flutes, and percussion. This setting is of a quite different nature when compared to the Waigali vocal polyphony. The parts are not intertwined but are virtually independent voices applied to the basic rhythm.

As such, it has somewhat of a 'symphonic' setting: the vocals are organized in two groups: a call-response choir and a duo singing a two-voice rhythmic chant. According to a comment made by Ferdinand on tape, the lead singer is also performing the percussion rhythm ("de-ge-dek") – a stick striking a piece of wood. The audible output of the two flutes are inseparable resulting in a continuous melody. The two flute players adhere to a recurring motif with minor variations. The length of the motif is longer than the 4-bar period of the song resulting in a continuous rhythmic displacement.

In the display below the call-response choir is noted in the top line.

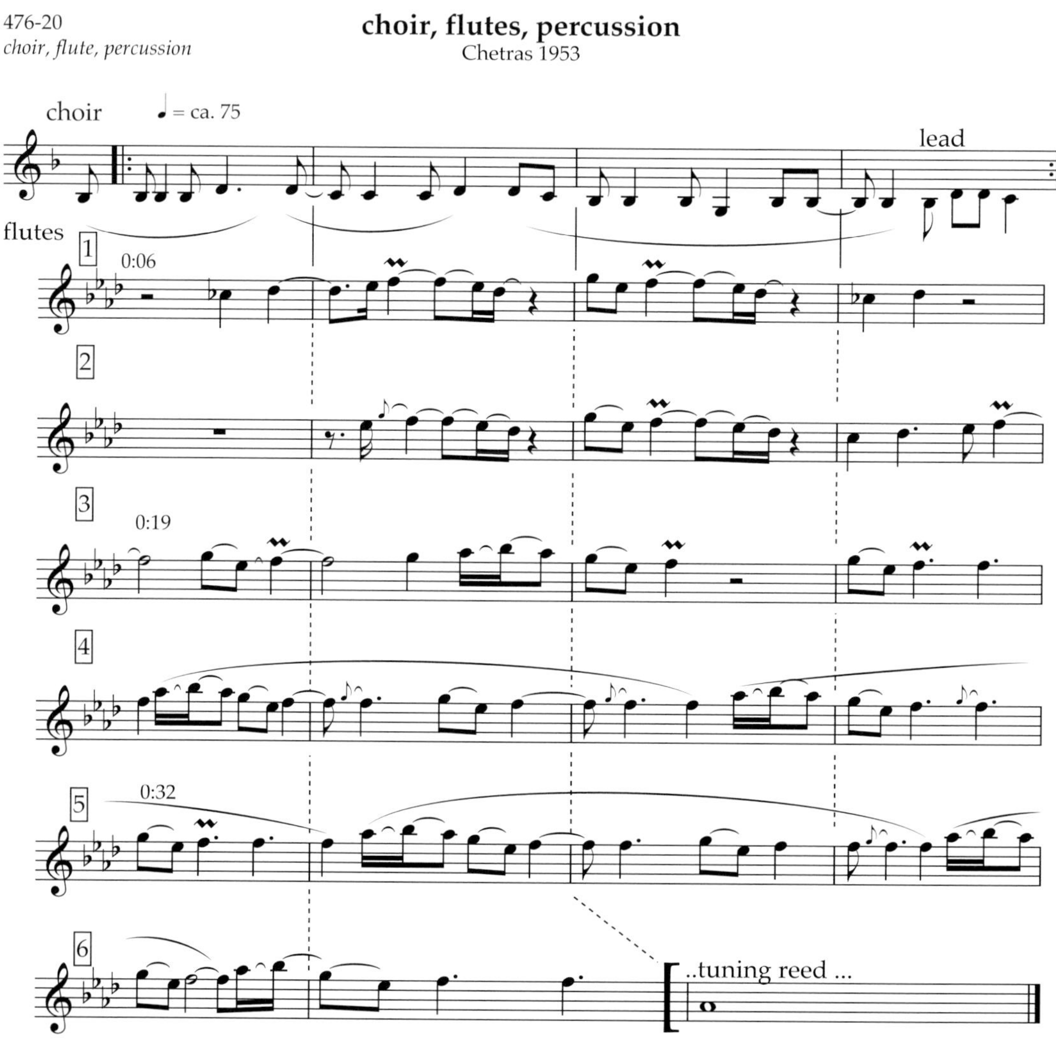

Polyphonic song arrangement with flutes and percussion in a night camp in Chetras, Oct. 1953. Music example 3.

The rhythmic chant at the end of the recording is transcribed as:

476-20
voices in rhythmic chant

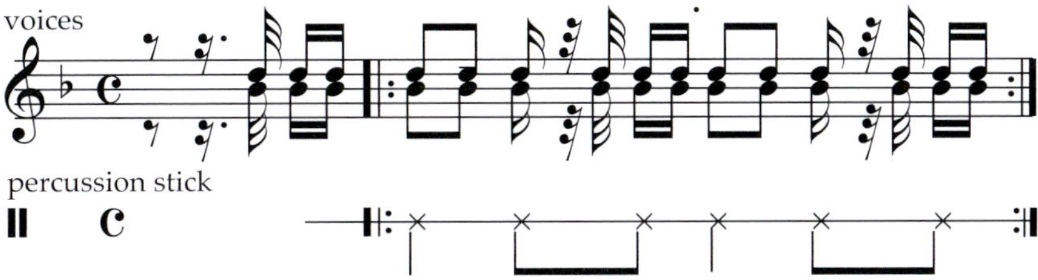

An extraordinary instrument, the *urba*, was encountered in several villages in Parun and twenty-three recordings with four different players were collected. This rather comprehensive documentation is accounted for in this author's book[12] and is not discussed in detail in the present context.

Urba, a 4-string lute used in Parun and played with a pick. Photo: Peter Rasmussen.

Dancer in Kushtos, 1953. To his right the five-hole flute player. The assembly claps – the drum is not visible in the photo. Photo: Peter Rasmussen.

Kushtos

This village played an important role for the three expeditions in Nuristan. During the initial mission, it was entered from Waigal valley through a mountain pass. Waigal valley and its villages had been investigated one by one with an exit in the south following the Pech river. Kushtos became the transit point to Parun valley which could be reached from the north by the mountain pass Kunjanida. Lennart's friendship with Abdullah Wakil (1897-1972)[13] the leading elder – the *mäläk* – was crucial for his future connections with Nuristan. During the 1950s, Wakil became a member of the parliament in Kabul as the representative for the Kunar region – Eastern Nuristan. He was himself a singer and composed his own songs. He was invited to Aarhus when Moesgaard Museum was launched in 1970. In 1964, Kushtos was the point of departure upon leaving, and in 1970, the first village visited on that occasion.

The documentation of the music from Kushtos in 1953 and 1964 is comprehensive, with twenty-five and thirty-five recordings respectively, while only one song was recorded in 1970.

A monophonic funeral song appears in Lennart's film *In the Land of the Pagans*.[14]

In the following, a typical dance song will be discussed.

Often dance sessions start out with the assembled choir singing a long held unison tone to the drum accompaniment, frequently in the rhythmic meter of 6 / 8. At certain points during the performance this choir's long held note recurs. All along, whistling and yelling in falsetto are vividly expressed, probably to encourage the dancers. All the participants are men.

Satar, a 4-string lute, appears in recordings from Bashgal and Parun.

A typical song, which was recorded in several versions, consists of an easy to pick up melody, where every second verse is sung on the vocales "na-na-na", giving an opportunity to sing along without knowing the text.

The melody consists of four song lines, where the first and third are repeated according to melody. The first repeated line has two similar phrases to an identical set of rhythms, and the third repeated line continues the rhythm of the initial melody; while the contour is constantly descending, ending up by repeating notes an octave below the starting note.

The drum is played on all four beats.

Kushtos 1953, popular dance song. Music example 4.

The ending of the song line is a recurring phenomenon in a number of songs (marked in blue in the example above). Although drum accompaniment is ever present, often a five-hole flute appears, and in some cases a *satar*.[15]

A satar was brought back to Aarhus for the museum and is currently still in the Moesgaard ethnographic collections.

Notes

1. Klimburg 1999, 58.

2. Musik aus Nuristan. Musique de la zone interdite du Nuristan. See references.

3. Strand about the war Kamdesh-Kushtos: "Flow from highland water resources, including winter snowpack and monsoonal rainfall, has decreased over the last 40 years. Forests have suffered moderate dieback from lack of water. In the LanDay Sin Valley the communities of Kombrom (Kamdesh) and KShtorm (Kushtoz) went to war over water resources in 1998, resulting in the destruction of KShtorm and the dispersal of the KShto people." http://www.mei.edu/content/social-change-eastern-nuristan. Middle East Institute, April 23, 2012 (On-line Journal).

4. The music to for the examples is accessible at the homepage of the author. [http://christerirgensmoller.dk/21_nuristan/polyphonic_choir.html

5. In the Edelberg film *Kafiristan – hedningernes land* (*Kafiristan – land of the pagans*) on Moesgaard's web page in the Afghanistan section (http://www.moesmus-afghanistan.dk/?p=998), and on YouTube (https://www.youtube.com/watch?v=metEbNdmovA&feature=youtu.b) Drums and dancing appears at :(links to the exact time of appearance): first excerpt at 34:00. http://www.youtube.com/watch?v=metEbNdmovA&t=34m0s, second 35:12. http://www.youtube.com/watch?v=metEbNdmovA&t=35m12s, third at 43:00. http://www.youtube.com/watch?v=metEbNdmovA&t=43m0s

6. [Editor's note: the man on the right is Amir Shah from Berimdesh. He was a famous maker of musical instruments and made a *saringi* now in the Pitt Rivers Museum, Oxford. See p. 87 in *Nuristan* by Edelberg and Jones].

7. Edelberg 1979, 120.

8. The full video appears at the web address accessible at: https://docs.google.com/file/d/0BwsuV_bMv582VUtFQXlVNnpoRzA/edit. The link has been delivered by Abdul Wahid Nuristani (see footnote 9).

9. Edelberg's field notes designated "Maihak."

10. The songtext of the song was transcribed and translated in 2016 by my personal contact, Abdul Wahid Nuristani, who is a junior economist in the Ministry of Aagriculture in Kabul.

11. In the introduction to the Edelberg film (see fn v), a Paruni song appears. This song is a call-response song by a group of men repeating the names of a number of pastures.

12. Irgens-Møller 2009, 182.

13. See the webpage of Mas Rogers: http://www.innerself.com.au/archive/articles/sa/sa003/asa003-immortality_light.html).

14. At 35:53 this song (473-08) appears. Direct link: http://www.youtube.com/watch?v=metEbNdmovA&t=35m53s.

15. This instrument is still a common Kalash accompaniment instrument. In an introduction to recording 473-13, Ferdinand announces that he was told that the instrument originated in Kashgar (in Xingjiang). According to local perceptions, this means
Chitral – the home of the Kalash, north of Nuristan, and closely related in regard to
population and culture. The satar appears on a CD from 1999 "Musiques Kalash –
Songs of The Hindukush.Musique Kalash" (see reference, five pieces with the instrument are accessible in half-minute samples on: (http://www.allmusic.com/album/paki-
stan-sounds-of-the-hindu-kush-mw0000052129.)). Also, on this album, the first track
contains dance music with the same character as that of the Kushtos documentation.

List of references

The music recordings are supplied with catalogue numbers with the acronym EAL (Edelberg Arkiv Lyd), Edelberg Sound Archive. The photos, has have EAF (Edelberg Photo
Archive) as a reference.

Alvad, Thomas in collaboration with Lennart Edelberg (1953) "The Nuristân harp". *Afghanistan* (Kabul), 8, no 3: pp. 34-44.

Alvad, Thomas (1954) "The Kafir Harp." In: *MAN – A monthly Record of Anthropological
Science*: pp. 151-154.

Alvad, Thomas (1979) "Die Musik Nuristans." In: *Nuristan*, Lennart Edelberg and Schuyler
& Jones: pp. 141-147. Akademische Druck- u. Verlagsanstalt: Graz.

Baily, John (2001) "Afghanistan." *In: The New Grove Dictionary of Music and Musicians*,
p. 189. The New Grove Dictionary 2nd edition: London.

Castenfeldt, Svend (1999) "Bjergfolk i Hindukush og på Moesgaard." In: *Menneskelivets
mangfoldighed. Arkæologisk og antropologisk forskning på Moesgaard*, edited by Ole
Høiris, Hans Jørgen Madsen, Torsten Madsen og Jens Vellev. Højbjerg: Moesgaard
Museum: pp. 47-54.

Edelberg, Lennart (1949) EA 375. *Dagbog III. Afghanistan* (July 29-30): pp. 37-49.

Edelberg, Lennart (1953-55) *Etnografisk feltarbejde. Afghanistan, spec. Nuristan.* Fra
Lennart Edelbergs dag- og notesbøger: VII. Nuristan: pp. 16-17.

Edelberg, Lennart (1956) "Fra Kafirhytte til Ildtempel." In: *Næsgaardsbogen.*

Edelberg, Lennart and Lis Gramstrup (1971) *Index to Sir George Scott Robertson The Kafirs
of the Hindu-Kush. London 1896 and 1900. With a map by Lennart Edelberg.* Jutland
Archeological Society: Højbjerg (59 pages).

Edelberg, Lennart (1972) "Some Paruni Myths and Hymns." In: *Acta Orientalia*, 34: pp.
31-87.

Edelberg, Lennart & Schuyler Jones (1979) *Nuristan.* Akademische Druck- u. Verlagsanstalt: Graz.

Edelberg, Margot (2004) Interviews. Unpublished. Moesgaard Museum archives.

Irgens-Møller, Christer (2005) "Remnants of an eradicated culture." In: *The DSCA journal*,
no 2. (Oct 2005). Web based periodical on dsca.dk (Danish Society for Central Asia).

Irgens-Møller, Christer (2009) *Music in Nuristan.* Jutland Archaeological Society: Højbjerg.

Jettmar, Karl (1974) *Cultures of the Hindu-Kush. Selected papers from the Hindu-Kush
cultural conference held at Moesgaard 1970.* Edited by Karl Jettmar in collaboration with
Lennart Edelberg. Franz Steiner Verlag: Wiesbaden.

Klimburg, Max (1966) *Afghanistan. Das Land im historischen Spannungsfeld Mittelasiens.* Österreichischer Bundesverlag für Unterricht, Wissenschaft und Kunst: Wien und München.

Klimburg, Max (1999) *The Kafirs of the Hindukush. Art and Ssociety of the Waigal and Ashkun Kafirs. Vol. I-II.* Franz Steiner Verlag: Stuttgart.

Morgenstierne, Georg (1951) "Some Kati Myths and Hymns." In: *Acta Orientalia Vol. 21:* pp. 161-189.

Morgenstierne, Georg (1967a) *"Some Folk-songs from Nuristan."* In: *To honor Roman Jakobson* , Vol. 2: pp. 1378-1392. De GruyterMouton: The Hague and Paris.

Morgenstierne, Georg (1967b) "The Languages of Afghanistan." In: *Afghanistan: Historical and Cultural Quarterly XX:* pp. 81-90.

Morgenstierne, Georg (2005) Website http://www.nb.no/baser/morgenstierne

Robertson, George Scott (1896) *The Káfirs of the Hindu-Kush.* Lawrence & Bullen: London.

Strand, Richard (1997-2015) Richard Strand's Nuristan site. http://nuristan.info

Strand, Richard (2012) Middle East Institute, April 23. (Online-line Journal) http://www.mei.edu/content/social-change-eastern-nuristan.

Recordings

Musik aus Afghanistan. Nuristan (1968)

Recorded by H.M. Gressl. Adevaphon. Akademische druck u. Verlagsanstalt. Graz 1976. Recordings and liner notes by. H.M. Gressl, Hochschule für Musik und darstellende Kunst.

Locations: Kamdesh. Waigal, Wama. Includes: dance music, polyphonic choirs, wadzh solo, men's song in collective improvisation, plus women's choir in the polyphonic style,. Additionally, a men's song from Wama.

Musique de la zone interdite du Nuristan (1968)

Recorded by Yves Sommavilla in co-operation with Francois Denis. Barclay 920 086.

Location: Wamdesh. Includes: two dance sessions with clapping, shouting, whistling, drums and flute. Plus one choir song with drum and clapping; according to the liner notes, the song.

Chants et musiques de Pakistan et Afghanistan (Kafiristan, Nuristan, Chitral) (1998)

Albatros B00004VFCS (not available).

Eight tracks are recordings taken at Waigal; of these, three are the polyphonic standard, two with flutes and drums, one with wadzh solo and one is a "proki wadzh alol.". The two remaining tracks are presumably Kalash-recordings.

(Can be heard in half-minute samples are available on http://www.alapage. com/-Fiche/Musiques/385653/CD/chants-et-musiques-de-pakistan-et-afghanistan).

Pakistan: Musiques Kalash – Songs Of The Hindu-Kush. (1999)

Recorded by Thomas Vater. PLAYA SOUND PS 65221.

Includes five pieces with satar, either solo or as accompaniment for singing. One of these (track 2) bears an affinity to the documentation from Kushtos. One track (5) is a song of the elders – slow with long notes.

3. The languages of Edelberg's Nuristan and environs

By Peter Bakker, Kristoffer Friis Bøegh
& Yonatan Ungermann Goldshtein

Introduction

This study was inspired by Lennart Edelberg's research results in Nuristan. In 1970, he co-organized a conference on the cultures of the Hindukush held at Moesgaard, Aarhus. The grand old man of Nuristani language studies, Georg Morgenstierne, attended the conference, where he presented his ideas on the history and development of the languages of Nuristan (published as Morgenstierne 1974). In 2016, a conference was devoted to the life and work of Lennart Edelberg, again at Moesgaard, and this conference inspired us to reconsider the question of the phylogenetic position of the Nuristani languages.

A direct source of inspiration was also to find an answer to the question of the connection between the Kalashamon language as spoken in Chitral, Pakistan, with the small group of Nuristani languages spoken on the other side of the border in Afghanistan. One of these Nuristani languages in Afghanistan is also called *Kalaṣa-alâ* (or *Waigali* or *Wai-alâ*) and the similarity of the language names does not appear to be accidental. Also building terminology from Nuristan, as found in Edelberg's (1984) book on Nuristani buildings, is very similar to that used in Kalashamon (Taj Khan Kalash, personal communication); moreover, pre-Islamic topographic terms in certain regions of Nuristan are rather similar to those found in the Kalasha valleys in Pakistan. Such links, possibly the result of hitherto unreported contact, may cast new light on the histories of the languages and peoples of Nuristan and its environs. In evaluating potential linguistic connections – be they genealogical or contact-induced – we take an analysis of linguistic data as our point of departure.

In the following, we first provide an overview, based on available literature, of the languages of Nuristan as well as neighboring regions from geographical and linguistic points of view. We then summarize earlier proposals as to their internal and external classification, providing the reader with the background information needed to evaluate the relevance of our own comparative work. Next, based on different lexical data sets (words), we present our two comparative studies of the languages of Nuristan, the Dardic languages, and some other Indo-Iranian languages spoken in Southeastern Afghanistan, North India, and North Pakistan. For these analyses, we make use of software developed for visualizing evolutionary patterns as well as other similarities in biological species, or other entities subject to change through descent with modification (e.g., languages). Such phylogenetic algorithms have been utilized successfully in historical-comparative linguistics, since the first decade of the twenty-first century (see Bowern & Evans 2015). The specific techniques applied in the present study have previously been used for the internal classification of the languages of Chitral in North Pakistan (Bakker & Daval-Markussen 2016). Finally, we discuss some grammatical peculiarities of the Nuristani languages, before concluding the study.

Nuristan and its languages

Nuristan is a geographical term that refers to a province of Afghanistan. The Nuristan region is indicated on Map 1. Several but not all of the languages spoken in that province are labeled as Nuristani languages. Nuristani languages have been suggested to be a special subgroup of languages since Morgenstierne (1932) and more recently on the basis of a more extensive database – especially as argued by Strand (1973). Their arguments are mostly based on sound changes and differences with Indic and Iranian languages.

The Indo-European (I-E) language family comprises a large set of some 450 languages. It can be proven that these languages are historically related in that they all go back to one original language spoken six to ten millennia ago somewhere in Central Eurasia. The following main branches are usually distinguished: Romance / Italic, Germanic, Balto-Slavic, and Indo-Iranian (I-I). The languages of Nuristan and the adjacent areas of Chitral in Pakistan all belong to the I-I branch of I-E. Specialists distinguish between two and four branches of I-I: all agree about Indic and Iranian, but some also distin-

Map 1. Afghanistan with Nuristan highlighted in red. (Source: Wikimedia Commons).

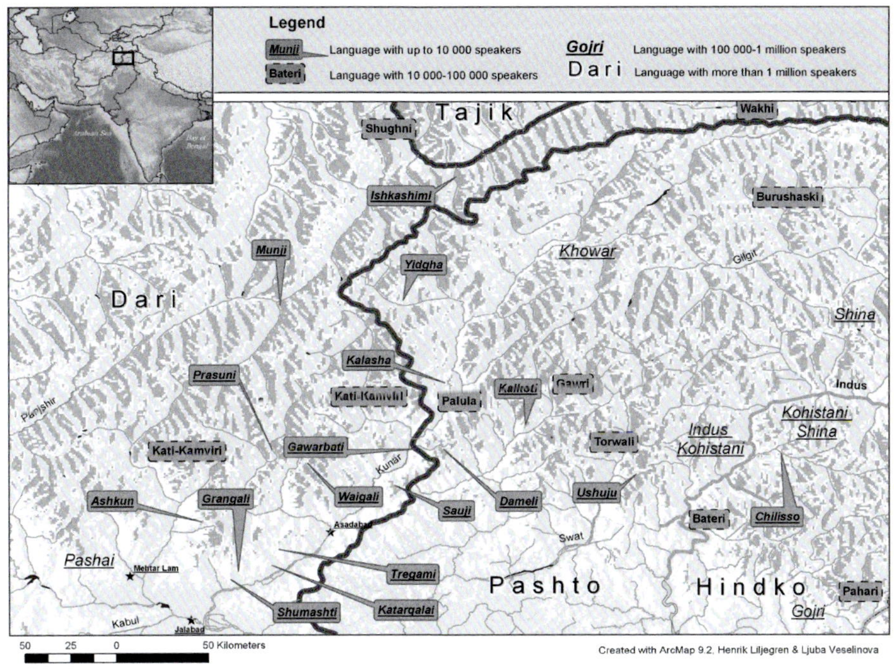

Map 2. Languages of the Hindukush region (from Liljegren 2016, 14).

guish a Dardic group and some also a Nuristani group. Our focus is on the Nuristani group.

Usually, some five or six languages are considered to be part of the Nuristani group. The names (labels) for the languages, however, are quite different from author to author.

Map 2 (from Liljegren 2016, 14) shows the relevant region with its languages, including not only the Nuristan region in Afghanistan but also the adjacent region of Pakistan. From north to south, the five Nuristani languages indicated on the map are: Prasuni, Kati-Kamviri, Waigali, Ashkun, and Tregami.

Earlier proposals for the classification of Nuristani languages

Linguistic classification

A number of earlier classifications of Nuristani languages have been made. The languages were first suggested to be a distinct subgroup by Morgenstierne (1932) on the basis of his fieldwork. There have been several proposals with regard to the position of the Nuristani and Dardic languages within the I-I branch of I-E. Morgenstierne (1961) was perhaps the first to propose that the Nuristani languages were a separate branch that was on a par with Indic and Iranian. The oldest overall classification of the languages is probably Grierson (1906), and many subsequent classifications were based on it. It is, however, now universally rejected. Since the 1970s, scholars such as Fussman (1972), Morgenstierne (1973), Strand (1973, 2016), and Edelman (1983, 1999) have proposed classifications. The most recent sources seem to accept six different Nuristani languages. An exception is Strand (2016), who distinguishes five languages: he considers Prasun and Kati-Kamviri as dialects of the same language. We now proceed to the classification of the Nuristani languages within I-I.

Morgenstierne's observations are almost exclusively based on the lexicon and especially on sound changes. Since the split between Old Indic and Old Iranian, "… the Kafir [Nuristani] languages have suffered such loss of final syllables, so that the possibility of showing old differences is very slight" (Morgenstierne 1973, 332, our translation). There are, he argues, no features distinguishing Dardic, as a whole, from the rest of the I-I languages. Dardic, then, is simply a convenient term to denote aberrant I-I hill languages. On the basis of the archaisms in Nuristani languages, Morgenstierne states that "we must regard the Kafir [Nuristani languages] as the remnant of a particular branch of [I-I], as much as it has been superimposed on Indian elements" (Morgenstierne 1973, 338, our translation).

Glottolog (Hammarström et al. 2017) classifies Nuristani languages as a separate subbranch of the I-I branch of I-E. Thus, I-I is split into three branches: the two large branches, Indo-Aryan (218 languages) and Iranian (94 languages), and one small branch of six Nuristani languages. The Dardic languages are not listed as a subgroup at this level.

In the Automated Similarity Judgment Program (ASJP) project, which is an automatic language classification on the basis of a forty-item wordlist and an algorithm to measure similarities between languages, the Dardic languages appear as a separate subgroup together with Nuristani languages.

Hock (2016a, 13-14) has recently summarized the question from the standpoint of an historical linguist. He offers three arguments for Nuristani languages being a separate branch of I-I, beside Indic / Indo-Aryan and Iranian. Nuristani languages did not undergo a certain development called RUKI. They preserved the dental affricates of the Proto-I-E palatovelars and de-aspirated the voiced and voiceless aspirates of I-I. He also discusses some criticism of these ideas.

Migration history

Morgenstierne (1973, 342) laments the difficulty in drawing conclusions about the early history of the *Kafirs*. However, it appears certain, he argues, that they have been living in their isolated mountain valleys for a very long time. He goes on to speculate that the ancestors of the speakers of the Nuristani languages were the oldest immigrants into the region: "They would then have been pushed back into their mountain valleys by the later, more powerful and numerous Indo-Aryans, and have remained there ever since" (Morgenstierne 1973, 342-343). Scholars like Burrow (1973) have proposed that Nuristani languages arrived in the region some 2300 years ago, before the Vedic populations. As the oldest archaeological remains in the Western Himalaya have been dated to an age of ca. 4000 years ago, the Dardic / Nuristani immigrants could not have been the first inhabitants (Kogan 2005, cited in Kuz'mina 2007).

Strand, while recognizing the archaic nature of Nuristani languages, does not believe that the speakers of Nuristani languages settled the valleys before the invasion of the Indo-Aryans into South Asia, but he relies on oral history according to which they fled into the Western Himalayas from Khorasan and other areas of Afghanistan around the year A.D. 1000 (https://iranicaonline.org/articles/nurestani-languages-archive).

Conclusion: Nuristani, Dardic, and Indo-Iranian

The conclusion we can draw from the above discussion is that the Nuristani languages should be considered a separate, third, group within the I-I branch of I-E. The age of the separation of Nuristani from I-I is subject to discussion.

There is a consensus that the Dardic languages are not a separate group within I-I, beside Indic, Iranian, and Nuristani, but a subbranch of Indic. However, the ASJP lists the Dardic and Nuristani languages as one subbranch. There is otherwise agreement about which languages belong in this branch of Indo-Aryan, except that *Glottolog* includes Sindhi-Lahnda languages in the same overall group as the Dardic languages.

Kalasha in Chitral and Kalasha-Ala in Nuristan

One of the issues we want to shed light on is whether there is a close connection between the Waigali language in Nuristan, also called Kalasha-Ala or Wai-alâ and the Kalashamon speaking Kalasha in Chitral, Pakistan. The first language is classified as a Nuristani language, the other as a Dardic language. The complexity of the situation is outlined by Strand (1973, 299-300), who names several groups with this ethnonym:

> The appellation Kalaṣa appears among other ethnic groups in addition to the Kalaṣa of Kalaṣüm. Informants from Sǝṛu and Kordar claimed that they were Kalasa, and although I was not able to verify these claims, I was told by a Kom informant [Mohammad Azam of Kun] that the Kalasa "are the same tribe" as the people of Sǝṛu and Kordar. The Kalaṣ of Čitrāl have a tradition that they spent some time in the Wāygal Valley before entering Čitrāl (Morgenstierne 1965, 189; Siiger 1956, 34), and it is tempting to speculate that Kalaṣa originally designated a group of diverse tribes living in what is now south-central Nuristān.

In the next section, making use of lexical data sets, we will make use of computational techniques to shed light on these languages and their connections.

Lexical classifications of Nuristani languages

In this section, we report on the results of our lexical comparisons involving the languages of Nuristan and its neighboring regions, based on the application of computational classificatory techniques to two different data sets. We begin with a brief discussion of the results for the Nuristani languages in an automated, large-scale classification of the world's languages, based on yet another set of lexical features.

The first scholars to use computational techniques for classification that included Nuristani languages, were the people around the ASJP (ASJP; https://asjp.clld.org). It was their goal to make an automatic classification of the world's languages on the basis of forty words known to be quite resistant to replacement (see Brown et al. 2008; Holman et al. 2011). In their results, all Dardic languages except Kashmiri cluster together, and the two included Nuristani languages, Kativiri and Shekhani (Kamviri), as well as the Shina variety, Brok-Skad, are found in between Khowar and Kalasha, the two included Dardic languages of Chitral. In our two empirical studies, we include more Nuristani languages and larger numbers of words.

Methods and data

Since the 1980s, bioinformaticians have made use of computational clustering algorithms for reconstructing phylogenies (i.e., graphic representations of evolutionary relationships) from large sets of encoded character data (see Felsenstein 2004). Their methods were eventually carried over to other branches of science, including linguistics (see Bowern & Evans 2015; Borchsenius et al. 2017). A number of parallels between language development and biological diversification are discussed by Atkinson & Gray (2005, 514), two of the pioneers of computational phylolinguistics.

Following the established tradition of the Comparative Method, classification of languages is ideally based on both lexicon and grammar, especially shared forms, and on regular sound changes. There is a tradition in historical linguistics of taking cognacy in specific sets of words, most often a so-called Swadesh list, as the litmus test (see e.g., Wichmann & Grant 2012). We will investigate the position of the Nuristani languages on the basis of two different sets of lexical data. To this end, we make use of the Neighbor-Net algorithm

(Bryant & Moulton 2004) as implemented in the software SplitsTree 4 (Huson & Bryant 2006) to systematize and reveal data patterns in our study of the Nuristani languages' internal and external lexical affinities.

A classification based on Strand's extended word list

The point of departure for this first lexical study was the basic vocabulary material gathered by Richard Strand and presented on his website (Strand 1997-2016). He had a number of standardized lists of 207 different words for the following languages: Achareta Phalura, Pashai, Waigali, Sanuviri, Bash-kali, and Kamviri. The word meanings in the lists, which were tailored to be of specific relevance for Nuristani languages, are relatively culture-neutral (i.e., they denote concepts such as 'tree,' 'sun,' 'fire,' or 'blood' that can be expected to exist in very different languages and are assumed only rarely to be replaced by other lexical forms). To view the full list, consult Strand (1997-2016).

Drawing on a selection of published language descriptions and surveys (Back-strom & Radloff 1992; Decker 1992; Hallberg 1992; Morgenstierne 1945, 1952, 1954; Rensch et al. 1992; Strand 1997-2016; Buddruss & Degener 2015, 2017), we collected vocabulary items for a maximally inclusive sample, in addition to Strand's languages. This sample appeared to contain 91 languages / dialects spoken in the mountainous Hindukush region – both on the Pakistan and the Afghanistan sides. The full list of languages sampled with their ISO codes and their geographical locations are available from the authors.

We collected a total of 7,855 words based on Strand's 207 meanings. These data were then coded for cognate candidacy (cf. Dunn 2015, 192): If word A in language X, upon inspection, was assessed to most likely share its etymological origin with word B in language Y, then A and B would be assigned the same code; if words A and B seemed to derive from different ancestral forms, they instead received different codes (A would get '1' and B would get '2'), and so forth. The resulting matrix was analyzed with the Neighbor-Net algorithm.

Figure 1 shows our sample of 91 lects in a network. It should be read as a representation of relative lexical similarity between the different language varieties (the endpoint labels). The length of a line between two labels is proportional to the degree of lexical similarity between the corresponding languages / dialects: the longer the line, the more lexically deviant from the other languages. For instance, Shina, in the top of the graph, is represented

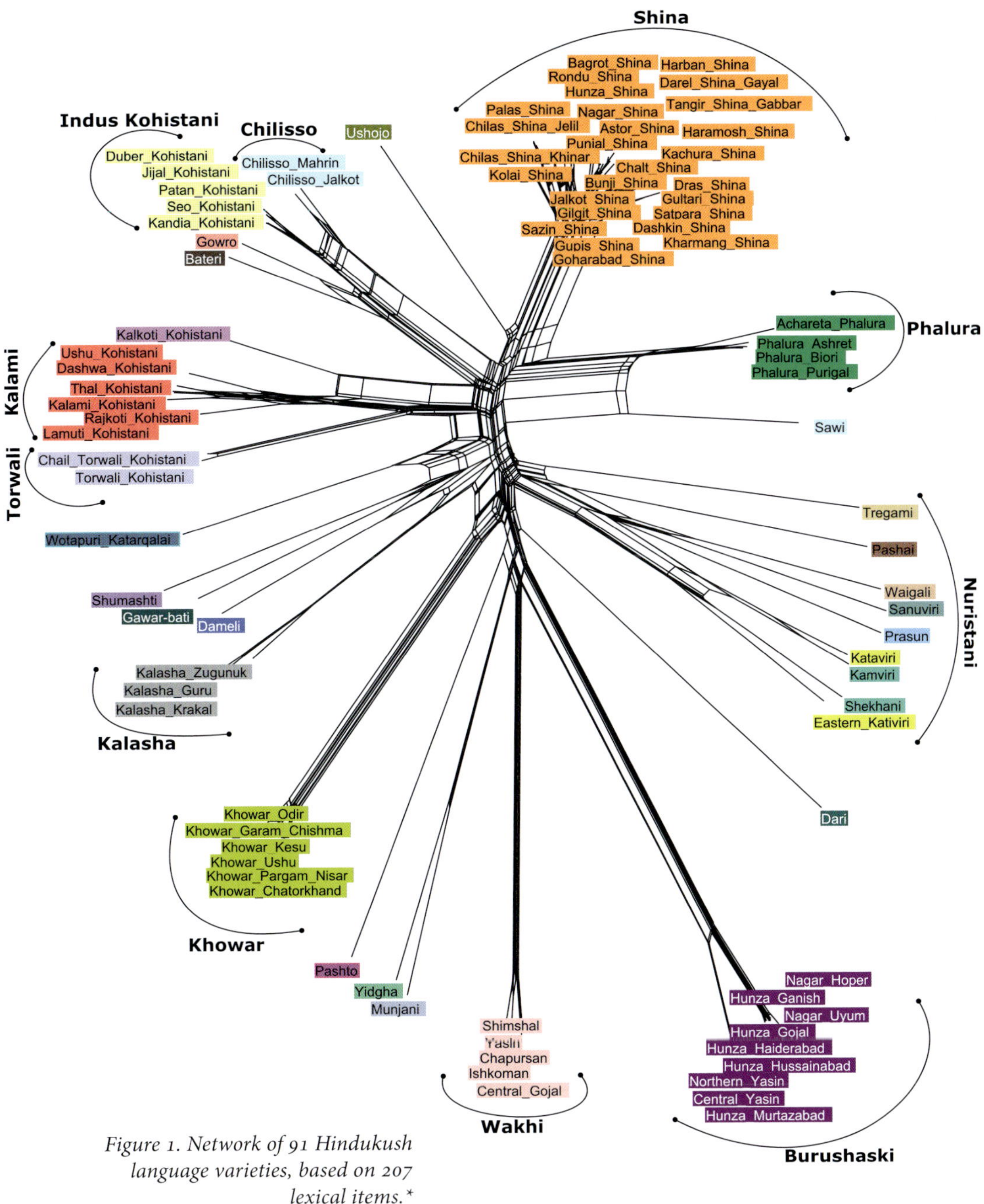

Figure 1. Network of 91 Hindukush language varieties, based on 207 lexical items. *

* In this and subsequent networks, languages (lects sharing one ISO code) are differentiated by color codes, in order to summarize the graph.

with many varieties that do not differ dramatically from one another. Similarly, the Chilisso varieties and the Kohistani languages appear relatively similar in their lexicon, while most of the Nuristani languages diverge more clearly from one another.

Lines connecting vertically across language labels that give a characteristically web-like visual impression indicate conflicting signals in the data. These represent contact influences and / or chance resemblances in form.

The Nuristani languages form a cluster (i.e., we find Tregami, Waigali, Sanuviri, Prasun, Kataviri, Kamviri, Shekhani, and Eastern Kativiri grouped together). However, one non-Nuristan language, Pashai (a Degano dialect), which usually is classified as Dardic and which neighbors the Nuristan region, is found among the Nuristani languages.[*]

As for the rest of the graph, we can find the subdivisions of the Dardic languages into Shina (with Shina proper as well as Phalura / Palula, Savi, Ushojo), Kohistani languages (Chilisso, Indus Kohistani / Maiya, Gowro, Bateri, Kalami, Torwali, and Katarqalai), Kunar languages (Shumashti, Gawarbati, Dameli), Chitral languages (Kalasha, Khowar). The only other Dardic language (besides Degano Pashai) at an unexpected position is Kalkoti, a Shinaic language that ends up in the middle of the Kalami Kohistani languages. See Liljegren (2013) for Gawri influence on Kalkoti.

In the bottom of the graph, we find the six languages that are neither Nuristani nor Dardic. Dari, Pashto, Yidgha, Munjani, and Wakhi are Iranian languages. The Burushaski dialects, a group universally recognized as an isolate, are found between Dari and the other Iranian languages.

Figure 2 shows a network where dialect clusters have been trimmed down to one representative lect from each group so as to test whether the clustering of Nuristani languages is replicated when held against a more well-balanced variety sample (Rijkhoff & Bakker 1998). The results of this operation corroborate the basic cluster of Nuristani languages. In conclusion, the special place of Nuristani in Indo-Iranian is confirmed. Further, we note that neither network discussed thus far, supported a particularly close lexical connection

---

[*] Below, we include a larger sample of Pashai lects. It will be shown that the result reported for Degano Pashai is not generalizable to the lexically diverse Pashai dialects.

between Waigali (or Kalaṣa-alâ) and the Kalasha dialects of Birir, Bumboret, and Urtsun (Chitral, Pakistan).

In Figure 2, the included Kalasha lect can be seen approaching the Nuristan cluster, but no clear lexical links obtain between these languages.

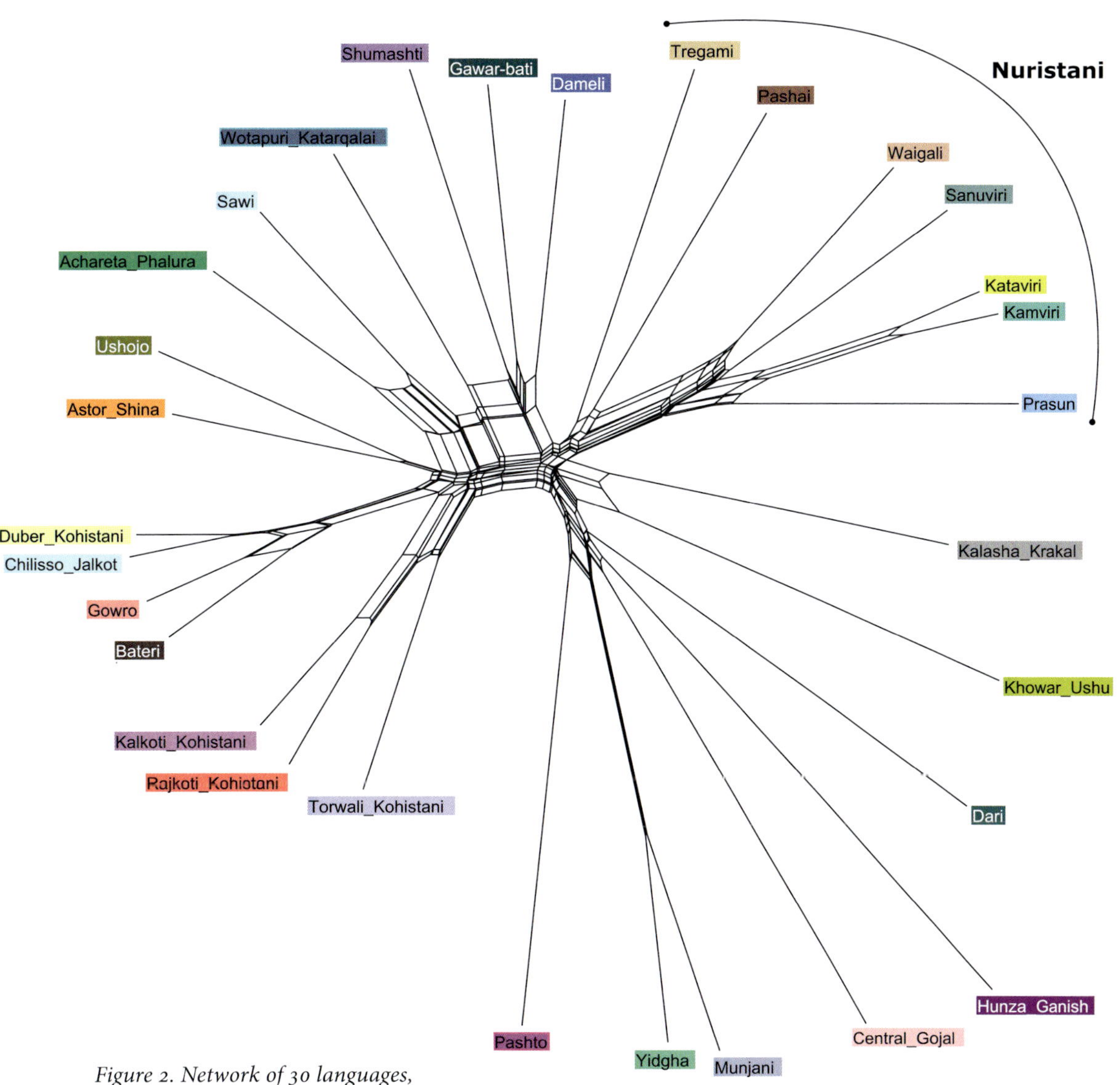

Figure 2. Network of 30 languages, based on 207 lexical items.

A classification based on Fussman's atlas data

We now turn to dealing with the data in Fussman's (1972) *Atlas linguistique des parlers dardes et kafirs*. On the one hand, these data have a high degree of reliability. On the other hand, the quantity is uneven. For some languages, less than a handful words are given. For others, almost the whole set is known. No attempt was made to fill the gaps, as we wanted to maintain the level of expert and consistent judgments of cognacy.

Fussman had 167 target words or phrases. They include the lower numerals, some body parts ('belly', 'kidney'), natural phenomena ('earthquake', 'river'), verbs ('to kill', 'to see'), animals ('mouse', 'scorpion'), fruits ('apple', 'apricot'), food ('rice', 'barley'), adjectives ('far', 'sharp'), kinship terms ('granddaughter'), the house and furniture ('bed', 'mirror'), some colors, etc. In short, there are both everyday words and more locally relevant terms. Compared with the data set utilized earlier, these words are more culture-specific.

134 languages and dialects were surveyed in Fussman (1972). For our analysis, we opted for a subset comprised of varieties with more than 100 of the 167 possible words recorded by Fussman, and that subset included all of the major Nuristani languages in eight varieties. The following Nuristani lects were included (we add the number of data points for each language between brackets): Ashkun (137), Ashkun spoken in Wama (144), Kati (130), Prasun (104), Tregāmī (141), Waigalī spoken in Kegal (130), Waigalī spoken in Waigal (143), Waigalī spoken in Zhönchigal (123). The full list of language names with Fussmann's abbreviations and ISO codes is available from the authors.

Fussman's expert judgment of cognacy as presented in his atlas (1972) was recoded into a numeric format. This made it possible to construct a matrix compatible with computational analysis. The resulting phylogeny, based on 4,940 data points, is presented in Figure 3.

The Figure 3 network elucidates the place of the Nuristani languages within the languages of the region, as surveyed by Fussman (1972). As in the networks discussed above, the Nuristani varieties show up in a cluster of their own (indicated on the graph). Note that the three selected Waigali lects (grouped together within the larger Nuristani cluster) again show little sign of lexical commonalities between them and the surveyed variety of Kalasha that is located between Khowar and Dameli and found on the left side of the network.

Morgenstierne (1973, 1974) had pointed out a number of Nuristani features in some of the Dardic languages, especially Dameli, but also Kalasha, Gawar-Bati, and Khowar. On the basis of the data, it appears that these four Dardic languages are indeed closest to the Nuristani cluster.

An evident difference between the Figure 3 network and the results discussed above is that the various Pashai lects here show up in the opposite end of the graph that is away from the Nuristani cluster. Note, however, that Degano Pashai was not surveyed in Fussman (1972).

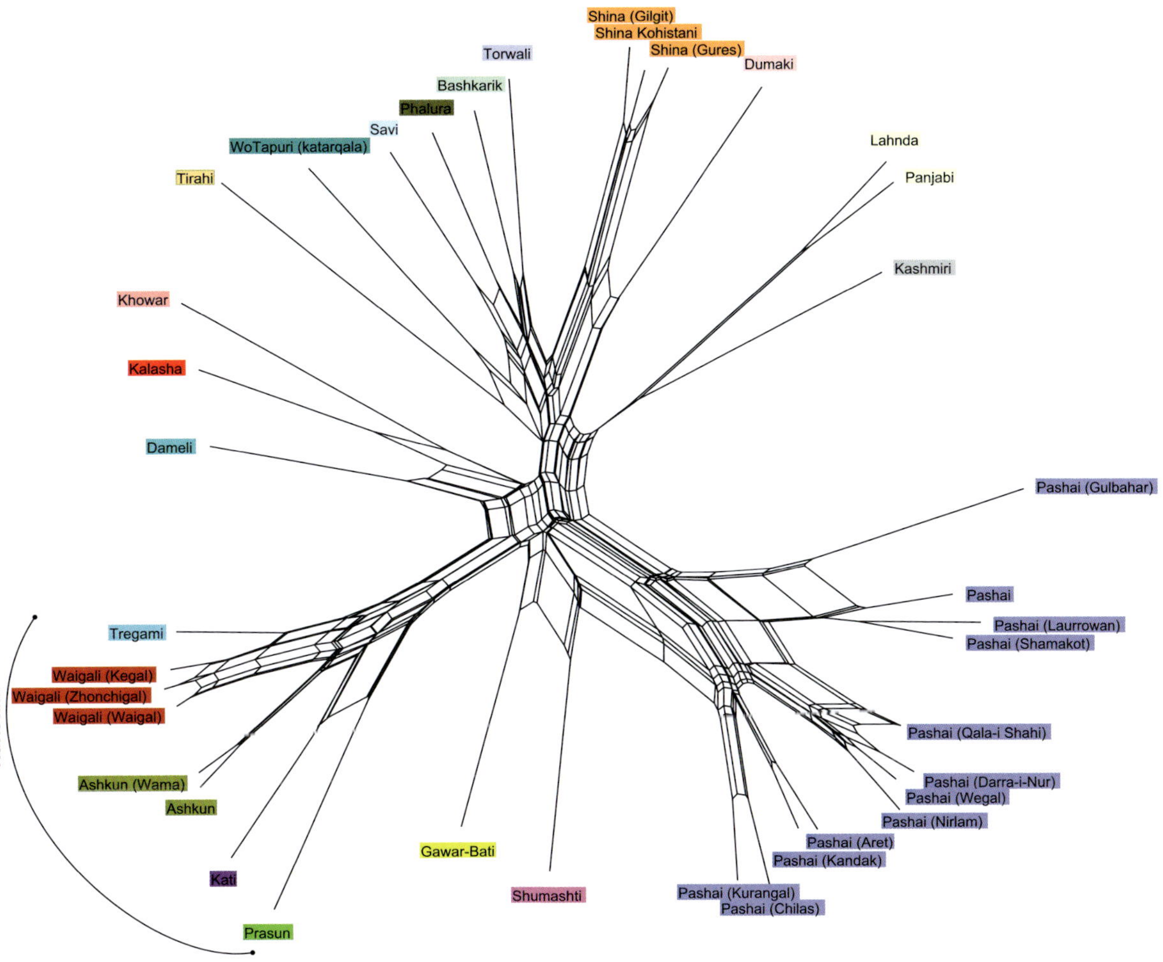

Figure 3. Network of 38 varieties, based on 167 lexical items.

Summary: lexical classifications of Nuristani languages

Our lexical comparisons, based on different data sets, source materials, and language selections, point consistently to the Nuristani languages comprising a unit, separate from the languages spoken in their environs. The results thus point to a separate history of the Nuristani languages, which were most likely an early split from I-I. This view converges with the views of specialists like Morgenstierne (1974), Hock (2016a), and Strand (2016).

On some grammatical aspects of the Nuristani languages

Good grammatical descriptions have been published for two Nuristani languages: Prasuni and Waigali. A recent publication by Buddruss & Degener (2017) includes more than 400 pages on Prasuni. For Waigali, two sources are worth referring to: Degener (1998) and Morgenstierne (1954). A small number of Waigali speakers have settled in Denmark, and Goldshtein initiated fieldwork with some of them. Unfortunately, the Nuristan region is particularly inaccessible not only due to physical barriers in the sense of high mountain ranges but also as a consequence of the continuously changing but almost always insecure socio-political situation in the region.

According to Van Driem (2007, 338), the Nuristani languages are not only "highly important from the point of view of understanding the population prehistory of South and Central Asia," but they also "exhibit numerous peculiar typological features of great interest to cognitive linguistics." According to Degener (2002, 106), though, the grammatical systems of Old Iranian and Old Indo-Aryan were "very similar and has been thoroughly recast" in both families. Moreover, in Degener's view, it is "hardly possible" to draw any genealogical conclusions from a comparison of grammatical traits. Indeed, specialists have written about the South Indian linguistic area or *Sprachbund* since at least Emeneau (1956). Whether Degener is right in claiming that comparison of grammatical features cannot inform our understanding of the genealogical relationships between the Nuristani languages and their neighbors stands as a question for future research.

We offer a brief discussion of two grammatical phenomena found in Nuristan: split ergativity and spatial orientation. Spatial orientation is one of the most outstanding characteristics distinguishing the Nuristani languages from related languages. Split ergativity was chosen because it is, on the one hand, a pronounced areal feature and, on the other hand, it shows internal variation within the Nuristani group. In ergative languages, subject and object are marked differently. In nominative-accusative patterns, known from European languages, the subject of the verb is invariant regardless of whether the clause has an object or not: 'he saw her' and 'he slept'. In ergative patterns, on the other hand, the subject of an objectless clause is like the object of a clause with an object: 'he saw her' and 'he slept'. Split ergative languages exhibit nominative patterns in the present tense, and ergative in the past tense.

Both the case marking of nouns and the system of verbal agreement in most Nuristani languages seem to exercise a split between a nominative and an ergative patterning.

Nuristani nouns have a set of markers for the core grammatical cases with the primary function of marking the grammatical relations of subject and object. These are often referred to as direct and oblique. In Waigali, Ashkun, and Kati, the direct case is used for subjects and the oblique for objects in the present tense, and vice-versa in the past tense. Only Prasun does not have this split system of case marking. Apart from that, the case systems of the languages vary considerably; Waigali has an additional ablative-instrumental, whereas Ashkun has a dative and an instrumental case.

As in other Indo-Iranian languages, the split patterning is not only determined by tense. It is also usually influenced by factors such as aspect, animacy, and definiteness (Bashir 2016, 454; Hock 2016b). A more detailed description of this interplay between various factors could inform us about the differences and similarities between the languages.

A striking feature of the Nuristani languages is the prevalence of overt marking of directionality and spatial orientation. One of the ways in which this is done is by an intricate system of verbal prefixes. In Prasun, where this phenomenon is frequent, a word such as 'to look' will combine with different prefixes depending on whether the subject is looking up, down, downward from the inside of something, and many more (Edelman 1983, 119). This feature seems to be prevalent in all Nuristani languages, though it appears to differ quite a bit with regards to its frequency and use as well as the directions and spatial orientations marked.

In short, the grammars of the Nuristani languages exhibit a number of very interesting features. Importantly, they have traits that appear to distinguish them as a group from the surrounding languages, and they display variation among themselves as well.

Conclusion

The results of our computational tests affirm that the Nuristani languages should be considered a separate group within the I-I branch. This is the case on the basis of lexical data (our work) and the studies by historical linguists about sound changes (e.g., Strand 1997-2016; Lipp 2009). We have not attempted to relate our findings to migration routes, but see some informed suggestions in Strand (2016), Kuz'mina (2007) and Burrow (1973).

The position of the Dardic languages is more ambiguous. The proposed subgroupings of Dardic languages put forward by others are to a large extent replicated in our results based on the application of computational clustering techniques, with some exceptions. Historical linguists have not found any unique Dardic innovations. But in the ASJP tree, the Dardic languages together with the Nuristani languages and the island Indo-Aryan languages (Vedda, Sinhala, Maledivian) are outliers within I-I and relatively close to Iranian. We intend to make a more detailed study of the classification (Bakker et al., in prep.)

In the beginning we asked whether Kalashamon of Chitral could be related with Kalasa-alâ, one of the Waigali varieties spoken in Nuristan. Our comparison leads us to reject the hypothesis at this point. It is more likely that one of the groups obtained the tribal name from the other (see e.g., Strand 1973, 2016).

Lennart Edelberg is one of the few who have been able to do fieldwork in Nuristan. His work focused mostly on anthropology, religion, history, and architecture. In this study, we have supplemented his work with information on the languages of this fascinating and under-researched region. In closing, we express our hope that fieldwork will become possible again in this part of the world.

Acknowledgements

We are grateful for the help we received from the following persons: Dino Rogic, Emily Jørgensen, Jacob Heath, Karen Nissen Schriver, Kasper Fyhn Jacobsen, Nina Gislinge, Rocio Lopez, Svend Castenfeldt, Taj Khan Kalash, and Zana Jaza. Further, we thank the State Library / Royal Library and Institute for Communication and Culture at Aarhus University for their support.

List of references

Atkinson, Quentin D. & Russell D. Gray (2005) "Curious parallels and curious connections – Phylogenetic thinking in biology and historical linguistics." In: *Systematic Biology* 54, no 4: 513-526. doi: 10.1080/10635150590950317

Backstrom, Peter C. & Carla F. Radloff (eds.) (1992) *Languages of Northern Areas.* (Sociolinguistic Survey of Northern Pakistan, Vol. 2). National Institute of Pakistan Studies and Summer Institute of Linguistics: Islamabad.

Bakker, Peter & Aymeric Daval-Markussen (2016) "Linguistic and genetic roots of the Kalasha." In: *In the Footsteps of Halfdan Siiger – Danish Research in Central Asia*, edited by Ulrik Høj Johnsen, Armin W. Geertz, Peter B. Andersen and Svend Castenfeldt: pp. 93-114. Moesgaard Museum: Højbjerg.

Bakker, Peter, Kristoffer Friis Bøegh & Yonatan Goldshtein (In prep.) "Classification of the languages of Nuristan."

Bashir, Elena (2016) "Agent marking." In: *The Languages and Linguistics of South Asia: A Comprehensive Guide*, edited by Hans Heinrich Hoch and Elena L. Bashir: pp. 450-459. De Gruyter Mouton: Berlin.

Borchsenius, Finn, Aymeric Daval-Markussen & Peter Bakker (2017) "Phylogenetics in biology and linguistics." In *Creole Studies – Phylogenetic Approaches*, edited by Peter Bakker, Finn Borchsenius, Carsten Levisen and Eeva Sippola: pp. 35-58. J. Benjamins: Amsterdam.

Bowern, Claire, and Bethwyn Evans, eds. (2015) *The Routledge Handbook of Historical Linguistics*. Routledge: London/New York.

Brown, Cecil H., Eric W. Holman, Søren Wichmann, and Viveka Velupillai (2008) "Automated classification of the world's languages: A description of the method and preliminary results." In: *STUF – Language Typology and Universals* 61: pp. 285-308.

Bryant, D. & V. Moulton (2004) "Neighbor-net: An agglomerative method for the construction of phylogenetic networks." In: *Molecular Biology and Evolution* 21, no 2: pp. 255-265.

Buddruss, Georg, and Almuth Degener (2015) *Materialien zur Prasun-Sprache des Afghanischen Hindukusch, Teil 1: Texte und Glossar.* Harvard University Press: Cambridge, MA.

Buddruss, Georg & Almuth Degener (2017) *Materialien zur Prasun-Sprache des Afghanischen Hindukusch, Teil 2: Grammatik.* Harvard University Press: Cambridge, MA.

Burrow, T. (1973) "The Proto-Indoaryans". In: *Journal of the Royal Asiatic Society* (N.S.) 2: pp.123-140.

Decker, Kendall D. (1992) *Languages of Chitral.* (Sociolinguistic Survey of Northern Pakistan, 5.) National Institute of Pakistan Studies, Quaid-i-Azam University and Summer Institute of Linguistics. Islamabad.

Degener, Almuth (1998) *Die Sprache von Nisheygram im afghanischen Hindukusch.* Harrassowitz Verlag: Wiesbaden.

Degener, Almuth (2002) "The Nuristani languages". In: Nicholas Sims-Williams (ed.), *Indo-Iranian languages and peoples* (Proceedings of the British Academy 116), pp.103-117. Published for the British Academy by Oxford University Press: Oxford.

Dunn, Michael (2015) "Language phylogenies." In *The Routledge Handbook of Historical Linguistics*, edited by C. Bowern and B. Evans, pp. 190-211. Routledge: London & New York.

Edelberg, Lennart (1984) *Nuristani Buildings.* Jutland Archaeological Society: Højbjerg.

Edelman, Džoi Iosifovna (1983) *The Dardic and Nuristani languages* (Languages of Asia and Africa). Moscow: Nauka.

Эдельман, д. и. [Edelman, D.I] (1999) "Индоиранские Языки" [Indo-Iranian Languages]. In: J*azyki mira. Dardskie i nuristanskie jazyki*: pp. 10-12. Indrik: Moskwa.

Emeneau, Murray (1956) "India as a linguistic area." In: *Language* 32, no 1: 3-16. doi:10.2307/410649.

Felsenstein, Joseph (2004) *Inferring Phylogenies.* Sinauer Associates: Sunderland MA.

Fussman, Gérard (1972) *Atlas linguistique des parlers dardes et kafirs.* Paris: École française d'Extrême-Orient.

Grierson, G. A. (1906) *The Piśāca languages of North-Western India.* Royal Asiatic Society: London.

Grjunberg, A. L. (1999) "Zemiaki jazyk/dialekt." In: *Jazyki mira: Dardskie i nuristanskie jazyki, pp.* 123-125. Indrik: Moscow.

Hallberg, Daniel G. (1992) "The languages of Indus Kohistan." In: Rensch, Calvin R., Sandra J. Decker, and Daniel Hallberg, *Sociolinguistic Survey of Northern Pakistan 1: Languages of Kohistan* (series ed.: Clare O'Leary). Summer Institute of Linguistics: Islamabad.

Hammarström, Harald, Robert Forkel, Martin Haspelmath, and Sebastian Bank (eds.) (2017) *Glottolog 3.0.* (Accessed 2017-11-16). Max Planck Institute for the Science of Human History: Jena.

Hock, Hans Henrich (2016a) "The languages, their histories, and their genetic classification." In: *The Languages and Linguistics of South Asia: A Comprehensive Guide*, edited by Hans Henrich Hock and Elena L. Bashir: pp. 9-240. De Gruyter Mouton: Berlin.

Hock, Hans Henrich (2016b) "Agreement marking." In: *The Languages and Linguistics of South Asia: A Comprehensive Guide*, edited by Hans Henrich Hock and Elena L. Bashir: pp. 465-477. De Gruyter Mouton: Berlin.

Hock, Hans Henrich, and Elena L. Bashir, eds. (2016) *The Languages and Linguistics of South Asia: A Comprehensive Guide.* De Gruyter Mouton: Berlin.

Holman, Eric W. et al. (2011) "Automated dating of the world's language families based on lexical similarity." In: *Current Anthropology* 52, no 6: pp. 841-875.

Huson, D. H., and D. Bryant, (2006) "Application of phylogenetic networks in evolutionary studies." In: *Molecular Biology and Evolution* 23: pp.254-267. doi: 10.1093/molbev/msj030

Kogan A. I. (2005) *Dardskie Jazyki. Geneticheskaya Kharakteristika* [Dardic languages. Genetic Characteristics]. Vostochnaya literature: Moscow.

Kuz'mina, Elena E. (2007) *The Origin of the Indo-Iranians.* J.P. Mallory (ed.). Brill: Leiden.

Liljegren, Henrik (2013) "Notes on Kalkoti: A Shina Language with strong Kohistani Influences." In: *Linguistic Discovery* 11, no 1: pp. 129-160.

Liljegren, Henrik (2016) *A Grammar of Palula.* (Studies in Diversity Linguistics 8.) Language Science Press: Berlin.

Lipp, Reiner (2009) *Die indogermanischen und einzelsprachlichen Palatale im Indoiranischen. Band I: Neurekonstruktion, Nuristan-Sprachen, Genese der indoarischen Retroflexe, Indoarisch von Mitanni. Band II: Thorn-Problem, Indoiranische Laryngalvokalisation.* Winter: Heidelberg.

Morgenstierne, Georg (1932) *Report on a Linguistic Mission to North-Western India.* Instituttet for Sammenlignende Kulturforskning: Oslo.

Morgenstierne, Georg (1945) "Notes on Shumashti, a Dardic dialect of the Gawar-Bati type". In: *Norsk Tidsskrift for Sprogvidenskap* 13: pp. 239-281.

Morgenstierne, Georg (1952) "Linguistic Gleanings from Nuristan." In: *Norsk Tidsskrift for Sprogvidenskap* 16: pp. 117-135.

Morgenstierne, Georg (1954) "The Waigali Language." In: *Norsk Tidsskrift for Sprogvidenskap* 17: pp. 146-324.

Morgenstierne, Georg (1961) "Dardic and Kâfir Languages." In: *The Encyclopaedia of Islam,* New Edition, Vol. 2, Fasc. 25. Leiden: E. J. Brill: pp. 138-139.

Morgenstierne, Georg (1965) "Notes on Kalasha." In: *Norsk Tidsskrift for Sprogvidenskap* 20: pp. 183-238.

Morgenstierne Georg (1973) "Die Stellung der Kafirsprachen." In: *Irano-Dardica,* by Georg Morgenstierne: pp. 327-343. Ludwig Reichert Verlag: Wiesbaden.

Morgenstierne Georg (1974) "Languages of Nuristan and surrounding regions." In: *Cultures of the Hindukush: Selected Papers from the Hindu-Kush Cultural Conference held at Moesgaard 1970,* edited by Karl Jettmar, in collaboration with Lennart Edelberg: pp. 1-10. Steiner: Wiesbaden.

Rensch, Calvin R., Sandra J. Decker & Daniel G. Hallberg (eds.) (1992) *Languages of Kohistan. (Sociolinguistic Survey of Northern Pakistan, Vol. 1).* Islamabad: National Institute of Pakistan Studies and Summer Institute of Linguistics.

Rijkhoff, Jan, and Dik Bakker (1998) "Language Sampling." In: *Linguistic Typology* 2, no 3: pp. 263-314.

Siiger, Halfdan (1956) *From the Third Danish Expedition to Central Asia: Ethnological Field-Research in Chitral, Sikkim, and Assam: Preliminary Report.* Hist. Filol. Medd. Danske Videnskabernes Selskab 36, no 2. København: Ejnar Munksgaard.

Strand, Richard (1973) "Notes on the Nuristani and Dardic Languages." In: *Journal of the American Oriental Society* 93, no. 3: pp. 297-305.

Strand, Richard (2016) "Nûristânî." In *The Languages and Linguistics of South Asia: A comprehensive guide,* edited by Hans Henrich Hock and Elena L. Bashir: pp. 66-72. Berlin: De Gruyter Mouton.

Strand, Richard (1997-2016) "Nuristan: the Hidden land of the Hindu-Kush." http:// nuristan.info (Accessed 2017-15-11).

Van Driem, George (2007) "Endangered Languages of South Asia." In: *Handbook of Endangered Languages,* edited by Matthias Brenzinger: pp. 303-341. De Gruyter Mouton: Berlin.

Wichmann, Søren, and Anthony P. Grant (eds.) (2012) *Quantitative Approaches to Linguistic Diversity: Commemorating the Centenary of the Birth of Morris Swadesh.* John Benjamins: Amsterdam/Philadelphia.

4. The Kafir Temple in the Parun Valley

By Svend Castenfeldt

This is the story of a magnificent temple in the Hindukush mountain range that was destroyed many years ago; a fabled temple, and the undisputed center of the old *Kafirs* religious and cultural life, which later fell into oblivion. And it is the story of a remarkable collaboration between friends and foes to reveal its secrets. The story begins with the British intelligence officer, George Scott Robertson, who visited the secluded area known as Kafiristan ('Land of the Heathens') first in 1889 and again in 1890-91 as one of the first Europeans known to have ever reached this area.[1] In the Parun Valley he saw the temple, which, shortly after, was completely destroyed. The actual story begins with great scholars of the Hindukush such as Wolfgang Lentz and his friend Lennart Edelberg; and it ends – at least up to now – in the research archives of Moesgaard Museum.

October 1947. The botanist Lennart Edelberg was one of four members of the 'first wave' of Henning Haslund-Christensen's grand expedition – the Third Danish Expedition to Central Asia, 1947-52. Lennart left his wife, Margot, and their newborn daughter, Vibeke, behind in Denmark, in order to carry out fieldwork in Afghanistan. He embarked on an extraordinary adventure together with the physician and zoologist Knud Paludan, the historian of religions, Halfdan Siiger, and the explorer and traveller of Mongolia, Henning Haslund-Christensen. Haslund was the leader of the Third Danish Expedition to Central Asia that had ethnographic research among its objectives. Together these scientists formed the spearhead of the expedition; the second wave of scholars was to arrive at the expedition's HQs in Kabul in 1948. This second group included botanist Mogens Køie, his wife and assistant Aase Køie, the geographer Johannes Humlum, and the zoologist Niels Haarløv.

The HQ in Kabul, Afghanistan, 1948.

In Kabul, Haslund trained the expedition members on where to find and how to buy artefacts for the National Museum of Denmark in Copenhagen, which was one of the expedition's main purposes. Local men were hired for practical assistance, and the scientists prepared their fieldwork plans in different locations in Afghanistan, in order to start as soon as spring arrived. Lennart's first journey to Nuristan in the summer of 1948 was in the company of Mohammad Akbar and Knud Paludan. They were searching for traces of the ancient Kafir culture, which had been prevalent at one time in the province now called Nuristan ('Land of Light').

It was thought that the old Kafir religious beliefs that existed in the Afghan province of Nuristan until about 1900 might offer a unique glimpse into the very early Indo-European past, as its predecessors shared origins with the first Europeans. Since the region was isolated by the remote Hindukush, it was thought that this isolation might have preserved ancient cultural practices. One thing is beyond question: Few visitors from the outside world had visited Kafiristan and survived to tell the tale. One of those who not only survived but also wrote about it, was the British intelligence officer, George Scott Robertson. Robertson's book *The Kafirs of the Hindukush* was one of the few books that Lennart was able to find about pre-Muslim Kafiristan (Robertson 1896). This book would assist him in his search for traces of ancient cultural practices in the region. Ever since its publication in London in 1896, it has been an important source of information, as it provides ethnographic data regarding the now almost vanished Kafir culture.

Robertson was the only Westerner known to have seen the temple before its destruction in the village of Kushteki in the Prasun or Parun Valley in Kafiristan. Shortly after Robertson's visit, it was destroyed by Muslim invaders and a majority of the 100.000 Kafirs were forcibly converted to Islam following the invasion of Kafiristan by the Afghan Emir, Abdur Rahman. A number of the Kafirs fled to the three valleys of the Kalasha on the other side of the border in the kingdom of Chitral in British India (since 1948, Pakistan). The last of those exiled Kafirs converted to Islam in the 1930s. During Afghan raids on the Kafirs, which lasted three years, the army of the Afghan emir destroyed the religious center of the Kafir faith – the grand temple in the Prasun (also Parun) valley. After the invasion and conversion, the area was renamed Nuristan. The temple as well as details of how it was constructed had been hidden in darkness for a long time. But Robertson had seen it in the 1890s.

Kafiristan had a widespread reputation of being a dangerous place. However, as a British intelligence officer and medical doctor, he had important qualities and qualifications to enter it, just a few years before the emir's raid, which forever changed the destiny of the area. Robertson made his first contacts in Kafiristan in 1889, and he later managed to stay among the notorious Kafirs for more than twelve months. With him, he brought a camera and took photos on glass plates. One of the important sites in his photographic record was the temple in the village of Kushteki. Leaving Kafiristan after twelve months, he used donkeys to carry his equipment. But, alas, the donkey that was carrying the glass photographic plates lost its life crossing one of the many turbulent rivers that led back to British India. All the glass photographic plates were all lost as well.[2] After returning to England, Robertson asked the artist A.D. McCormick to make drawings of the temple based on his descriptions and sketches. One hundred years later, this resulted in the construction of a model of the Kafir temple in Aarhus, Denmark; this came about thanks to the initiative of the Kafiristan Group inspired by three competent researchers, among them, Lennart Edelberg.

1935. Nazi Germany planned an expedition to Afghanistan. Fifteen researchers were selected to engage in a mission, which would take them from Germany to Afghanistan and further on to British India. Their orders were to find the 'original grain,' which is believed to have been eaten by the early Indo-European populations. They were told they might find it in the mountains in a place between the fire (the sun) and the ice. If successful, reintroducing the original grain to Europe where grain was believed to have degenerated through the centuries, the Aryan population of Germany would gain strength in the Nazi efforts to conquer and master the rest of the world. At least, such was the argument of the group of Nazis known also as the *Thule Gesellshaft* (Thule Society). The society had been formed in Munich right after World War I, where the German Workers' Party, which was later transformed by Adolf Hitler into NSDAP, the Nazi Party, sponsored its activities. The society was clearly occultist, and it has been argued that Hitler incorporated some central members of the society and their ideas into the Third Reich – including, apparently, the theory of the 'original grain.'[3] The expedition plan was to set out for Afghanistan, and then go through Nuristan to British India, but the expedition also had other purposes – spying for Nazi Germany. Some of the expedition members were botanists – but not all of them. And none of them had mastered the languages necessary to carry out the expedition. But there was a German teacher in a German gymnasium in Kabul, who had studied several versions of different Iranian languages. This man was Wolfgang Lentz. He was asked to join the expedition, as an interpreter. He managed to borrow a Rolleiflex 6×6 camera with which he took around 2000 excellent photos, which are now in the ethnographic collections of Moesgaard Museum.[4]

Early 1940s. World War II was underway and a young couple – Lennart and Margot Edelberg – were employed to study the seagull population on a small island, Jordsand, in the Wadden Sea. In the nearby harbor of Esbjerg, however, the Gestapo was keeping an eye on their activities, thinking that the young Danish couple were communicating by radio with the British; they suspected that they had radio equipment with which to send messages to England regarding the whereabouts of German battleships and other activities on Denmark's west coast. The Germans sent investigators to check on the young couple, and in the process of digging for hidden radio equipment on the beaches, they disturbed the seagull colonies. They found nothing, however, to support their suspicions and the Nazis withdrew. But they, too, had been under observation. Close to the island of Sild, there was another German garrison, but these were ordinary troops – not SS, like those who ransacked Jordsand. An officer from the garrison from Sild suggested that Margot and Lennart had better leave the island before the SS-troops returned. They followed this advice, and the experience was never forgotten.

Early 1950s. When the war ended, Lentz contacted one of his old school comrades, the architect Albert Schäfer. Both had grown up in the German city of Hameln. Schäfer had served in the German army during the war as commander of a German gunboat based at the island Helgoland in the North Sea; later on, this fact would have implications for the account of the temple in the Prasun valley. Lentz and Schäfer began a year-long discussion about the temple that Lentz had heard of from the local population during the German expedition in 1935. He got the idea that this temple might be nothing less than a gigantic solar observatory. What sparked that idea? When Robertson saw the temple in 1891 he was not allowed to enter it. But he found a hole in the wall that allowed him to peek inside – and what he saw was extraordinary. He saw two large wooden statues: one depicting Imra, the god of creation, sitting on a horse, and one depicting Disni, the goddess of fertility, sitting on a stool.

On the western wall of the temple hall, he also saw chess-like squares and paintings that might indicate the passing of the agricultural year. Lentz, who was also a specialist on primitive calendar systems,[5] had studied the descriptions by Robertson, and he formed the idea that sunlight passing through the hole in the eastern wall would fall on different areas according to the season.

Schäfer began working on the problem but was hindered by a lack of essential details in Robertson's description. A possibility then presented itself; Lentz had heard of a Dane who had participated in the Danish expedition to Nuristan in 1948 and who was now planning to return. The Dane was Lennart Edelberg. Lentz went to see Lennart in Ribe, and it was decided that Lennart should make measurements of the temple ruins upon his return to Nuristan. Thus, in the autumn of 1953, this time as a member of the Danish Scientific Mission to Afghanistan and together with the ethnographer Klaus Ferdinand, Lennart made his way back to Afghanistan.

Back in Presungul (Parun / Prasun), Lennart made the required measurements and he also had the good fortune to meet some old men who were able to tell him that in wintertime an important ritual was carried out in the temple by the Kafir high priest. Lennart learned from his informants that this ritual focused on offering praise to the sun, which has divine powers. In the middle of the temple room, the high priest burned wet twigs in the fire place, releasing thick smoke; the shaman then went into a trance and singing began, accompanied by the sound of Kafir music instruments: lutes, harps, wadz, and drums. All of this was in honor of Imra, the Kafir god of Creation. In the middle of it all, one of the assisting priests removed a small panel covering an even smaller opening in the wall, allowing the sun to enter the dark and smoky temple. The highlight was reached when the sunray illuminated the lapis lazuli, a semi-precious stone, which adorned yet another god, Mahandeo. This annual event was crucial to Kafir ritual life, because it meant that the sun was returning and would thereby secure life and crops in the coming year. As Lentz would have understood it, the Kafir conception of time was circular – not linear; accordingly, he was able to put some of the puzzle together.

This account, which Lennart heard from the old men, who as young boys witnessed the ritual, is remarkable. One of the men was able to sing the old praises to Imra for Lennart, who recorded it all on tape. This recording, which is in the archives of Moesgaard Museum, is extremely rare, if not unique. The old man's song is a voice from the past, just as is the temple itself. Lennart continued his measurements of the temple ruins. He had brought with him measuring equipment that he had tested in the marshlands around Ribe back in Denmark, and he had a precise list of questions sent by Schäfer. The measurements were then sent to Germany, where they almost served to confirm Lentz' theory. But a major problem appeared in the Schäfer's calculations: he concluded that the roof must have been very heavy, requiring many pillars to support it, and thus preventing the sun beams from reaching the figure of Mahandeo inside.

In 1954, after his return to Europe from the expedition, Lennart continued the discussions about the temple with Lentz and Schäfer. In 1957 they presented their preliminary findings at an orientalist congress in Munich. They continued to try to solve the mystery of the temple, and in that process something unexpected happens. Lennart and Schäfer somehow began to discuss World War II – and this abruptly terminated their collaboration. Separately they continued the work, but now only via Professor Lentz. Subsequently, Schäfer refused to let Lentz show his drawings to Lennart, telling Lentz that they were burned. And both Lentz and Lennart believed him.

1986. Klaus Ferdinand had accompanied Lennart to Nuristan in 1953. By the 1980s, he was head of the ethnographic collections at Moesgaard Museum and lecturer in anthropology in Aarhus University. He hired me to work as a research archivist in the early 1980s. One day he asked me to go to visit Lentz in Marburg, Germany, in order to fetch the remainder of his research materials, which Lentz had donated to Moesgaard in 1970 during the First International Hindukush Cultural Conference. In the early 80s, due to his advanced years and failing eyesight, Lentz had decided that it was about time to hand these materials over to Moesgaard, as he had promised in 1970. Schuyler Jones had assisted him in sorting and preparing the material. Klaus had gone to Marburg in the early 1980s to collect the documents but found he did not have sufficient space in his car for all the material, so he arranged that I should go, accompanied by a student of ethnography to assist, in the summer of 1986.

Going through the documents included in the first batch of the Lentz research material and Lennart's papers that had also been donated to Moesgaard Museum after Lennart's untimely death in 1981, it became clear to me that there was a possibility of continuing their work with the help of modern technology. To this end a research team called the Kafiristan Group

Drawing of the vanished temple on the cover of pamphlet prepared by the Kafiristan Group.

was formed in Aarhus in 1984. The aim was to better understand the temple in Parun Valley.

So, the student and I were on our way to see Lentz in Marburg. However, before visiting him, we went to visit Schäfer's house in Hameln. The Kafiristan Group did not believe that the drawings had been burned – only that Schäfer wanted to hide them from Lennart. With us we had the address of a local newspaper in Hameln, which another member of the Kafiristan Group, a retired military officer, had found. We also brought with us an article, prepared by the group, that was to be published in the newspaper; it is a tribute of Schäfer's achievements in his work with the local architecture in Hameln and for his work on the temple in Kafiristan. The newspaper immediately accepted the article, and it was subsequently published. We then got something that we also needed: the address of one of Schäfer's daughters, who happened to be living with her family in her childhood home in Hameln. She was pleased to have seen our recently published praise of her father's work in the local newspaper, and we were welcomed heartily. After some discussion and inquiries, she produced her father's temple drawings; these were the very drawings that Lennart and Lentz had presumed Schäfer had destroyed many years earlier. With those drawings kindly given to us by Schäfer's daughter, we drove on to Marburg.

When we arrived at Lentz's home in Marburg, I asked the student to have a chat with Professor Lentz outside on the balcony in order to prepare a surprise for him. Then I placed Schäfer's long-lost drawings on the large dining room table. Lentz, needless to say, was more than thrilled to see the drawings, which he had long believed to be lost. Unfortunately, Lentz did not see the ongoing work we carried out in an effort to complete the study of the Kafir temple, as he passed away a few months later. We had, however, collected the remaining documents, which completed the important Lentz donation to Moesgaard Museum.

Back in Aarhus, the Kafiristan Group then had access not only to Lentz's research materials, plus those of Lennart's on the buildings of Nuristan, and Schäfer's drawings – we also came in contact with specialists in the Aarhus School of Architecture. There all the relevant information were added to the latest available technology of the time, and based on those results a model of the temple was made. It is satisfying to know that now, almost 130 years since Robertson saw the original and decades after Lennart, Lentz, and Schäfer collaborated in an attempt to solve the mystery of the now long vanished Kafir temple in the Parun Valley, its architectural secrets have been revealed in Aarhus: *the main room in the temple was round.* That is the only explanation of how the walls of the building were able to support the heavy roof, and that also reveals how sunbeams could fall upon the lapis lazuli set in the image of Mahandeo, thereby ushering in a new year in the Kafir calendar.

Notes

1. The Gilgit Mission led by the British officers Lockhart and Woodthorpe had visited the upper Bashgal valley in the course of their 1885-1886 expedition. The 448-page report of that expedition, The Gilgit Mission, was never published. It was printed as a secret report in 1889 and was, therefore, not available for study.

2. Photographs from Robertson's first visit to the Bashgal Valley in the autumn of 1889 did survive, and these were used by A.D. McCormick to make some of the illustrations that appear in Robertson's book.

3. The Russian scientist Nikolai Ivanovich Vavilov had carried out botanical fieldwork in Afghanistan in 1924. He considered that the 'original home of wheat' may well have been in the Himalayas because of unique botanical evidence. See his 1929 publication *Zemledicheskiy Afghanitan (Agricultural Afghanistan).* This may have been the excuse for the German expedition. Wolfgang Lentz quickly found that the expedition members were Nazi spies.

4. See his *Zeitrechnung in Nuristan und am Pamir,* Berlin, 1939.

List of references

Robertson, George Scott (1896) *The Káfirs of the Hindu-Kush.* Lawrence & Bullen: London.

5. Working on the exhibition "Nuristan and the Kalash area" in 1970

By Flemming Bau

Having just arrived at the Prehistoric Museum in Aarhus at the beginning of 1965, my first assignment was to send a camera to Afghanistan to replace Klaus Ferdinand's camera that had been broken during his fieldwork among Afghan nomads. It was impossible to predict that, almost ten years later, I would have an opportunity, as exhibition curator, to join a study trip to Afghanistan together with twelve students of ethnography, Ole Høiris, and Klaus Ferdinand (Bau 2010, 209). The Prehistoric Museum was closely connected with the Institute of Prehistoric Archaeology and Ethnography, as it was named after 1963, at Aarhus University. In 1965, both institutions were located in The Old Hammel Railway Station in Carl Blochs Gade in Aarhus. As a conscientious objector with an educational background in visual art/graphic design, I had relocated from the forest section of the Kompedal camp to the many facetted workplace of the museum. During the previous two years, the museum had carried out comprehensive excavations in the central parts of Aarhus city in close proximity to the cathedral. My assignment during the excavations was to measure and to sketch the numerous excavated artefacts.

The restoration of the main building at Moesgaard Manor was completed in 1966, and the museum moved from Aarhus to the newly renovated premises. The craftsmen were still working at full speed to renovate and make changes to the old farm buildings – the stables and the barn, which had been turned into exhibition galleries. A brand new exhibition gallery was constructed to house a permanent ethnographic exhibition. In December 1966 I was about to be discharged, as my time as a conscientious objector was ending. The museum leadership, however, decided to employ me to continue my work in a newly created job as illustrator at the institute.

Figure. 1. The great panoramic view in the exhibition "Nuristan og Kalash-området" from 1970 with ancestor statues left and god statues right. Photo: Preben Dehlholm.

It was not until 1969 that we seriously engaged ourselves in the detailed planning of a new permanent exhibition on the ancient history of Denmark. Regarding the ethnographic section, it was decided that the newly built exhibition gallery should house the outstanding collections from Nuristan and the Kalash area in Afghanistan and Pakistan (Castenfeldt 1999, 52). The old exhibitions at the premises of Aarhus Museum in Vester Allé were packed up in 1968-69. Some of the more difficult artefacts to transport to the new premises were the runic stones, which were placed in the new galleries with the help of a crane on January 17, 1969.

We faced an enormous task; 1500 m^2 were waiting to be designed in about a year and a half; of these, around 200 m^2 were allocated to ethnography. The Head of the Ethnographic Collection, Klaus Ferdinand, gave the task to

Lennart Edelberg, who in collaboration with the professor of history of religion at Aarhus University, Halfdan Siiger, was responsible for the academic content, planning and texts of the exhibition (Ferdinand 1999, 38).

Expeditions to Nuristan and the Kalash area had been taking place since 1948. Lennart was focusing on Nuristan, and Halfdan Siiger was concerned with the Kalasha in Chitral. These people still practiced an ancient religion, while being surrounded on all sides by Muslims. During 1895-98 the Afghan Amir, Abdur Rahman, forcibly converted the inhabitants of Nuristan to Islam.

In July 1970 during preparations for the exhibition, Lennart together with his wife Margot, his daughter Miriam, and Ulf Timmermann went to Nuristan to collect additional material for the museum. At that time, a large diorama with some ancestor memorial statues was being built, and part of a traditional house from Nuristan had almost been completed in the gallery. The original decision that the entire exhibition should be devoted to an exhibition on Nuristan and the Kalash area was changed; the museum leadership had decided that half of the space should accommodate an exhibition about Greenland, which accordingly was planned and built. Jens Rosing was assigned the academic responsibility for this part of the exhibition (figure 1 and 2).

The architect C.F. Møller, who had designed the buildings at Aarhus University, was also assigned the task to lead the renovation of Moesgaard Manor. In the old buildings housing the stables and barns, he chose to achieve a special theme in the galleries by letting the walls appear roughcast and whitewashed and set on with stone flooring. In the newly built galleries he chose raw timber constructions in pine to support the ceiling panels. These design and material choices permeated both the archaeological and ethnographic galleries.

Figure 2. The Nuristan house from the 1970 exhibition. Photo: Flemming Bau, 1989.

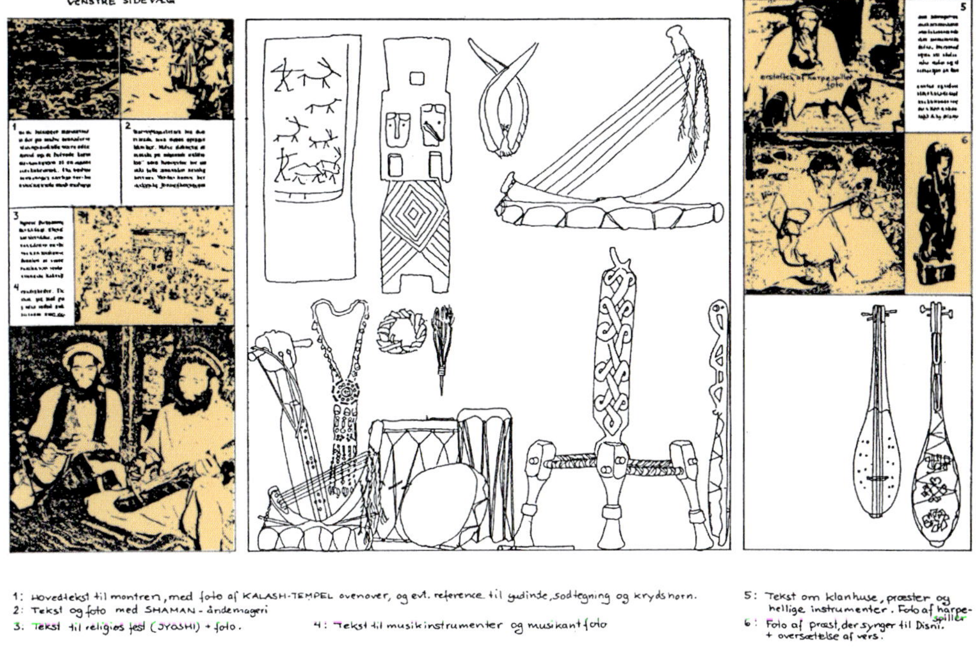

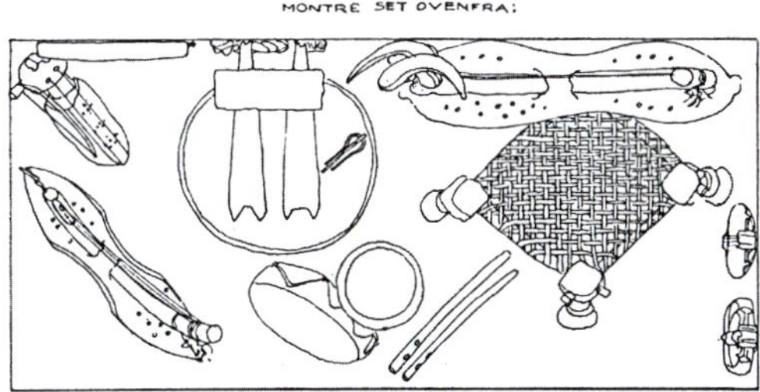

Figure 3. Layout of the display case with artefacts explaining religion and cult in Nuristan and the Kalasha area. There are photos of the Kalash temple, shamans and musicians. Among the instruments are 'wadzh' (harp) and 'sarangi' (string instrument).

Framed by two of these sloping-timber constructions, we built up a plateau with newly acquired ancestor effigies (*gandau*) from the Kalash area and deity effigies on loan from Musée Guimet in Paris. The entire wall behind the installation consisted of a large photograph from the heathen past of Nuristan – that is from the time before their conversion to Islam in 1896 (Ferdinand 1970, 13). The diorama was supposed to work as a visual attraction, as it was installed at the end of a glass hallway that the museum visitors passed through before entering the area devoted to Danish antiquities. Approaching the tableau, visitors could see a Nuristani house, or rather the upper part of a house (*ama*), a living room with four columns. The large end wall behind the house was covered with a giant photograph showing the village of Wama, where the houses were built up a steep mountain side – a collage made from Lennart's photographs taken in 1948. Collected implements, utensils, and music instruments were placed in exhibition cases standing on the floor, which formed a room divider between this exhibition and the Greenlandic exhibition.

We divided the material into an overall narrative about daily life (i.e., the keeping of animals, working in the fields, and hunting). The collection consists of both hunting tools and milk jars and goat skins for churning. Another theme focused on religion and cults. Both the horn chair and the tripod table with the silver cup had a particular importance in the culture of the *Kafirs* (Edelberg 1965, 189). The same is true for the musical instruments such as the harp (*wadzh*) and a stringed instrument (*sarangi*) (figure 3 and 4).

Personally, I have never liked white text labels in an exhibition, as I find them disturbing to the overall impression. Neither do I like the labels often seen in museums with one long text placed somewhere in the display case or on the glass side of the case – with a reference number placed next to the artefact. In both the archaeological and the ethnographical exhibitions, I introduced captions printed directly on the colored cardboard background on which the artefacts were placed. Thus, there was information placed in close proximity to the actual artefacts.

As a communicator and designer of the exhibitions, it was by its very nature my job to make sure that the different topics were grouped in a natural way into certain small narratives, and that they were supplied with texts, which were neither too long nor too complicated. Lennart had a particular knack for writing vividly and pedagogically – one of the reasons for this was probably his experience as a teacher at Ribe Cathedral School. Halfdan Siiger, an incredibly knowledgeable man, had a harder time letting go of the academic writing tradition to which he was accustomed at Aarhus University, and that led to a number of rewritings. Before giving my editing suggestions to Siiger, I reviewed them all with Lennart, who, with a great deal of authority, was able to comment on various aspects regarding religion and cult. Thereby, we tossed and turned many of the concepts and ethical challenges one faces when the subject is about faith and values.

Lennart had a high regard for the Nuristanis, and he was anxious to show a great deal of respect to them when communicating to others information

Figure 4. Hunting, animal husbandry and the making of grain and milk. Photo: Preben Dehlholm.

about their lives. He sent me a copy of the magazine *Frit Danmark,* which in the previous year had published an article of his called "Besættelse" (Occupation). In this he describes a small episode that took place during his first expedition: "In 1948 I enjoyed a week of extensive hospitality in an American USAID camp in Afghanistan. I was allowed to make boxes for the shipment of ethnographic material to the National Museum in Copenhagen out of odd waste materials at the camp. A young, kind, American engineer – with whom I shared a bedroom – supervised the employed Afghan workers. They asked me what I was doing, and I answered them in the level of Persian I was able to speak after a few months' stay in the country. Afterwards, they turned to the American engineer and said: This man is trying to speak to us in Persian – why don't you do the same? He answered: 'I am an American…'"

During his many travels around Nuristan, Lennart made many friends. One of them was particularly important – also for the preparations of the 1970 exhibition, namely Abdullah Wakil from Kushtooz / Keshtagrom. Abdullah Wakil was originally an artisan, called a *bari* in Nuristan. Nuristani society consisted of farmers, herdsmen, and artisans, but these bari did not enjoy a high social status (Edelberg 1981-84, XII). In his publication *Nuristani Buildings*, Lennart recounts a conversation with Abdullah: "One day we were talking about the fact that Nuristani farmers' sons in Kabul do not even call their craftsman compatriots by name – merely bari. If one asks, 'Why do you only call him bari?,' they reply, 'Because he is bari!' It was on this occasion that Abdullah said something that I have often thought about since. He said, 'Yes, but things in Nuristan will never be good until we are all bari!'"

In 1965, Abdullah Wakil was presented with the Order of Dannebrog by King Frederik IX, which was recommended by Klaus Ferdinand and Lennart. As evident from the official document, he is a former member of the Afghan National Assembly and that means that his position in Kabul was at least acknowledged (Nuristani & Klein 2012).

During the summer of 1970, Lennart and Abdullah went to Denmark (Edelberg 1981-84, XII). The exhibition had to be completed, purchased artefacts needed to be included, and the arrangement of the Nuristan house needed to be under the guidance of Abdullah Wakil. The house was built as a replica of the first floor of a house, the *ama,* but only 80 per cent of the size of the original. The reconstruction workers at Moesgaard, Egon Hansen and Viggo Thomsen, produced most of the building elements from measurements and photos provided by Lennart. Original wood-carved columns and household effects were a part of the furnishings (Ferdinand 1984, 214).

Shortly before the official inauguration of Moesgaard's exhibitions, we celebrated the completion of the Nuristani house. Abdullah sacrificed one of our Gothlandic sheep, and the ceremony included food and wine in the house – the wine was not enjoyed from Nuristani silver cups but from Danish wine glasses.

Figure 5. *The inauguration dinner in the Nuristani house before the exhibition opening. Abdullah Wakil sits next to Egon Hansen – and behind him sits Inga Kjærum. Photo: Preben Dehlholm.*

Figure 6. Crown Princess Margrethe, who opened the new exhibitions in Moesgaard September 10th 1970, is given a guided tour in the newly opened Nuristan house by Lennart and Abdullah Wakil. This photo is visible in the photo from the home of Abdullah's son (figure 9).

The exhibition was officially opened by Crown Princess Margrethe, who in 1964 as a student of archaeology had participated in the Slusegård excavations on Bornholm under the guidance of Moesgaard's leader Ole Klindt-Jensen. Lennart and Abdullah Wakil received her at the Nuristani house with goatskins over their shoulders and orders displayed on the chest – including the Order of Dannebrog.

The two exhibitions *Nuristan and the Kalash area* and *Greenland* were on display until 1989. Working together with Svend Castenfeldt, Inge Meldgaard, and Mytte Fentz, I arranged a new exhibition that took up the entire gallery space: *Mountain cultures of the Hindukush*. The Nuristan house and the background panorama photograph continued to be on display (Bau 2010, 147).

Epilogue

While working on this account, I was taken to an unexpected place that gave me a new perspective on the story of Lennart and the 1970 exhibition. Searching on the internet, I stumbled onto the article "One Afghan's Three-Generation Quest for Peace". The article gives an account of Abdullah Wakil, his son Khalilullah Nuristani and his grandson Kakail Nuristani (Nuristani

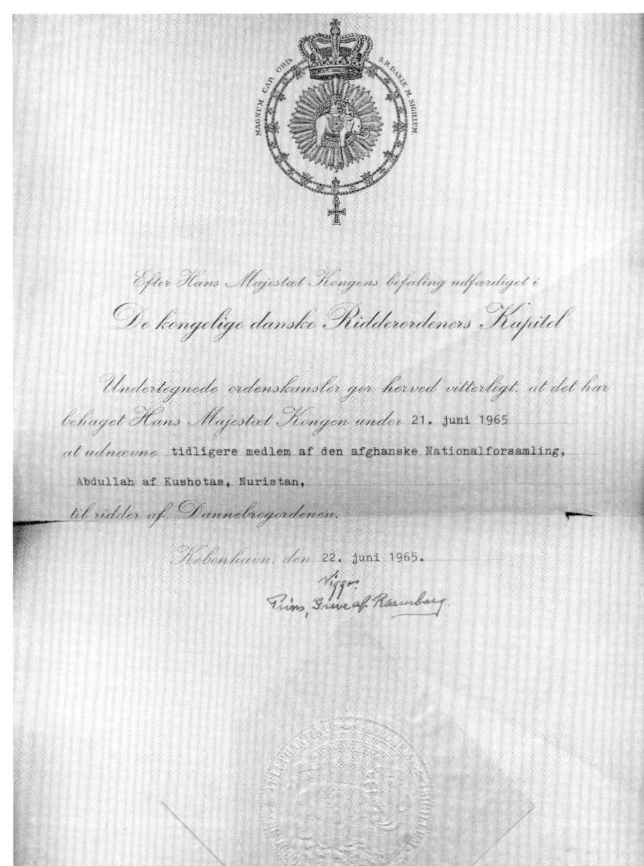

Figure 7. The document that accompanied the presentation of the Order of Dannebrog on June 21st 1965.

& Klein 2012). By coincidence, I met Birte Høj Pedersen at a party. She was a student of archaeology at Moesgaard around 1969-70. I told her about this account, about the three generations of Afghans, and about a photo I had seen in the article on the internet that pictured Abdullah Wakil with the Order of Dannebrog in front of the Nuristani house in the exhibition. The article itself was Birte's account about a visit with the son of Abdullah (Khalilullah) in 1984 – in his house in Chitral in Pakistan. There he was, living in exile out of fear of the Soviets, who had invaded Afghanistan. He had been active in one of the previous governments under the leadership of Daoud. And on a wall in his house, just below the ceiling, were two framed photos of his father thanking king Frederik IX for the Order of Dannebrog, and having Klaus Ferdinand by his side, and another photo of Abdullah with Lennart and Crown Princess Margrethe from the opening of the exhibition.

Khalilullah had obtained asylum in the US, where he tried to raise support from the US to act on the situation in Afghanistan; in fact, he also persuaded the boxer Muhammad Ali to finance the purchase of weapons in the struggle against the Soviets, but apparently the money ended up among a different branch of the mujahedin than he had planned. After this he had left for Chitral, where he became chief consular officer for Nuristan (Ismail Sloan). Later on,

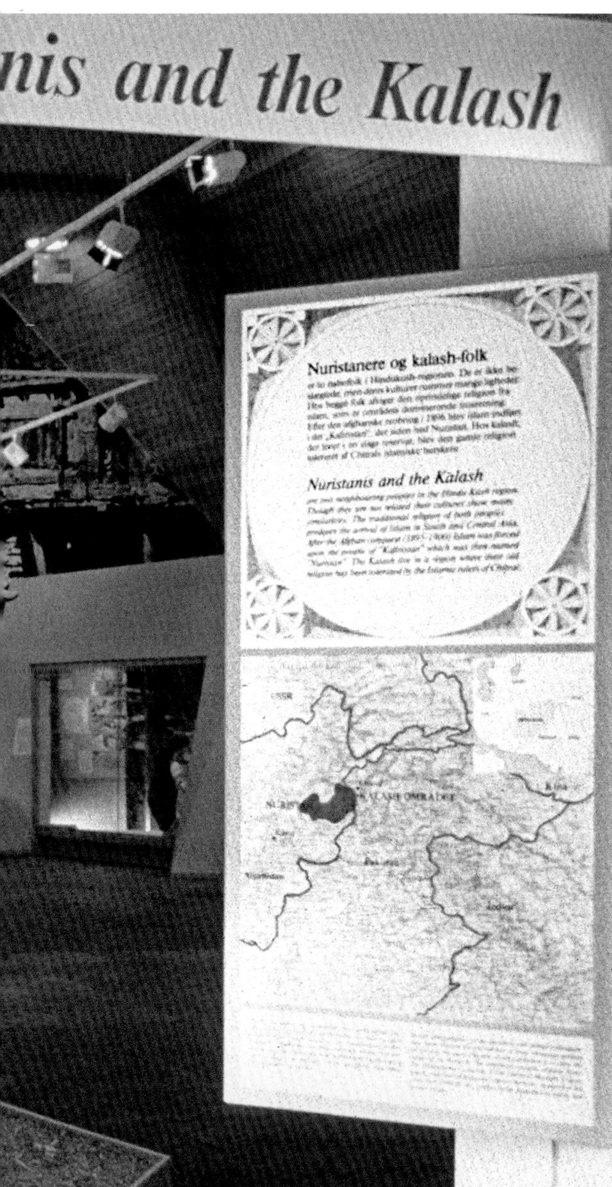

Figure 8. Scene from the exhibition 'Bjergfolk i Hindukush' from 1989, which was a reworked version of the 1970-exhibition. Finally, the extraordinary collections were presented in the entire exhibition gallery. Exhibition cases and walls were made with sloping fronts and plateaus in order to give the audiences a sense of being in the mountains. Photo: Flemming Bau.

his daughters Laila and Zainab were accepted by a university in Canada, and his son Kakail studied at the American University of Afghanistan in Kabul. The account of Kakail Nuristani told to Adam Klein in May 2012 about his family caused comments from many people. I will, in short, quote a few that are relevant for this chapter – those that give an impression of Lennart's activities and significance.

Figure 9. Visit at Abdullah Wakil's son, Khalilullah, November 1984. At the top there are two photos of Abdullah with the Crown Princess Margrethe. Photo: Birte Høj Pedersen.

Figure 10. In one of the photos, Abdullah Wakil is thanking King Frederik 9th for the Order of Dannebrog, while Klaus Ferdinand is watching. To the right the decoration that he received is on display among other decorations. Photo: Birte Høj Pedersen.

Miriam Kathleen Edelberg, Ølstykke, Denmark. June 18, 2012

Dear Kakail Nuristani. I incidentally came across your article, because I was googling my father, Lennart Edelberg. You see, in my childhood Afghanistan became my other homeland because our home was decorated with so many things which my dad had brought home from his many expeditions to Afghanistan, Nuristan. Furthermore, he always gave his talks and slide shows to us children at home before performing in public, so we knew every photo and all details in each slide by heart. My older sister, my father, and mother visited Kushtoz in 1964. Together with my mother and father and my fiancé I visited your grandfather and his family in Kushtoz in the summer 1970, and in Kabul we also met your father. Abdullah joined us upon our return to Denmark, and he stayed in our home for more than a month before he went back home. My mother is now 91. On her wall is still a photo of your grandparents. I have so many wonderful memories of Afghanistan. Your article has left a deep impression. Yours sincerely Miriam Edelberg

Kakail Nuristani Kabul, July 12, 2012

I thank you all for your heartwarming comments.

…Our family, beginning with my grandfather, dedicated their lives to change just that. But three generations thus far have achieved nothing more than hollow promises. Ms. Edelberg, your father has done far greater service to the poor people of Nuristan than all the governments of Afghanistan put together, for which we the people of Nuristan will always be indebted. Sadly, we can't offer to invite you to the place where you had been as a youth, Kushtooz, as it was completely burnt down 14 years ago, and since we have been struggling, battered, and abandoned to keep our identity alive…

Laila K Nuristani Toronto, Canada July 19, 2013

I heard that history repeats itself and it does. I truly admire my brother's article with his professor. It is piece of art. I really appreciate and enjoy the comments by the readers. Some readers are names that we grow up with specially Ms. Mariam K Edelberg. Some day my dream will come true, I will go to Denmark and see Nuristani treasure as Wall Pictures. So. Thank you for living in our hearts.

I will end this chapter with a quote from Khalilullah Nuristani's letter to Birte Høj Pedersen – spelled exactly as in the letter:

…HOW ARE YOU AND WHAT ARE YOU DOING, DID YOU SAW, MY FATHER FRIENDS, MR CALLAUS FER DENAN, IHAVE NOT HIS ADDRESS. HOWS THE LIFE IN DANMARK, YOU ARE HAPPY WITHIT.

WE ARE SO SORRY TO TELL YOU THAT WE ARE NOT VERY HAPPY, YOU KNOW WILL. THAT GOD LISS ROUSSAIN ARE GAIVING US MUCH TRABLES KNOW IN NURISTAN HAVE FIGHT GOUSE ROUND, THADMOUR DARIS ROUSSAINS OR BOMING UOR WELIGES AND OUR HOUSES, AND KILLING, OUR CHILDERENS,… 9.6.85

List of references and relevant literature

Bau, Flemming (2010) "Afghanistan – et styldte formidlingsarbejde." In: *Fortællingens rum. Dansk Tidsskrift for Museumsformidling nr. 30*: pp. 208-221. Forlaget Hikuin: Højbjerg.

Bau, Flemming (2010) "Bjergfolk i Hindukush – Moesgård." In: *Fortællingens rum. Dansk Tidsskrift for Museumsformidling nr. 30*: pp. 147-150. Forlaget Hikuin: Højbjerg.

Castenfeldt, Svend (1999) "Bjergfolk i Hindukush og på Moesgård." In: *Menneskelivets Mangfoldighed. Arkæologisk og antropologisk forskning på Moesgård*, edited by Ole Høiris, Hans Jørgen Madsen, Torsten Madsen and Jens Vellev: pp. 47-54. Moesgård Museum: Højbjerg.

Ferdinand, Klaus (1999) "Den etnografiske samling på Moesgård." In: *Menneskelivets Mangfoldighed. Arkæologisk og antropologisk forskning på Moesgård*, edited by Ole Høiris, Hans Jørgen Madsen, Torsten Madsen and Jens Vellev, pp. 33-46. Moesgård Museum: Højbjerg.

Ferdinand, Klaus (1971) "Etnografien på Moesgårdmuseet: samlingen og noget om at indsamle etnografika." In: *Kuml* 1970: pp. 13-30.

Edelberg, Lennart (1965) "Nuristanske sølvpokaler." In: *Kuml* 1966.

Edelberg, Lennart (1984) "Prologue." In: *Nuristani Buildings*. Jutland Archaeological Society: Højbjerg.

Ferdinand, Klaus (1984) "Nuristani building components in the Moesgaard Museum." In: Lennart Edelberg *Nuristani Buildings*. Jutland Archaeological Society: Højbjerg.

Nuristani, Kakail & Adam Klein (2012) *"One Afghan's Three-Generation Quest for Peace."* http://www.atwar.blogs.nytimes.com (*The New York Times*).

Sloan, Ismail *"Khalilullah Nuristani"*, http://www.anusha.com/khalil.htm

6. Through the eyes of Lennart Edelberg

By Christian Vium

The first time I saw a photograph by Lennart Edelberg was in the basement of Moesgaard manor in Klaus Ferdinand's office. Amidst a welter of material, I discovered a small box of indexical archive prints from one of Edelberg's expeditions. Each photograph – even those of vast landscapes were invested with an intimacy that one rarely sees in mechanically produced images.

Edelberg's curiosity and humanity shines through in his photography, which is full of invitations to embrace other people and places just as he himself did over a lifetime.

Rather than providing a scientific analysis of his photographic work, I have tried to remember my first meeting with Edelberg's work when I was a young student of anthropology about to visit Afghanistan for the first time.

Here are some words that come up when seeing through the eyes of Edelberg in a selection of his photographs from Nuristan made in the period 1948-1970.

EAF 297-116. Nuristan, 1953.

EAF 128-1167. Nuristan, 1964.

EAF 128-1039. Nuristan, 1964.

EAF 128-569 Nuristan, 1964.

EAF 128-1113. Nuristan, 1964.

EAF 128-984. Nuristan, 1964.

EAF 128-817. Nuristan, 1964.

EAF 128-978. Nuristan, 1964.

EAF 128-981. Nuristan, 1964.

EAF 128-807. Nuristan, 1964.

EAF 128-807. Nuristan, 1964.

EAF 130-492. Nuristan, 1970.

EAF 130-561. Nuristan, 1970.

white men in pressed shirts
on a dusty valley road in Afghanistan
gazing into the sky

a village
growing from the cliffs
blinding light and pitch-black shadows
which century are we in?

and then
this immaculate composition
of human bodies on a roof
women, men, children
a fragment of a moment opening up to other worlds
one could spend hours pondering the stories
of these people returning the gaze

inside a house
the light is caressing silhouettes
faces
hands
the intimacy of lived lives
still like sculptures
a solitary man
embraced by the light
what is he thinking of
what transpired in the moments before
the mechanical shutter of the camera broke
the silence

an assemblage of artefacts
in a dark interior
illuminated by a flash
ornamentations carved in wood
signs of a world beyond
metallic pots
ash

Outside
looking into
the darkness
an exquisite decorated wooden door
inviting
an opening
then she appears
enters the world anew
with healthy scepticism
who is this man that
took her picture?

a palette of ochre
harmony
wood and horns
more ornamentations
patterns

an intimate encounter
a mirror of happiness
I see you
the hand that invites
the smile and
the eyes
I can almost hear the sound
of your laugh

in this world
where all seems to be in place

it seems so long ago
somewhere else

it will be alright
he says
with his eyes
while she seems to see beyond
and into the future

the chandelier and
the water on the ground
what did they pray for

the herders
and the herd
somewhere
on top of the world

7. Kafiristan revisited
Kalasha – the so-called 'last Kafirs' of the Hindukush

By Taj Khan Kalash

It has been 122 years since the fall of Kafiristan. The remote isolated mountainous region of the Hindukush on the borders of Central Asia and India was called Kafiristan, meaning – the land of heathens, pagans, or infidels. In the winter of 1895 / 96, the Emir of Afghanistan Abdur Rahman conquered the region and converted the non-Islamic indigenous tribal groups to Islam. The religious conversion to Islam along with the introduction of Islamic rules and culture to these independent tribal peoples was achieved through the direct use of military force and indoctrination. This resulted in the gradual extinction of the former religion. After the conquest, Kafiristan was renamed Nuristan – the land of light – and annexed to Afghanistan. A group of non-converts to Islam, who were also called Red Kafirs, managed to flee the mayhem through the snow-bound passes into the neighboring Muslim principality of Chitral (under British rule then, now part of Pakistan) and sought refuge. The Muslim ruler relocated these so-called Kafir families among another non-Islamic indigenous population called the Black Kafirs in the border valleys of Chitral.

All the pre-Islamic tribes of the Hindukush mountains had been known to outsiders for centuries by the Arabic term *Kafirs* – meaning non-believers. The use of the misnomer Kafir for the pre-Islamic groups of the region has been pervasive in Hindukush literature. Colloquially the use term carries various damning religious connotations and negative sterotypes. The Kafirs are painted as feard bounty hunters, thiefs and godless people. In colonial times a racial element was added to the term Kafir as Aryan race. This led to thier new romanticism as wild, white and liberated pagans in popular culture. Prior to the twentieth century, very little was studied about the history, material culture, languages and religious practices of these so-called Kafirs.

Two members of the Third Danish Expedition to Central Asia (1947-52) went to the Hindukush area: Lennart Edelberg went to the then Islamized Nuristan, and Halfdan Siiger went to the non-Islamized Kalash Kafir area in Chitral, Pakistan. They both collected artefacts and carried out valuable ethnographic fieldwork. Their work thus laid the foundations of research into the pre-Islamic past and material cultures of the peoples of the Hindukush. Their research substantially contributed in dismantling the unfounded narratives prevalent in both eastern and western imagination about the hindukush mountain peoples as primitive and lawless savage cultures. For centuries the Kafir label and a negative sterotypes about the Hindu Kush peoples resulted in their subjugation, humiliation and cultural annhilation. Lennart and Siiger provide a scientific base for Hindukush researchers and compassionate perspective on the mountain region as an ecologically, culturally and linguistically unique enclave of ancient cultures.

In this chapter, I reflect upon the invention of Kafiristan and on Siiger's ethnography of the Kalash Kafir religion. I also discuss the continued portrayal of the Kalasha people in non-academic popular literature as the 'last Kafirs' of the Hindukush, meaning 'infidels' and 'primitive people.' The term Kafir was first used by Islamic conquerors for several non-Islamic ethnic groups in the Hindukush, and their tribal territories, labelling them Kafiristan in the Middle Ages, a name later adopted by Western writers in the nineteenth century. (Beveridge 1922; Burnes 1838; Biddulph 1977 [1880]; Ghufran 1962). This terminology, replete with Islamic and European meanings, continues to influence public discourse and popular thinking regarding the pre-Islamic religion, culture, society and racial ancestry of the non-Islamic Kalasha people of Pakistan as well as other populations in the area. As a result of century-old Western scholarship alongside non-expert cultural views, these terms are regularly perpetuated and reused in popular literature (travelogues, journals, magazines, novels and on the internet) about ancient Kafiristan. In manifold ways, this has increased the popularity of the Kalasha, the last non-Islamic group. On one hand, it has stimulated the growth of ethno-tourism and the perceived heritage of the Kalasha valleys, and on the other, it has triggered threats of attack from the Taliban and raids from Nuristan across the border from Afghanistan which are meant to 'cleanse' Kalash Kafir culture. I discuss the impact of this Kafir label on the pre-Islamic tribes of the Hindukush and the survival of Kalasha culture in the former Muslim principality of Chitral. I will also contrast the

Kalasha people's political and social status and treatment within the former principality with their status and treatment in the modern Islamic Republic of Pakistan as a minority religious group.

The Kalasha collections at Moesgaard and meeting Svend Castenfeldt

In 2008, I was invited by Svend Castenfeldt to visit the Moesgaard Ethnographic Museum in Aarhus to view the Hindukush archives and the collections from Nuristan and the Kalash Kafirs of Chitral. Aarhus University, connected to Moesgaard Museum and its ethnographic collections, has a long tradition of research in Central and East Asia. Halfdan Siiger carried out fieldwork among the Kalash in Chitral, and among the Lepchas in Sikkim in 1948 (see Johnsen et al. for an assessment). Lennart worked in Nuristan (e.g. Edelberg & Jones 1979 and Edelberg 1984), while Henning Haslund-Christensen was based mainly in Mongolia but also visited the Eastern Himalayas (see Prince Peter 1954 and Frederiksen 2001). Much of the work these three men conducted had its roots in the Third Danish Expedition to Central Asia in 1947-52. Danish ethnographers and linguists have since continued their studies in Pakistan. For instance, Svend Castenfeldt, Mytte Fentz, Jan Heegard, and Ida Mørch carried out fieldwork in the Kalasha valleys during the late twentieth century and published their findings.

The main purpose of my visit to Moesgaard was to provide language consultancy on the manuscripts of Prof. Halfdan Siiger for a future publication to be entitled *The old Kafir religion and society*. My job as a Kalasha language consultant was to transcribe and translate Kalasha and other local terms, and provide possible interpretations of documented Kalasha phrases and their intended meanings. It was the first time a Kalasha had had the opportunity to see the museum's Kalasha material since it was added to the collection in 1948.

I felt a deep sense of wonder and curiosity about these remnants of our cultural past that had been collected and preserved outside of the Hindukush. Svend had informed me in advance that, besides Siiger's manuscripts and field notes, there were also 300 old photographs of the Kalasha (then called the Kalash Kafirs) and various objects of material culture including ancestral effigies (Castenfeldt 2003).

All this was very exciting. The materials Svend had mentioned were in special storage rooms, and he had obtained exclusive permission from the museum's directors for them to be studied by a Kalasha. We entered the underground storage rooms using special cards and security codes. I had never been in a place like this. It felt as if the Kalasha materials had a lot of value to the museum. The storage rooms were kept under special temperature conditions and light adjustments in order to prevent any possible damage to the materials. It was remarkable to witness how much work and care had gone into their cataloguing and preservation. We spent hours unpacking Kalasha objects. I was amazed to see the old hand-spun black-woolen robes of Kalasha women, which perhaps had earned them the name *Siah posh*, or Black Kafirs, i.e. 'wearers of the black robes' (Burnes 1838, Ghufran 1962). There were traditional wooden utensils, ornaments, and leather shoes as well.

Everything I touched generated a feeling of the Kalasha past. In one room, the most precious possessions of Kalash Kafir material heritage were standing tall and intact through time: the *Gandaw*s, the ancestral effigies of the Kalasha. Only a few of them have been preserved, and most of those are in Aarhus.

It was then time to inspect the more intangible aspects of Kalasha heritage. Svend had photocopied and arranged all copies of the documents in their folders on a round table in his cozy living room. A large lamp hung from the ceiling, shedding bright light on the manuscripts. Svend's living room was filled with a large collection of owl figurines made of different materials, including some carcasses that had been stuffed and mounted. The owls watched us while we sat across the table from each other. Occasionally, when Svend took a backseat, it felt as if his face in the dim background transformed into an owl reminiscing about the past. It was surreal and magical. We were engaged in the past of the Kalasha, and it was a subject that Svend knew well. He also knew and had met almost all the scholars who had worked in the Hindukush from the mid-nineteenth century. In his eloquent archaic English, Svend would tell me stories of the many misadventures of European travelers in the Hindukush as well as details of the intentions and unmet expectations of those expeditions. His very particular demeanor made me feel the vital presence of the past. Svend is the living connection to the great scholars of the Hindukush as well as to the region's storytellers. He had been a student and assistant of Siiger's, and had cared for Siiger's unpublished Kalasha manuscripts for seventy years. After seeing the wealth of ethnographic material and Siiger's fieldwork notes, I realized why Svend wanted to publish them. He also told me that he had been waiting all these years for a Kalasha to come and provide insights into matters that were unclear to him in the notes. I felt especially privileged to be fulfilling this role. I spent one month with Svend working on the fieldwork notes. Later, I made two more trips to Aarhus. The work on these transcripts is still in progress but will hopefully be finalized soon.

While working on these ethnographic materials and having seen this Kalasha material heritage up close as well as the texts produced by Siiger and Castenfeldt, it was natural that I began to compare this archival past with the Kalasha's present situation. The Hindukush, both the Afghan side and the Pakistan side, owe a lot to researchers like Lennart Edelberg and Halfdan Siiger.

Religious profiling of the Kafirs, 'scientific' racism, romanticism and the Kalasha

By 'revisiting Kafiristan' I mean reviewing the past of the tribal peoples of the Hindukush as viewed, named, observed, created, destroyed and preserved by outsiders. As mentioned above, the Arabic term Kafir means 'unbeliever' or 'infidel.' Its extension, Kafiristan ('land of unbelievers'), is clearly a religious categorization without racial, linguistic, or cultural distinctions.

Yet, linguists have used it while discussing languages in the region, even in recent times (Fussman 1972; Morgenstierne 1973). This term is not employed to describe other non-Islamic populations, e.g., Hindus on the Indus plains. Retaining the term solely for the pre-Islamic tribes of the Afghan-Pakistani mountain regions suggests an additional identification of a primitive and wild people without a holy scripture, prophets, or an omnipresent God, i.e. primitive people without an awareness of or belief in Abrahamic religion (Lockhart 1896; Curzon 1926; Alauddin 1992; Gharzai 1960).

The term Kafir was imported into European writing along with secondary information and popular ideas about tribal societies from Muslim sources. This appears to be principally due to the region's lack of accessibility. The British military officer Robertson, who actually spent one year in 1889-1890 among the pre-Islamic tribal groups in the unconquered land of Kafiristan, retained the Muslim title in his book *The Kafirs of the Hindu-Kush* (1896).

Robertson ventured into Kafiristan through the Muslim principality of Chitral which had been conquered in the late sixteenth century. The local Kafir population had then been converted to Islam, with the exception of the Kalash Kafirs of Chitral, who were instead subjugated and made to pay *jizya* (Islamic tax for being non-Muslim) to the Muslim ruler. The Kalasha resisted conversion to Islam and continued practicing their pre-Islamic culture and traditions. These Kalash Kafirs of Chitral were the first Kafirs Robertson encountered on his way to the independent Kafirs.

Robertson had a very low opinion of the Kalash Kafirs of Chitral. He saw them as a degenerated and servile race, while he held the independent Kafirs in high regard. Robertson considered these unbelievers to be the 'True Kafirs.' The idea that the Kalash of Chitral were less worthy Kafirs than their independent neighbors is quite interesting – both groups were clearly unbelievers, and 'primitive' according to the Islamic use of the word. In contrast, for the European explorer, it becomes clear that Kafir indicated qualities of bravery, savagery, and independence. Perhaps the imperial spirit of the time appreciated warlike behaviour. However, we also get a glimpse of Robertson's view of the Kalasha religion as an 'idolatrous cult.' This provides an indication that his ideas about the Kalash Kafirs were informed by Muslim views of the Kafirs as idol worshippers (Robertson 1896).

Robertson and contemporary European intellectuals seem to have enlarged the meaning and use of the term Kafir by adding positive and negative values to it. A further classification of the inhabitants of Kafiristan as 'Black Kafirs' and 'Red Kafirs' that was based on their attire and attitudes appears frequently in the literature. These labels also appear in the local language as 'Siah posh Kafirs', 'Saffed posh' (i.e., wearers of black robes and white robes); in contrast, the term 'Red Kafirs' only appears in Western texts. The use of the term Kafir in religious scriptural contexts classed all non-monotheistic groups as idol worshippers or heathens, without taking account of linguistic, cultural or racial identity markers.

This religious profiling sanctioned Islamic domination, religious conversion, and the subjugation of Kafiristan in 1895 / 96. Abdur Rahman, Emir of Afghanistan from 1880 to 1901, had clear political and religious motives to conquer, subjugate and bring the light (*nur*) of Islam to the people he perceived as still residing in the darkages. Therefore, after conquering Kafiristan – the land of darkness, he chose to rename it Nuristan – the land of enlightenment. (Katz 1982; Dupree 1971).

The acquisition of Kafiristan by the Emir of Afghanistan in 1896 represents not only an indigenous land grab by invasion but also marks the taking away of native religion, material culture and thought, with the strict and forced imposition of Islamic ways of life upon the Kafir tribes.

The survival of the Kalash Kafirs in the adjacent area of Chitral under British control reveals the different ways local Islamic rulers treated the non-Islamic populations. The Kalash Kafirs of Chitral state were regarded as merely a small and insignificant contingent of enslaved and humiliated peoples in the grand geo-political theater of the late nineteenth century. (Cacopardo & Cacopardo 2001; Parkes 1983). Yet they survived the forced Islamization, while fallen Kafiristan was mythologized as the land of God-deniers, heathens and hedonists.

With the end of Kafiristan, Robertson's independent warrior Kafirs had been either killed, or subjugated and rebranded, and their homeland had been annexed by Afghanistan. Some 'Red Kafir' families from the Bashgal region in Nuristan in Afghanistan fled and sought asylum as refugees among the Black Kafirs of Chitral in the late 1800s. These Red Kafirs were allowed to resettle in the Kalash Kafir valleys of Mumuret (Bumborate) and Rukmu (Rumbur). In Kalasha oral narratives, the Red Kafirs from invaded Kafiristan are called Tsatruma and their homeland Tsatrumdesh. They were deployed as Anwal – border guards, for the protection of the Kalash Kafirs against raiders from Afghanistan and Nuristan. This gives the impression that the Muslim rulers of Chitral at that time had no Islamization agenda directed against the Kafirs under their rule (Wazir 1974).

The fleeing refugee Kafirs, forced out by religious conversion, were resettled in the Kalash region, but within a generation they gave up their traditional religion and converted to Islam. This rapid voluntary conversion of Red Kafir refugees to Islam in the Kalasha valleys is interesting, but historical sources shed no light on it. The prime interest of Western scholarship appears to have been Kafiri religion, and, more pertinently, grief over its loss before it could be properly studied (Jettmar 1982). In addition to religion, there appears to be a great interest in the genetic ancestry and biological characteristics of the Kafirs and their origins, due to their perceived European characteristics (see e.g., Trail 1996 and Bakker & Daval-Markussen 2016 for a study of supposed traces of European languages).

The Kafir label evoked mystery for European audiences, while for Muslims of the time it evoked loathing and provided religious legitimacy for domination, subjugation and conversion. The inhabitants were portrayed as primitive, blasphemous, unbelieving idol worshipers with dark souls and immoral ways of life. In the popular imagination of Westerners, a more mixed image prevailed: the Kafirs of the Hindukush were rather archaic Aryans, hedonists, noble savages, promiscuous pagans drinking wine and dancing freely. Kafirs in European narratives tend to become unbelievably beautiful, part white, familial and culturally relatable even while residing in the distant past (Elphinstone 1839, Pincott 1884).

The popularity of the idea of Kafirs-as-Aryans was so widespread that there was even a German expedition to the Hindukush during the time of the Third Reich, in order to trace the migration roots of the Aryan race and the original grains they had cultivated (Castenfeldt, personal communication). It appears that there was a subtle degree of racial attachment to the presumed whiteness, Aryan, or Macedonian origins of the Hindukush tribes, which remains in the background of the Hindukush literature and has become a major point of interest in modern popular literature concerning the Kalasha (see Wood 1997)[1].

Scholarship and the Kalasha

The last Kafirs of Chitral thus became a living cultural sample of the lost Kafiristan frontier. Kafiristan does not seem to be a real country either, despite the '-stan' suffix. Kafiristan appears to be an idea and an umbrella term implanted on a few tributary tribal territories where different ethnic tribes lived and fought each other and ambushed intruders entering into those areas. But Kafiristan had no common army or united tribal front against foreign aggression. Studies of the former Afghan Kafirs reveal that there were several distinct groups that spoke very different languages (see e.g., Fussmann, 1972; Strand, 2001, 2013, 2016; Bakker et al., this volume) and had varying religious and cultural practices (see e.g. Jettmar 1975, 1986; Jettmar & Edelberg 1974; Katz 1982; Jettmar 1986; Cacopardo & Cacopardo 2001).

By the twentieth century, the Kafir label had become synonymous with the Kalasha, including attributes of all former Kafirs. One of the focus areas for the new Western scholarship at this time concerned the study of the lost Kafir religions as preserved by the Kalash Kafirs (Jettmar 1975, 1986 and the work of Siiger).

Halfdan Siiger was the first European researcher to conduct a detailed ethnographic field study of the religious behaviour and culture of the Kalash Kafirs of Chitral (e.g. 1950, 1951, 1963). The Kalash Kafirs were at the time a minor ethnic and religious minority numbering approximately three or four thousand people inhabiting relatively isolated mountain valleys in what is now Pakistan.

According to Siiger, the Kalash Kafirs were soon to lose their shamanistic religion and their distinct cultural characteristics. This was due to incipient conversions to Islam and the arrival of new Muslim settler communities in their valleys. In view of the lost religions and cultures in Kafiristan, it may be safe to state that the Third Danish Expedition in 1948 among the Kalasha as well as the collection of their heritage materials was an act akin to salvage anthropology. Siiger was on a mission to record the beliefs of the adherents of the last pre-Islamic religion of the Hindukush, before their likely absorption into Islam.

Siiger's ethnography in the Kalash Valleys

Halfdan Siiger arrived in the Kalash Valleys in Chitral in the spring of 1948, a few months after British India gained its independence and was about to be split into the two states of India and Pakistan. Chitral was then still a Muslim principality, which had yet to work out its complete succession to the new Islamic nation state of Pakistan. Chitral became part of Pakistan in 1969. Siiger stayed in the Kalasha valleys with his interpreter Wazir Ali Shah, who was assigned to him by the *mehtar* (ruler) of Chitral. Wazir was not a speaker of Kalasha, but he communicated in Khowar (the *lingua franca* of Chitral) with their Kalasha consultants and he then interpreted their answers in English to Siiger. Many local terms in Siiger's ethnography appear to be of Khowar origin.

Siiger refers to the Kalasha as Kalash Kafirs, which was the established name in Western scholarship regarding Kafiristan. Nonetheless, it is the first time we observe that the Kalasha religious tradition was explored for itself, beyond the so-called Kafir label, as an indigenous form of animism and a shamanistic religion. Siiger's ethnography laid the academic foundations for the study of the so-called Kafir non-believers. Siiger was able to witness and document the ecstatic experiences of Kalasha shamans known as *dehar*. He was also able to document sacred places and shrines in the Kalasha landscape that were dedicated to the spirit world. Siiger identified and visited a total of twelve large open-air shrines, eight *jestak han* (female Jestak temples), six *bashalis* (menstruation houses for women, as well as birthplaces), four *mandaujaw* (open-air cemeteries with ancestral effigies), and a number of wine cellars in Biriu. He identified Zhoshi, Uchau, Pu and Chaumos to be the great cyclical religious festivals of the Kalasha. During these ceremonies, rites were performed and petitions made to the spirit world. He also mentions forms of distributive feasting among the egalitarian Kalasha as a means of achieving higher social and political status. Siiger further observed that the Kalasha erected effigies in honor of their ancestors. These ancestral effigies were also erected at the entrance of the valleys as guardian spirits.

According to Siiger, the Kalasha religion was fundamentally a form of shamanism based in a sacred landscape. "Every Kalash who lives heart and soul in his culture – as most of them do – is well aware that he moves about in a world controlled by different extraordinary (supernatural) powers who exercise their influence through certain spheres (qualities) inherent in the Kalash country and way of life" (see Siiger 1956).

Siiger described the Kalasha as agriculturalists and pastoralists. The highest form of belief resided in the supernatural – most importantly the Succi spirits (fairies) who communicated through the *dehar*. The Kalasha believed in a parallel spirit world and that, upon death, the Kalasha would join their ancestors in that spirit world. Siiger attended a Kalasha funeral in Batrik village where Rota Dehar, a shaman, underwent spirit possession. The Kalasha also followed a solar calendar for activities that centered on agriculture and animal husbandry. The non-sacred sphere included birth and menstruation – *bashali* and *mandaujaw*.

Siiger points out that the supernatural world, mythology, and legends of the Kalasha comprise many figures ranging from divine persons to demon-like beings. He stressed that the Kalasha had acquired and borrowed many elements from several other religions and cultures they had been in contact with. Still, on the level of practice, the Kalasha religion was distinct and based on ancestral traditions.

Transition of stewardship of the Kalash Kafirs to Pakistan

The Kalash Kafirs were ousted from their position of power in Chitral and were subjugated politically in the sixteenth century by Muslim conquerors from Central Asia. A majority of the Kalash population of Chitral converted to Islam, with the exception of a few peripheral valleys linked to the so-called 'true Kafiristan.' The Kalash Kafirs in these border valleys were left alone and could continue to practice their own religious traditions in return for *thangi* (taxes on crops and domestic animals) and *begar* (unpaid labor) (Loude & Lievre 1980; Cacopardo & Cacopardo 2001; Parkes 1983).

Siiger's visit in March 1948 to the Kalash Valleys coincided with the independence of British India. A new nation state based on religious identity, named Pakistan ('land of the pure'), had been established for the Muslim populations. Siiger's visit to Kafir country in the Muslim principality shows that the Muslim mehtar saw some value in the religion of the Kalash Kafirs, unlike the ruthless ruler of Afghanistan Abdur Rahman who destroyed Kafir material culture and imposed Islamic religion in Nuristan. (see Schomberg 1938; Snoy 1959; Jones 1974).

More detailed analysis of archival material may provide insights as to the reasons why the mehtar of Chitral decided to permit the territorial and cultural autonomy of the Kalasha as well as to what value the Kalasha found in their traditional religion. Despite subjugation and semi-slavery, the population desired to remain non-Islamic – even though all other non-Islamic groups in the Hindukush converted to Islam, voluntarily or involuntarily.

My impression is that Siiger was provided with the royal interpreter Wazir Ali Shah because the Muslim principality was aware of Western interest in the Kafirs and their ancient culture. Indeed, Kalasha were frequently asked to perform dances for visitors and dignitaries. In the case of Siiger, it may have been that the aim of establishing touristic, cultural or diplomatic relations with Denmark and other European countries is why the principality allowed the culture to be documented and studied by an expert. It is evident from Siiger's ethnography that the Kalash Kafir valleys were a restricted area for Muslim settlers and proselytizers. However, after the Muslim principality of Chitral was fully annexed to Pakistan in 1969, the mehtar's ownership of the Kalash Kafirs and their homeland was transferred to the newly-formed nation state. Siiger indicates that new Muslim immigrants had begun to settle in the Mumuret Valley and that the Kalasha started to convert to Islam there.

The Kalash Kafirs seventy years later

At the turn of the twentieth century mysterious stories of murder and raids in the Hindukush mountains started to appear in the world press. These stories in the press and popular media provide some evidence that the Kalash Kafirs survived as non-Islamic people in Pakistan well into the twenty-first century – contrary to the predictions of Siiger and others.

The first story, appearing in August 2002, concerned a European Yeti tracker and his teenage Kalasha servant who were brutally murdered in a remote village on the border of Afghanistan and Pakistan, where he had been living for several years.[2] The suspects were reported to have disappeared into neighboring Nuristan through the nearby Shawala pass. A will written by the slain Catalan / French / Spanish cryptozoologist Jordi Magraner surfaced at the regional office of the Deputy Commissioner in Chitral. In his last will and testament, Magraner stated that in such an event as death in the region, his body should not be returned to France but given an honorary pagan funeral. Consequently, the Kalasha of Kraka village in the Mumuret valley, as per ancient tradition, held the honorary funeral feast. They invited all the Kalasha villages, slaughtered goats, ate cheese, played drums, and danced around his body for two nights and three days. Singing ancient farewell songs, they gave honorary speeches and shared memories of the past fifteen years that Magraner had lived amongst them, recalling his pledge to protect their culture.

The eccentric life of Jordi Magraner among the Nuristanis and pagan Kalasha – including his supposed conversion to Islam and then becoming Kalasha; his meeting with Ahmad Shah Masood, nicknamed the Lion of Panjshir; the discovery of armor and antiques at his home; and his research on Himalayan snowmen – not only became part of local storytelling but it was also mythologized as an adventure novel for Western consumption[3] in a similar manner to Rudyard Kipling's famous story "The Man who Would be King" a century ago (Kipling 1952).

Then came the story of a Taliban raid from Nuristan and the abduction of another culture savior of the Kalasha.[4] The Greek teacher Athanasios Lerunis was kidnapped from his ethnological museum and Kalash School, the Kalasha Dur in Mumuret. The building is the most magnificent non-Muslim complex built in the modern history of the Hindukush. It was inspired by legends and an old speculative theory of descent: that the Kalasha are said to be the descendants of injured Greek soldiers from Macedonia who had been left behind in the Hindukush during Alexander the Great's military campaign (see Trail, 1996). The Kalasha Dur is a masterful combination of traditional Hindukush and modern architecture; it took ten years to build at the cost of three million euros raised in Greece. Athanasios wanted to restore the inferior social status of the Kalasha and train the locals to preserve their own heritage. The raid took place at time when the Kalasha of Mumuret had gone to the Birir valley to attend a funeral feast. A Chitrali Muslim guard provided by the government of Pakistan for security was murdered. The suspicions of this coordinated attack fell on the famous *bari* carpenters and laborers that he had employed to decorate the pillars of the Kalasha Dur. After spending six months in the Bashgal Valley as a hostage of the Taliban, Athanasios was retrieved in return for a ransom and prisoner exchange. In the time up to Athanasios' liberation, the Kalasha campaigned for his release, which received wide press coverage.

There was then the story of a Taliban attack on a Pakistani army post in Chitral that appeared in a Jihadist video, in which the Kafir Kalash were warned they would be attacked if they did not convert to Islam.[5]

In two raids over the past few years, Kalasha goat herders were reported to have been killed and their livestock stolen.[6] These raids on Kalasha shepherds took place in the pastures close to Nuristan. The identity of the raiders is not clear, sometimes they are called Taliban militants and other times simply referred to as insurgents. The raids typically take place in the summer months (May-September), when the Kalasha take their herds to pasture in higher regions of the mountains and when the passes are relatively accessible. The government of Pakistan took notice of these raids and sent special forces to the pastures, supposedly killing five raiders. The Kalasha were also advised to keep their livestock in the valleys. The Kalasha protested that this was state interference and an imposition aimed against the continuation of Kalasha religion; as mentioned earlier, Kalasha religion is based on pastoralism and raising goats.

Revival of Kalash Kafiristan in popular literature

In today's Pakistan, the Kalash Kafirs of the Hindukush mountains have ascended to the peak of their popularity. They have become a celebrity tribe raised from the ashes of fallen Kafiristan – a lost paradise of Western anthropology. The Kalash Kafirs largely owe this rise to fame to the ambiguities of the umbrella term Kafir, which was applied widely to all the polytheistic groups once thought to be one and the same group (see above). The Kalasha, representing the last remaining non-Islamic culture in the region, have apparently inherited the formerly recorded attributes of all the Hindukush Kafirs (see Khan 1975). Burgeoning interest in the Kalasha seems to have grown out of the wealth of social research and popular media that has created a demand for exotic literature on, and access to, the 'pagan Kalasha area' of Pakistan. Popular literature on the Kalash Kafirs has increased exponentially, due to the internet. Google search returns countless pages containing the terms Kafir, Kafiristan, and Kalash. Print media and internet websites regularly feature modern photojournalism showing non-veiled, colorful and black-robed, cowry clad, light-skinned, blonde, and blue-eyed Kalasha women, along with a narrative of their sexual liberation in opposition to conservative Islamic surroundings.

Siiger arrived in the Kalasha area in 1948 on foot through mountain passes from Chitral. Today access to the Kalasha valleys is made easier via government-built roads. In a climate of greater political instability and religious terrorism in Afghanistan, the frontier Kalasha also provide another story for journalists' audiences abroad. However, journalists and documentary filmmakers of the twenty-first century are often unaware of the complexities and ambiguities of the term Kafir and the varied contexts in which it has been used.

Their approach seems to have derived from early nineteenth-century literature on Kafiristan. This is evident in the reproduction of the old accounts – including the direct translation of Kafir as infidels, pagans, and non-believers and sometimes with an overtone of racial exclusiveness – in current social media and news stories about the Kalasha. These news articles tend to evoke an imagined past by placing the Kalasha in direct opposition to Islamic values. They highlight drinking and feasting, unveiled women, and general equality of the sexes.

Although, in academic literature, both anthropologists and linguists have dropped the old label 'Kalash Kafirs' because of its derogatory connotations, the term Kafir has in reality not fallen out of usage at a popular level (see Loude & Lievre 1988; Parkes 1983; Trail & Cooper, 1996; Cooper 2005; Heegard 2002; Di Carlo 2007). With its varied cultural meanings, it also continues to be used by intolerant Muslims and Islamist groups in their anti-Kalasha religious rhetoric.

By way of illustration, here are some recent headlines referring to the Kalash in international news media:

"Pakistan: Kalash valley of wine and festivals under threat," *BBC News.*

"Taliban targets descendants of Alexander the Great," *Telegraph.*

"Pakistan's Pagan Valley," *Men's Journal.*

"In the land of infidels," *Dawn News.*

"A little-known Pakistani tribe that loves wine and whiskey fears its Muslim neighbors," *Washington Post.*

"Earthquake was Allah's wrath for Kalash community's immoral ways," *Express Tribune.*

"No Relief for Kalash in Pakistan's Valley of Infidels," *Voice of America.*

"Kalasha; the happiest people in Pakistan?" CNN.

"Kalash: An odyssey of the heart," *Dawn News.*

"The Lost Children of Alexander the Great: A Journey to the Pagan Kalash People of Pakistan," *Huffington Post.*

[See full references in the bibliography.]

There is currently no consensus on the degree to which Kalash culture has managed to retain its non-Islamic characteristics in the seventy years since Siiger's ethnography. Siiger's research provides a sound basis for studying the past and present of the Kalasha traditional religion, in contrast to the contemporary views discussed above and fantasies of the Kalasha by popular media in Pakistan and abroad. The image of the Kalasha by outsiders in popular literature indicates that views of Kafirs created in the Middle Ages continue to exist and are perpetuated in popular media coverage on Kalasha history

and culture. The mortuary rites also reported in news stories provide some reason to establish that the practice of indigenous religion has not died out.

As a Kalasha, my personal assessment is that the Kalasha have maintained the traditions reported by Siiger in his ethnography. A new ethnographical study of the Kalasha, however, will be necessary to reveal the impact of Islam and globalization on indigenous Kalasha religious traditions since the creation of Pakistan.

Funeral feast of the author's grandfather, 2013. Photos: Taj Khan Kalash.

Pastoralism vs. tourism

The traditional funeral rites of the Kalasha attended by Siiger in 1948 in Batrik village and the Kalasha funeral rites of today demonstrate the continuity of Kalasha traditional religion and its distinctly non-Islamic character. Unlike Islam, traditional Kalasha religion had no eschatological conception of heaven or hell, nor did it have a concept of a judgement day. It would be interesting to see how these beliefs concerning the afterlife (or lack thereof) have been transformed.

Since Siiger's research, there have been several other important anthropological studies of Kalasha customs and ways of life. These have generated a new corpus of anthropological literature specific to Kalasha culture and religion (see Fentz 2011; Parkes 1983; Cacopardo & Cacopardo 2001). These studies have also shown that Kalasha religion is a tradition-based practice rather than possessing a dogmatic character; it is an ancient way of life designed around agriculture and pastoral activities.

The annexation of Chitral also increased the vulnerability of Kalasha religion with the arrival of Muslim settlers who desired to put an end to the Kafir Kalash religion. The first incident occurred in Darasguru village in 1969 after the incorporation of Chitral into Pakistan. A Muslim mob confiscated the dead body from a funeral proceeding and demanded an end to Kalasha funeral rites. However, the new civil administration in charge of Chitral intervened, and the Kalasha were allowed to continue their traditions. This shows that the Kalasha did receive a form of state protection from the government of Pakistan. Allowing the Kalasha funeral of Jordi Magraner in Kraka is also an indication that the Pakistani government wishes to avoid state interference in Kalasha traditions.

The visit of the first socialist Prime Minister Zulfikar Ali Bhutto to Chitral in 1971, when he declared the Kalash Kafirs to be a unique Pakistani heritage community, appears to mark the beginning of a new chapter in the relationship of the Kalasha with the Pakistani state (see Alauddin 1992; Ali & Rehma 2001).

Siiger attended the great Kalash spring festival of Joshi at the end of April 1948. The fixture of the date of Zhoshi (spring rites) to May 15 in tourist brochures and in a touristic documentary made in 1976 by Pakistan state television suggests that the government has become interested in promoting the Kalasha area as a tourist destination. A tourist fee on the entrance to the Kalasha valleys was put in place for the development of the Kalasha people in the nineteen seventies. These actions indicate early attempts towards the recognition of Kalash heritage and development of the valleys. Without the protection and intervention of the government of Pakistan during times of extreme pressure to convert, it is unlikely the Kalasha could have survived in their traditional cultural form. At the same time, Kalasha religion and culture face the risk of extinction, due to growing conversions to Islam and a lack of natural resources to sustain Kalasha economic traditions (see Russell 2014; Kalash & Heegard 2016).

The government of Pakistan seems to have developed a continued interest in protecting Kalasha culture due to its commercial value and tourism potential in the last few decades, itself the cumulative result of 120 years of literature about Kafiristan. The construction of museums in the Kalasha valleys, along with funding for several other traditional and non-traditional infrastructural projects, points toward a concept that regards the Kalasha as artefacts to be exhibited to outsiders. The outcomes of these initiatives can also be viewed as a revival of so-called Kafir culture as sponsored by an economy-driven progressive Pakistan (see di Carlo 2007; Maggi 2001; Parkes 1983). This governmental support, seen as preferential treatment, has attracted the hostility not only of Muslim communities residing in the Kalasha valleys but also of militant Islamists in neighboring Nuristan. The idea that the Kalasha valleys represent a heritage site is also a source of jealousy and hostility in the arena for power dynamics among the Muslim communities living there. They see NGOs as well as Pakistani and foreign tourists as only interested in the preservation and development of the Kalasha. They feel angered by the support given to Kalasha by the government in creating and nourishing the performance of Kafir or pagan culture. In addition, the volatile Nuristan-Kalash border between Afghanistan and Pakistan has become an attack and escape route for criminals who evoke religious legitimacy for the disruption of the so-called last Kafir culture (see Zaidi 1985). This has led to murders, kidnappings, and the periodic raiding of Kalasha pastures. The government's policy of development of this rural area through excessive tourism and promotion could also be detrimental for the survival of indigenous pastoralism.

The Kalasha are now outnumbered in their own valleys by Muslim settlers and converts by a ratio of 30:70. The core of Kalasha religion, however, has survived due to the continuation of livestock and animal husbandry. The raids on Kalasha livestock from Nuristan and the lack of grazing pastures and agricultural lands due to increased migration of non-Kalasha into the valleys may eventually terminate this facet of the lived experience of Kalasha religion. The continuous existence of the indigenous religion and viewing the valleys as a tourist destination is a problematic issue that requires a deeper understanding of Kalash culture as regards its sustainability.

The Kalasha argue that goat herding and agriculture form the core of their ethos; without goats, all their celebrations and traditions will be unsustainable and lose meaning.

Concluding remarks

The fact that the Kalasha are the last non-Islamic group in the Hindukush ensures their place in popular imagination and in the encyclopaedia of existing world religions. The label 'Kafir,' translated as infidel / pagan, allows for generalizations to exist in perpetuating the Kafir or pagan legends and origin myths in popular literature.

Siiger's ethnography presents us with an image of an historical pastoral and agricultural society with its own indigenous religion. This Kalasha society was predicted to convert to Islam in the following years. However, this has not been the case. The survival of the Kalasha into the twenty-first century shows that they can survive as a distinct non-Islamic people and successfully maintain their traditions and customs. The grand funerary feasts, at which large amounts of goat meat and ghee is consumed, also indicate that the Kalasha have not made a complete transition from a predominantly agro-pastoral society, despite a growing tourism industry as well as the pressures of globalization and urbanization exerted upon them.

There also seems to be a lack of legislative intervention and incentive in creating favorable conditions for safeguarding the natural environment of the Kalasha region and for protecting Kalasha pastoralism as an economic / cultural activity. The main issue pertaining to the Kalasha people now is the potential loss of their traditional goat-based economy and the opening up of their homeland to non-Kalasha settlers.

The historical conditions under the mehtar's rule as described by Siiger shows that, prior to the succession of Chitral to Pakistan, the Kalasha area was a reservation within the principality of Chitral. The restoration of that same status may be necessary for the survival of Kalasha culture.

Afterword: Joining the collections at Moesgaard with my experience and ambitions as a Kalasha

Siiger's ethnography, manuscripts, and old photos are a unique and exceptionally valuable treasure for the Kalasha of the twenty-first century and need to be published for their greater benefit. It is important to remember that these materials are historical documents made by non-Kalasha experts about the Kalasha and their religious and social culture. In the Kalasha valleys, tradition and history have been transmitted orally from generation to generation. Since the Kalasha had no written language prior to 2001, access to publications concerning the Hindukush can provide a wealth of material and knowledge by which a new Kalasha generation can engage and study their past. Such materials would be inscribed with their own chosen names and terms and their own views on Kalasha history and culture; in the process, it would vitalize Kalasha identity, language, and culture.

I will always be grateful to Svend Castenfeldt, Jan Heegard, Peter Bakker, and Ulrik Høj Johnsen for opening up this world of Western scholarship on the Hindukush to me. I am grateful for Svend's continued interest in the region, his commitment to publishing Siiger's work on the Kalasha, and his passion for the history of Hindukush researchers.

Notes

1. https://www.huffingtonpost.com/brian-glyn-williams/pagan-kalash-people-of-pakistan_b_4811627.html
2. http://www.bigfootencounters.com/articles/jordi.htm
3. In the Land of Giants: Hunting Monsters in the Hindukush, Gabi Martinez.
4. http://www.bbc.co.uk/news/world-south-asia-13466250
5. http://www.telegraph.co.uk/news/6214794/Taliban-targets-descendants-of-Alexander-the-Great.html
6. https://arynews.tv/en/two-kalash-shot-dead-alleged-by-afghan-taliban/

List of references

Alauddin (1992) *Kalasha: the paradise lost.* Progressive Publishers: Lahore.

Ali, S.S. and J. Rehman (2001) *Indigenous Peoples and Ethnic Minorities of Pakistan: Constitutional and Legal Perspectives.* Curzon Press: Richmond, Surrey.

Bakker, Peter and Aymeric Daval-Markussen (2016) "Linguistic and genetic roots of the Kalasha." In: *In the Footsteps of Halfdan Siiger – Danish Research in Central Asia*, edited by Ulrik Høj Johnsen, Armin W. Geertz, Svend Castenfeldt and Peter B. Andersen: pp. 93-114. Højbjerg: Moesgaard Museum.

Beveridge, A.S. (1922) *The Babur-nama* in English. Translated from the original Turki Text of Zahiruddin Muhammad Babur Padshah Ghazi. Reprint London 1969.

Biddulph, John (1977 [1880]) *Tribes of the Hindoo Koosh.* Indus Publications: Karachi.

Burnes, Alexander (1833) "On the Reputed Descendants of Alexander the Great, in the Valley of Oxus." In: *JASB* 2: pp. 305-307.

Buddruss, Georg (1974) *Some Reflections on Kafir Myth.* HCC: 31-36 Wiesbaden.

Burnes, Alexander (1838) *"On the Siah-posh Kaffirs- with specimens of their language and costume."* In: JASB VII/ 1: pp. 325-333.

Cacopardo, Alberto M. and Augusto S. Cacopardo (2001) *Gates of Peristan: History, Religion, and Society in the Hindukush.* Instituto Italiano per l'Africa e l'Oriente: Rome.

Cacopardo, A.S. (2006) "Anthropomorphic representations of divinities among the Kalasha of Chitral (Pakistan)." In: *Acta Orientalia* 67: pp. 127-158.

Castenfeldt, S. (ed.) (2003) *Historical Kalasha Picture Book. Photos from the Kalasha People of Chitral, Pakistan, 1948*. Århus.

Cooper, G. (2005) "Issues in the Development of a Writing System for the Kalasha Language." PhD Dissertation, Macquarie University.

Curzon, Lord Marques of Kedleston (1926) *Leaves from a Viceroy's Notebook and Other Papers*. Macmillan: London.

Di Carlo, P. (2007) "The Prun festival of the Birir valley, Northern Pakistan, in 2006." In: *East and West* 57, no. 1-4: pp. 45-100.

Dupree, Louis (1971) *Nuristan: "The Land of Light" Seen Darkly*. The American Universities Field Staff, Asia, South Asia Series, XV/6: pp. 1-24.

Edelberg, Lennart (1984) *Nuristani Buildings*. Jutland Archaeological Society: Højbjerg

Edelberg, Lennart & Schuyler Jones (1979) *Nuristan*. Akademische Druck- u. Verlagsanstalt: Graz.

Elphinstone, Mountstuart (1839) *An Account of the Kingdom of Caubul*. Reprint of the Third Edition 2 vols. Karachi: 1972.

Fentz, Mytte (2011) *The Kalasha. Mountain People of the Hindukush*. Rhodos: Humlebæk.

Frederiksen, Kurt L. (2001) *Manden i Mongoliet: Henning Haslund-Christensens fantastiske liv*. Borgens Forlag: København.

Fussman, Gérard (1972) *Atlas linguistique des parlers dardes et kafirs*. École française d'Extrême-Orient: Paris.

Gardner, Alexander (1977) "A Scetch on Kaffiristan and the Kaffirs- usually Called the Seea Posh Kaffirs by Mohammedan Tribes around them" (1869). With an Introduction by Schuyler Jones. *Afghanistan Journal* 4, no 2: pp. 47-53.

Gharzai, Moh. Safar Wakeel (1960; A.H. 1339) *Nooristan* (in Persian). Kabul: n.p.

Ghufran, M. M. (1962) *NayiTarikh-e-Chitral*. Translated from Farsi into Urdu by Ghulam Murtaza. Public Art Press: Peshawar.

Heegård, J. (2002) "Linguistic and political aspects of alphabet-making for a threatened language." In: *17th Scandinavian Conference of Linguistics II*. [Odense Working Papers in Language and Communication 19], edited by C.-E. Lindberg and S. Nordahl, 161-176. University of Southern Denmark, Institute of Language and Communication: Odense.

Jettmar, Karl (1975) *Die Religionen des Hindukusch*. Mit Beiträgen von Schuyler Jones und Max Klimburg. In the series *Die Religionen der Menschheit* 4, no 1. Kohlhammer: Stuttgart.

Jettmar, Karl (1986) *The Religions of the Hindukush: The Religion of the Kafirs*. Oxford & 1BH Publishing Co.: New Delhi.

Jettmar, Karl and Lennart Edelberg (1974) *Cultures of the Hindukush. Selected Papers from the Hindu-Kush Cultural Conference Held at Moesgård 1970*. Beiträge zur Südasienforschung, Südasien-Institut, Universität Heidelberg. Franz Steiner Verlag: Wiesbaden.

Jones, Schuyler (1966) *An Annotated Bibliography of Nuristan (Kafiristan) and the Kalash Kafirs of Chitral, Part one*. In: [Historisk-filologiske Meddelelser, Det Kongelige Danmarks Videnskabernes Selskab, Vol. Hist. filos. Medd. Dann. Vid. Selsk. 41/3.] Ejnar Munksgaard: København.

Jones, Schuyler (1967) *The Political Organization of the Kam Kafirs. A Preliminary Analysis.* Hist.-filos. Medd. Dann. Vid. Selskab: København.

Johnsen, Ulrik Høj, Armin W. Geertz, Svend Castenfeldt and Peter B. Andersen, (eds.) (2016) *In the Footsteps of Halfdan Siiger – Danish Research in Central Asia.* Moesgaard Museum: Højbjerg.

Kalash, Taj Khan and Jan Heegård (2016) Dynamics of Cultural Survival of the Kalasha. In: *In the Footsteps of Halfdan Siiger – Danish Research in Central Asia*, edited by Ulrik Høj Johnsen, Armin W. Geertz, Svend Castenfeldt and Peter B. Andersen. Moesgaard Museum: Højbjerg.

Katz, David (1982) *Kafir to Afghan: Religious Conversion, Political Incorporation, and Ethnicity in the Vaygal Valley, Nuristan.* University of California at Los Angeles. (Doctoral dissertation).

Kipling, Rudyard (1952) "The Man who Would be King." In: *A choice of Kipling's prose.* sel. & intro. by W.S. Maugham: pp. 171-202. London Macmillan: London.

Lockhart, Colonel (1896) "Notes on Chitral, Gilgit, January 1, 1896." Unpublished manuscript.

Loude, Yves and Viviane Lièvre (1988) *Kalash Solstice: Winter Feasts of the Kalash of North Pakistan.* Lok Virsa, Islamabad.

Maggi, W. (2001) *Our Women Are Free. Gender and Ethnicity in the Hindukush.* University of Michigan Press: Ann Arbor.

Martinez, Gabi (2017) *In the Land of Giants: Hunting Monsters in the Hindukush.* Scribe Publications: Melbourn & London.

Morgenstierne, Georg (1929a) "The Language of the Ashkun Kafirs." In: *Norsk Tidsskrift for Sprogvidenskap* 2: pp. 192-289.

Morgenstierne, Georg (1952) "Linguistic Gleanings from Nuristan." In: *Norsk Tidsskrift for Sprogvidenskap* 16: pp. 117-135.

Morgenstierne, Georg (1954) "The Waigali Language." In: *Norsk Tidsskrift for Sprogvidenskap* 17: pp. 146-324.

Morgenstierne Georg (1973b) "Die Stellung der Kafirsprachen." In: Georg Morgenstierne, *Irano-Dardica*: pp. 327-343. Ludwig Reichert Verlag: Wiesbaden.

Parkes, P. (1983) *Alliance and Elopement: Economy, Social order, and Sexual Antagonism among the Kalasha (Kafirs) of Chitral.* PhD dissertation, Oxford University.

Parkes, Peter (1987) "Livestock Symbolism and Pastoral Ideology among the Kafirs of the Hindukush." In: *Man* (N. S.) 22: pp. 637-660.

Parkes, Peter (1991) "Temple of Imra, Temple of Mahandeu: A Kafir sanctuary in Kalasha cosmology." In: *Bulletin of the School of Oriental and African Studies* 54, Part 1: pp. 75-103.

Parkes, Peter (1992) "Reciprocity and Redistribution in Kalasha Prestige Feasts." In: *Anthropozoologica* 16: pp. 37-45.

Parkes, Peter (2001) "The Kalasha of Pakistan. Problems of Minority Development and Environmental Management." http://www.the-south-asian.com/June2001/ Kalasha3. html

Pincott, F. (1884) "The route by which Alexander entered India." *Journal of the Royal Asiatic Society of Great Britain Ireland.*

Peter, H.R.H., Prince of Greece and Denmark (1954) "The Third Danish Expedition to Central Asia: Its Work in the Himalayas." In: *The Himalayan Journal* 18. https://www.

himalayanclub.org/hj/18everest/13/the-third-danish-expedition-to-central-asia-its-work-in-the-himalayas/

Robertson, George Scott (1896) *The Káfirs of the Hindu-Kush*. Lawrence & Bullen: London.

Schomberg, R.C.F. (1938) "Kafirs and Glaciers." In: *Travels in Chitral*. M. Hopkinson: London.

Siiger, Halfdan (1950) "Som etnograf blandt de sorte kafirer. Erfaringer fra den 3. danske centralasiatiske ekspedition." Offprint No 295. Folkeuniversitetsudvalget: Copenhagen.

Siiger, Halfdan (1951) *Statuer af træ hos Kalash-kafirerne i Chitral – materiale fra Den 3. Danske Centralasiatiske Ekspedition*. In: Nationalmuseet Arbejdsmark.

Siiger, Halfdan (1963) "Shamanism among the Kalash Kafirs of Chitral. From the Third Danish Expedition to Central Asia." In: *Folk* 5: pp. 295-304.

Siiger, Halfdan (n.d.) "The Old Kalasha Society." [Unpublished manuscript given to the author by Svend Castenfeldt].

Siiger, Halfdan, S. Castenfeldt and M. Fentz (1991) *"Small functional items and regenerations of society: Dough figurines from the Kalash people of Chitral, Northern Pakistan."* In: *The History of Things. Essays presented to Klaus Ferdinand on his 65th Birthday, April 19th, 1991*. [*Folk* 33] pp. 37-46. Danish Ethnographic Society: Copenhagen.

Strand, Richard F. (2001) "The Tongues of Peristân." In: *Gates of Peristan: History, Religion and Society in the Hindukush*, by Alberto M. Cacopardo and Augusto S. Cacopardo: pp. 251-259. Instituto Italiano per l'Africa e l'Oriente: Rome.

Strand, Richard F. (2013) "Dardic and Nūristānī Languages." In: *The Encyclopaedia of Islam, Third Edition*, Part 2013-14: pp. 101-103. Brill: Leiden.

Strand, Richard F. (2016) "Nuristani". In: *The Languages and Linguistics of South Asia: A Comprehensive Guide*, edited by Hans H. Hock and Elena Bashir: pp. 66-73. Mouton de Gruyter: Berlin.

Strand, Richard F. (1983) "Local insurgency Versus the Peshawar Parties in Nuristan." Talk given at the panel *Afghanistan: The Resistance in the Fourth Year – Additional Views*. Forum on Afghanistan, Loy Henderson Conference Room, Department of State, Washington, D.C.

Trail, G.H. (1996) "Tsyam Revisited: a study of Kalasha origins." In: *Proceedings of the Second International Hindukush Cultural Conference*. Hindukush and Karakuram Studies, edited by E. Bashir & I. ud-Din. Oxford University Press: London & Karachi.

Trail, R.L & G.R. Cooper (1999) *Kalasha Dictionary – with English and Urdu*. Studies in languages of northern Pakistan, vol. 7. National Institute of Pakistan Studies, Quaid-i-Azam University & Summer Institute of Linguistics: Islamabad.

Wazir Ali Shah (1974) "Invasions Preceding the Conquest of Nuristan." *HCC*: pp. 24-25.

Woods, Michael (1997) *In the footsteps of Alexander the Great*. University of California Press; Television tie-in edition: Berkeley.

Zaidi, A. (1985) *Ethnic Cleansing of Kafirs in Pakistan*. Retrieved from http://www.gowanusbooks.com/kafirs.htm

Web articles

"Pakistan: Kalash valley of wine and festivals under threat," *BBC News.*

http://www.bbc.co.uk/news/world-south-asia-13466250

"Taliban targets descendants of Alexander the Great," *Telegraph.*

http://www.telegraph.co.uk/news/6214794/Taliban-targets-descendants-of-Alexander-the-Great.html

"Pakistan's Pagan Valley," *Men's Journal.*

https://www.mensjournal.com/adventure/pakistans-pagan-valley-20130612/

"In the land of infidels," *Dawn News.*

https://www.dawn.com/news/752908

"A little-known Pakistani tribe that loves wine and whiskey fears its Muslim neighbors," *Washington Post.*

https://www.washingtonpost.com/world/asia_pacific/a-little-known-pakistani-tribe-that-loves-wine-and-whiskey-fears-its-muslim-neighbors/2016/08/15/9a8483aa-5273-11e6-b652-315ae5d4d4dd_story.html?utm_term=.c99d52656803

"Earthquake was Allah's wrath for Kalash community's immoral ways," *Express Tribune.*

https://tribune.com.pk/story/988585/earthquake-was-allahs-wrath-for-kalash-communitys-immoral-ways/

"No Relief for Kalash in Pakistan's Valley of Infidels," *Voice of America.*

https://www.voanews.com/a/no-relief-for-kalash-in-pakistan-valley-of-kafirs/3446943.html

"Kalasha; the happiest people in Pakistan?" *CNN.*

http://travel.cnn.com/mumbai/life/kalasha-happiest-people-pakistan-261067/

"Kalash: An odyssey of the heart," *Dawn News.*

https://www.dawn.com/news/1185154

"The Lost Children of Alexander the Great: A Journey to the Pagan Kalash People of Pakistan" *Huffington Post.*

https://www.huffingtonpost.com/brian-glyn-williams/pagan-kalash-people-of-pakistan_b_4811627.html

Village house in Balanguru. Sketch by Birgitte Glavind Sperber 1984.

8. Nuristan in Kalasha myth, history and life

By Birgitte Glavind Sperber

It was a dark night in the Kalasha Valley of Rumbur on December 30, 1983.[1] I had gone back to the guest room to take a nap after sitting inside a house where for the entire night the villagers of Balanguru sang prayers to a sacred white crow that a shaman had seen generations earlier.

Suddenly, the ground started swaying from side to side, first in my dream and also after I woke up and went outside. Dogs howled, the mountains roared, people were hugging their babies or turning around with raised arms: *bhónjaw* – earthquake. The magnitude of the earthquake was 7.2 on the Richter scale. It lasted for more than five minutes and caused many casualties. The epicenter of this devastating earthquake that night in 1983 was the district capital, Chitral. It was probably for the first time since the siege of Chitral in 1895 that Chitral was mentioned in the world press. Most of the modern buildings in the area were damaged.

The Kalasha houses were still standing, clinging to the mountainside on top of each other. The Kalasha men linked their hooked fingers to explain to me how their buildings had horizontal beams notched at the corners as well as round boulders and flat stones in between so they could vibrate horizontally without collapsing. The construction of the Kalasha houses is similar to many of the houses that Lennart Edelberg worked on for his future book on Nuristani buildings,[2] while, from January 1967 until the summer of 1968, I was his substitute teaching biology and geography at the Ribe Katedralskole and became his friend. During the earthquake, in awe, I felt the power of the huge tectonic plates pushing against each other and forcing up the mighty Hindukush, Karakorum, and Himalaya ranges. However, that explanation does not fit the mythical world of the Kalasha. Qazi Khosh Nawaz and Saifullah Jan told me many myths during that time, and these made me aware of Kalasha's history and magic whenever I walked through the valley. It was not

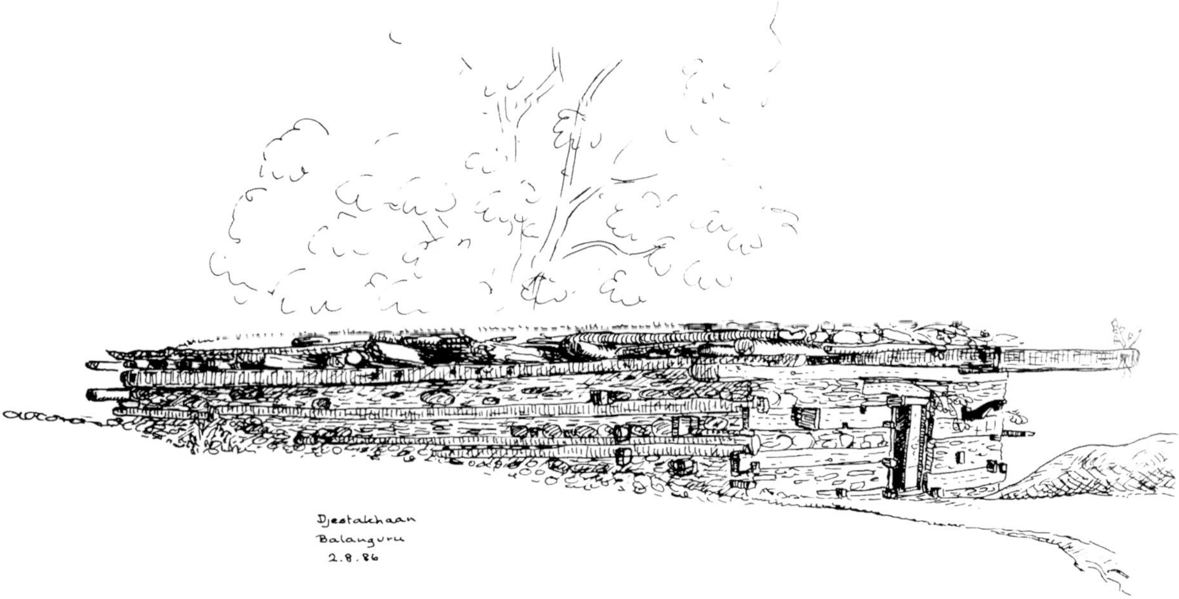

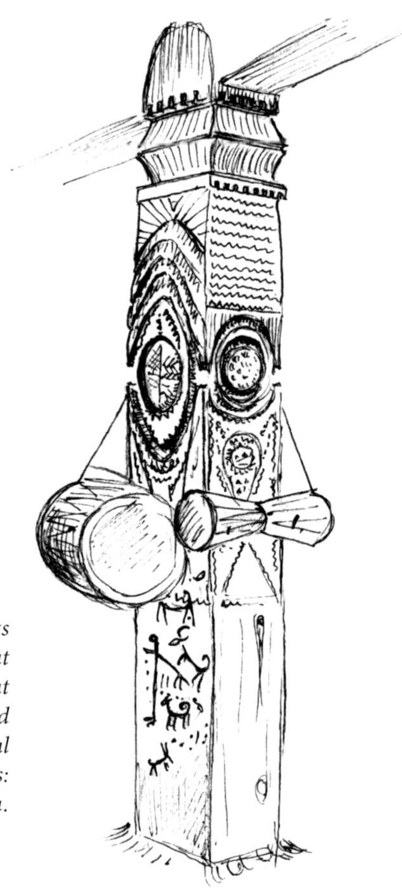

The former clan temple in Balanguru and one of its carved pillars. The drums are used for dancing at the festivals and funerals for men. Some of the goat paintings that boys make on the temple walls and columns at Kutramo night during the winter festival Chawmos can be seen below the big drum. Sketches: Birgitte Glavind Sperber 1984.

tectonic forces that caused the earthquake: in the world below, the gigantic bull Melbará was shaking his head.

The bearer of this oral tradition, Khosh Nawaz had told me where the carved designs in the temple came from:[3]

The Earthquake Myth

All the carvings in our clan temples and at the shrines of Sajigor and Mahandeo come from Wet Desh in Nuristan.

Once all our gods lived there, in the big temple Mahandelhán, the house of Mahandeo.

There, suddenly an iron pillar appeared. It was full of these carvings, we call Rikhíni.

The pillar was called Palaloi thū.

We believe there is world below.

We call that world Palalói, which means underneath.

We believe that this pillar came directly from the world below and up into the temple in Wet Désh.

Through a shaman, our god Balimaín directed us to copy these designs and carvings.

Now that temple and the iron pillar do not exist anymore. They have destroyed it.

All around Palalói there is a huge snake – into the earth around the entire world. That snake holds the world together. If that snake was not there, the world would fall apart. The iron pillar in Wet Désh came from where the snake's head and tail meet – in the middle of the world.

To carry this world, to keep it above the world below, there is a gigantic bull named Melbará. On its head this bull carries a pillar that supports the world so it does not fall down. Hundreds of people take care of this bull, feeding him all the time, so he does not move. If they don't feed him – even for one minute – he shakes his head.

That is the earthquake, Bhónjaw.

Later, some phrases from Roberston's book sent shivers down my back:[4]

A short distance from the temple, in short thick grass near the river, is the famous hole. . . . The old story was that everyone looking down the hole saw the nether world and died forthwith.

So, in Nuristan there actually was a hole down to the underworld.

There was also an iron pillar:

Close by the temple, in a house in the village, there is a miraculous iron bar placed in its present position by Imra himself. Its guardians conducted me with some reluctance into the apartment where the bar was said to be buried under a heap of juniper-cedar branches.[5]

The connection between the temple and the iron pillar reveals that the temple mentioned in the Kalasha myth must have been the temple described by Robertson, Parkes,[6] and later by Castenfeldt,[7] and confirms that temple was situated in Presungul.

In Kalasha religion, iron is pure. So is juniper, which is used for purification rites. That the iron bar was buried under juniper indicates that it was sacred.

Years earlier, I had read Lennart's lovely book *Furrows in the Ancient face of Asia* in which he writes:

> It is strange to imagine that in winter a man dressed up as a buck will run about in one of their remote villages – one's thoughts might go to the Norse Yule buck. Again and again, one asks oneself: Are we facing not only an ancient Indian culture trait, but also our common Indo-European culture traits? (My own translation).[8]

The Kalasha myth tells:

> All around Palalói there is a huge snake – down in the earth around the entire world. That snake holds the world together. If the snake were not there, the world would fall apart.

This made me want to use Lennart's words: "One's thoughts might go to the Norse…" but rather than to the 'Yule goat' to the Midgard serpent.

Actually, in old Vedic culture, the big snake Vritra surrounds the mountain world and is slain by Indra with his thunderbolt.[9]

The goat ritual in Nuristan reveals that goats were essential there – just as they are in Kalasha life and religion. The following myth links the origin of the goat culture to Nuristan. I have recorded it from two elders and have combined their versions here to illustrate that the myth is commonly known and told:

The Goat myth as told by Bahdur and Khosh Nawaz

B: Having goats is a very sweet thing.
Without goats in the world there would be no life.

KN: The first goat came from over there (East).
It went from country to country.
It was called Gadameshtak.
Everywhere, the goat asked: "What will you do to me?"
"We will look after you well," they said.

B: "When you die, we will bury you."
The goat did not agree. She continued walking.

KN: The goat also crossed the Shandur Pass and came here.
When she came down the mountain, from one teat came blood
and from one teat came milk.
That is why there are lines there in the rock – red and white.
Then she crossed the big Gangalwát Pass (into Waigal in Nuristan).
In the country there, the goat also asked how she would be treated.
She asked the elder of Waigal.
"We will look after you," he said.
"You can look after me and eat my milk products, but what about when I die?" she said.
"When you die – whether you are thin or fat – we will crush walnuts to mix with your
meat – and eat it."
"We will also chew your bones," they said.
"We don't throw them on the ground."

B: "Here, they really respect me," the goat said and she stayed there.
Also now in Waigal there are goats with two heads and one body.
They really are there now.
There are also goats with one head and two bodies.

KN: The goat with two heads on one body can eat a lot and get very fat.
That was the story of the goat, sister.

In old Nuristan, people worshipped many gods, among them Gish, the god
of war. They honored warfare – among each other and against the Kalasha.
The myths, the oral history and the life stories of the Kalasha are full of
episodes of Nuristanis coming to steal goats in particular.

In 1983, Saifullah Jan told me:

At the end of September six years back, there was a rattle at my door in the middle of
the night.

Worried people said that the Nuristanis had made an armed attack on our shepherds
in the high pastures and had stolen all our flocks of goats and sheep – around 3000
animals.

We took up arms and rushed away.

We were about 40-50 men from this village chasing the robbers who had a head start.

We passed the Gangalwát pass into Nuristan and crossed another pass too.

The Nuristanis were on their way to cross a third pass with our flocks ahead of them.

We went on top of that pass and started shooting.

There were three days and nights of gun battle.

My rifle was old and unable to hit.

I just shot 4-5 times to frighten the Nuristanis and left the rifle there.

I was exhausted, my shoes were broken. I was just wearing my thin cotton clothes and sandals.

I was leaning on a rock when a Pakistani border policeman, who had followed us, came by. He lent me his rifle and ammunition belt.

However, it was no longer necessary to shoot. We had won.

At least five Nuristanis were killed – two by my father-in-law, who gained great honor and the title "Man-killer".

Normally, we Kalasha must not kill.

We drove the flocks back.

After having crossed the second pass, we made a big fire and slaughtered 5-6 goats that we ate, because we were so hungry. However, we did not bring any salt with us.

As we passed the Gangalwát pass, our entire population received us with cheers.

It was great luck that the fact that Saifullah's father-in-law was a man-killer remained a secret to the authorities. Otherwise, he might have faced what happened to another big man, Gulab Din, whose widow Láchik told me the following story:

My husband was a big man.

One night a long time ago, Nuristani robbers came into our house.

My husband and his two brothers defended themselves and in the darkness they happened to kill a robber.

At the Chitral court, they were given the choice between the death penalty and conversion – So we became Muslims, but in my heart, I am still Kalasha.

Nuristani thieves occur in many myths as well, like this one told to me by Khosh Nawaz in 1983:

The Shepherd Noné

Noné was a shepherd from Birir.

He was in love with a girl in Shishikú[10] – it is near Drosh and was Kalasha at the time.

In the daytime he watched his goats but when darkness fell he brought them into the cattle house and went down to see his girlfriend in Shishiku.

At the time there was no bridge, so he had to ford the river.

His father advised him not to do it: – You might drown!

Noné never listened, and eventually, he drowned in the river.

Robbers came and took the goats towards Nuristan.

There were lots of bucks, and a bird had built a nest between the horns of one of them.

The robbers stole the goats at night.

Just before they reached the pass, the bird started whistling.

Then the Nuristanis believed that some men were after them and they ran away.

The goats returned to their house. When the father saw the animals returning alone, he walked along the river all the way down to Naggar where the plains are.

There he found his dead son. He brought him home and arranged a funeral for him.

(The myth continues).

(Khosh Nawaz 1983)

In 1979 the Soviets invaded Afghanistan and millions of refugees poured into Pakistan; some also went to Chitral. During the years of Soviet occupation, the Nuristanis needed the Kalasha valleys as a passageway between their homeland and the refugee camps in Chitral. After the Soviets left in 1989, again the Nuristanis started robbing and even kidnapping. In 2009 the Greek volunteer Athanasios Lerounis, who had projects in the valleys, was held hostage in Nuristan for seven months. In 2009, Nuristanis stole flocks from Rumbur, but the animals were recaptured. In 2012, Nuristani thieves killed a young Kalasha shepherd and stole flocks from Bomburet. There have also been other serious incidents: In 1993, a bomb was thrown down the chimney of Saifullah Jan's guest house where he was sleeping. His brother was killed. In 2002, a Spanish man, Jordi Magraner, was murdered in his home in Bomburet. Both cases remain unsolved.

As the Nuristanis are what we call 'the usual suspects', Kalasha think the deeds were done by Nuristanis – either from Nuristan itself or from the Nuristani villages constructed in upper Bomburet and Rumbur on land the British gave to Nuristanis who fled from conversion in 1895 but later converted.

In everyday life, though, there are peaceful relations between the two peoples. When Nuristanis walk down the valley, they often have a meal in a Kalasha household. When Kalasha go up the valley, they often have the same.

The Nuristanis do not understand the language Kalasha, whereas most adult Kalasha understand and talk Nuristani (probably Kati) – a useful strategy among the inferior Kalasha. Furthermore, the Kalasha value the Nuristani craftsmen and employ Nuristanis for the finest work. For example, a Kati living in Ayun was hired to make the carvings for the new clan temple in Balanguru. The capitals from the old pillars were re-used. Also, the two exchange goods – the Kalasha trade grain or money for the low stools with seats made from woven skin straps.

From the Nuristanis, the Kalasha buy the goatskin shoes that are now only used for the dead. The Kalasha honour their dead with funeral feasts lasting up to three days. They sing praises and give long eulogies about the deeds of the deceased and the ancestors going back many generations. In this way oral history is passed on to the next generations.

The Nuristanis and the Kalasha of the same valley can be united, as they were in Rumbur during the big court case against Ayun village that claimed the forests of the valley. In 2002, a big Mela was held in Bomburet – a kind of Valley Olympics. It was amazing to see the Nuristanis as skilled archers and demonstrating Buzkashi. The Nuristanis of Rumbur won the most cups and medals and were received with cheers by the Kalasha of Balanguru in Rumbur when they passed through the village on their return.

According to myth, shamans brought several of the Kalasha gods from the big temple in Nuristan. They wanted to come to the Kalasha valleys, as they foresaw the conversion of the future Nuristan. I have collected such myths about Praba and Warin in Birir, the female goddesses Kushumai, Jestak and Jatch, and the important Sajigor, whose shrine is in Rumbur.[11] This myth tells how Sajigor came to Rumbur from Nuristan. It was given to me in 1983 by Khosh Nawaz:

The Sajigor Myth

Once, Raja Wai was the king of the Kalasha. He lived in Bomburet.

One day he went out hunting. He returned at night, and in the darkness, by a mistake, he slept with his daughter Rajanoor. He had done something very bad and in the same night, he went to Mahandeo to sacrifice a bull and pray. Afterwards, Raja Wai forbade all men in Bomburet to make love to their women for the next three years.

When the three years had passed, all the women went to the daughter of Raja Wai asking for permission to start again. She went to her father and told him that now all women wanted to make love again, and he gave his permission. The very same night all men made love to their wives.

Nine months later, 180 baby boys were born on the same night. They grew up into big strong men and Raja Wai made them soldiers. With this army, he entered Nuristan.

He fought; killing many people, and took along as slaves 60 women, who were widows after the men he had killed.

In the Gangalwát Pass between Nuristan and Rumbur, they reached a level place named Kobrúnt. Here Raja Wai ordered the widows to dance for him. They were very sad, as they had lost their husbands, so they got upset and danced while weeping, and cursing him. Then the shaman Naga Dehár appeared.

He said to Raja Wai:

"You have not done well. Send the women back to their villages. You shall go back into Nuristan to the place called Mamadewaná where the god Sajigor resides. You shall ask him to come along with you into Rumbur."

Raja Wai did all this.

He stayed for three days in Mamadewaná and afterwards, he returned to the pass.

Again Naga Dehár appeared. He entered into a trance and he raised his hands like this.

In his hands now two arrows appeared – a red one and a black one.

The shaman shooting.[12]

THE RELIGIOUS WORLD VIEW OF THE KALASH

A simplified model

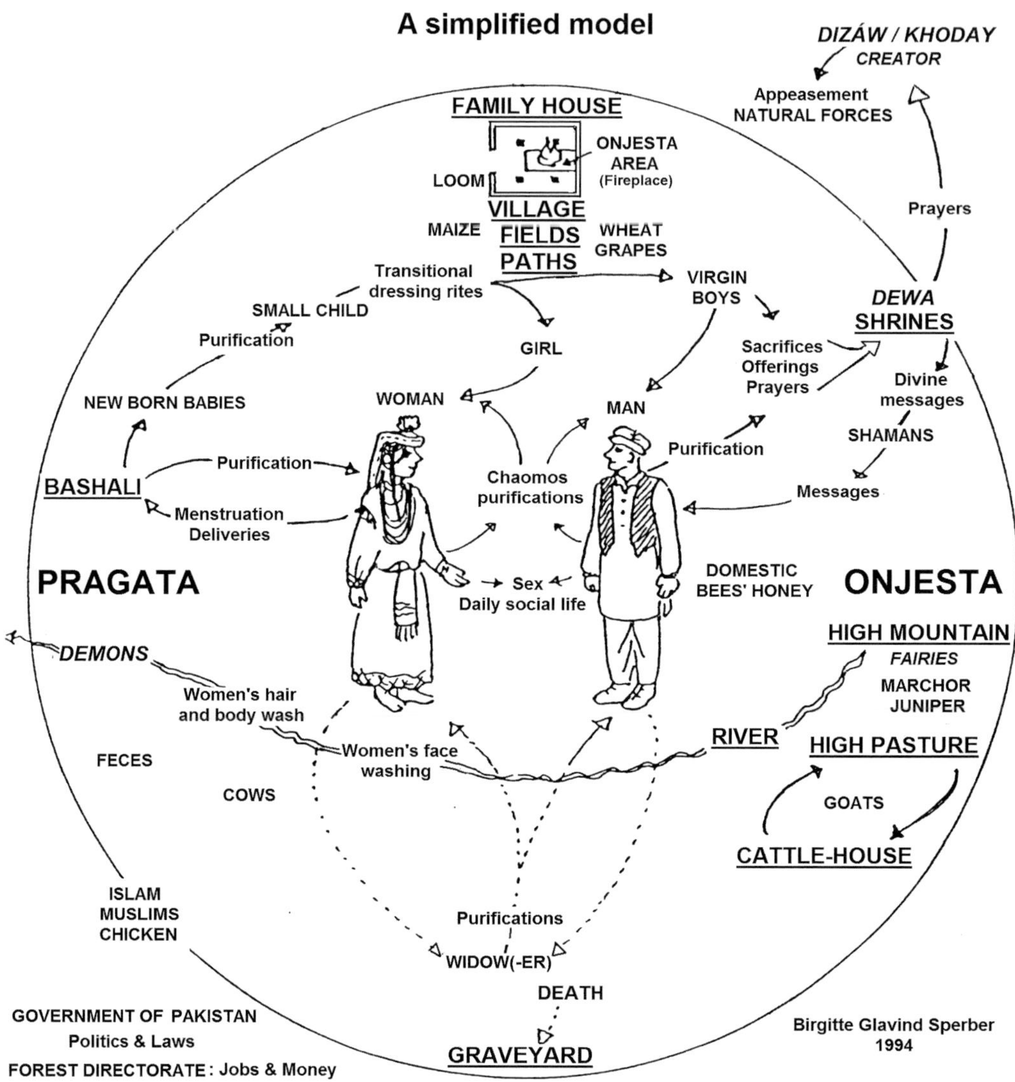

The religious world view of the Kalasha.

With his bow he shot them down into Rumbur and told to the people around him:

"Go down and look for them. Where you find the red arrow, you shall place Sajigor, and where you find the black one, you shall build the Basháli. (the birth and menstruation house)"

Then they went down into the valley.

Raja Wai had ordered the soldiers to search for the arrows.

The red arrow landed at a big holly-oak.

When the soldiers had found it, they told the king, and he placed Sajigor at that place.

Also the shaman appeared there and gave instructions.

The soldiers had 180 daggers they had used in the battle. These daggers were placed in the wall of Sajigor's altar. The first sacrifice at Sajigor was nine bulls and nine bucks.

That is how they installed Sajigor.

It is also said that the soldiers counted the leaves of the holly-oak and sacrificed as many animals as there were leaves.

Afterwards, they found the black arrow; at that place they built the Basháli of the valley. (At the time there lived another tribe in Rumbur called Balalik).

After the completion of Sajigor and the Basháli, Raja Wai returned to Bomburet.

There he asked his cousin Banguta and his son Adabók to move to Rumbur.

They settled in Grom.

They took care of Sajigor, said prayers and made sacrifices for him.

Adabók became the ancestor of our clans here in Rumbur.

It happened sixteen generations back.– – –

Sajigor foresaw that Nuristan would be converted to Islam, and that these valleys would be the last refuges for the gods.

That is why he wanted to come to Rumbur.

Sajigor is the god for everything – for health. He helps by keeping enemies away. He secures the growth of our people and things like that.

(Khosh Nawaz 1983)

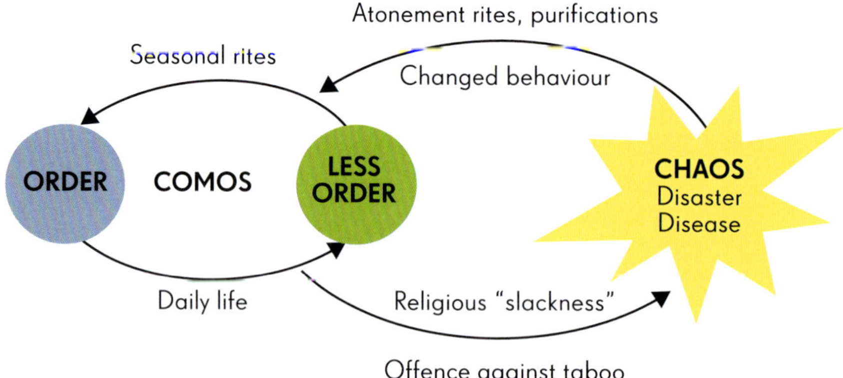

A model of cosmos and chaos.

The Kalasha world is divided into spheres of pure and impure, and this is reflected geographically in daily life and in the religion. Many actions are done to avoid defilement (interpreted as chaos) or, as in this case, to re-establish order by purifications.

In the Sajigor myth, the shaman Naga Dehár shoots the two arrows to indicate where the altar – the purest ónjesta place in the valley – and the Bashali – the most impure *prágata* place in the valley – must be placed. Symbolically, he establishes the religiously dualistic world – divided into spheres of pure and impure. The myth can be seen as a kind of founding myth.

In the myth the king commits incest – a serious violation of a religious taboo. He tried to atone for his sin by conducting sacrifices and prayers at Mahandeo. However, this was not enough. In the Kalasha community, an individual's violation of taboo can lead to collective punishment. Raja Wai's incest was so severe that collective action was necessary: The collective long-term celibacy can be interpreted as a collective catharsis. Over the three years without a close contact with the impure women, the men became more and more pure. After three years, special children were conceived: All were boys with unique strengths.

King Raja Wai's time was a golden age. The Kalasha dominated the southern part of Chitral [13]. They had a strong ruler who could wage war on Nuristan. Around the sixteenth century, Islam penetrated the area and Muslim rulers took control until 1947 when the area was included in Pakistan. The Kalasha were pushed into the side valleys of Chitral where their culture gradually died out, sometimes by force:

How Islam came to Shishikú

Once there was a king in Chitral. His name was Katúr.

When he was born he was placed in the care of the people in Shishikú Valley. They were Kalasha at the time.

In those days it was the tradition that when a prince was born he was given to someone who would later become an ally ("Milk brother").

When Katúr had grown up he became a king after his father but as he was in love with a girl in Shishikú, he went there often for a visit.

Once when he went there he told the people in Shishikú:

'Listen. I have been cared for by you. Now that I am grown up, I feel ashamed that you are Kalasha, when I am Muslim. You must convert –

Otherwise, I will beat you, I will kill you – I will use all my power!'

The people in Shishikú said to him:

'We will do it, but please let us first celebrate our spring festival, Joshi, one last time, before we convert.'

So the king went off again.

In the spring, when the Kalasha were celebrating Joshi, on the last day of the festival, he came with his army and with all his power.

He gave the soldiers orders to surround the dancing ground, where the Kalasha were dancing in a long chain – all boys, all girls – all together.

The dancing ground was by a high cliff with a precipice down to the river on one side. While dancing, the Kalasha sang:

'Oh God! Now this village is going to end!' And they all danced off the cliff, into the river and drowned –

Only a few had been left and were converted.

This is how Islam came to Shishikú.

(Khosh Nawaz 1983)

During the harsh rule of the Katúrs, the Kalasha were a people with no formal leader, only different clans. In case of a crisis, a Jirga may be organized. The Kalasha had to pay tribute to the king and were forced into bonded labor for the king and were exposed to harassment and theft by the authorities, as remembered by many elders.

So, when Pakistan came into being in 1947 the Kalasha were relieved. Now the glorious past exists in people's memories alone. It is remembered by the old shield laid beside a dead man at his funeral.

It is remembered in eulogies given at funerals, as for example in this extract from a funeral in Birir, in 1985.

> Bravour to you, grandson of Rashimúk.
>
> The world is like this – sometimes it makes you cry and sometimes laugh.
>
> Your ancestor was a wealthy man.
>
> With many people from Birir he crossed the pass into Nuristan.
>
> When reaching Wet Désh, he killed at lot of enemies.
>
> And he destroyed all of Nuristan.
>
> When he had done so, he went to Mahandelhán (Mahandéo's temple) in Wet Désh. He offered to sacrifice humans for Mahandeo but Mahandeo did not reply.
>
> Then he prayed to Mahandeo:
>
> "I will bring you to Birir and sacrifice goats and bulls for you."
>
> At that, Mahandeo laughed and said:
>
> "At every fall you shall sacrifice a goat and a bull for me."
>
> Your ancestor agreed and those days he brought Mahandeo over here and made these sacrifices for him.

Many Kalasha trace their ancestry back to the glorious Raja Wai who ruled Nuristan in pre-Muslim times. Thus, words like these could be recited at most funerals. All around the Kalasha Islamic fundamentalism is growing, also in Nuristan. I hope the two peoples with common roots will live in tolerance and peace with each other in the future and that the Kalasha will continue to exist as a people with a unique culture and religion.

In gratitude to Lennart Edelberg and to the great carrier of Kalasha tradition Qazi Khosh Nawaz.

Birgitte Glavind Sperber and Khosh Nawaz in 2006. It was a tremendous loss for the Kalasha when Khosh Nawaz sadly passed away in May 2015.

Notes

1. The approximately 4000 Kalasha living in the District of Chitral in three valleys along the Afghan border "… offer the only living example of Indo-European 'paganism' or, we may say, of a 'tribal' Indo-European religion. …It is indeed the only religion practiced by speakers of an Indo-European language that was never absorbed by any of the great historical religious traditions – Buddhism, Hinduism, Zoroastrianism, Islam – that have molded the thoughts and the social organizations of all other peoples belonging to that large linguistic family. The sole non-Islamized island in the vast Muslim Ocean extending from Turkey to India, the Kalasha are the last shred of a vast and multifarious polytheistic world, predominantly of Indo-European language, that occupied a large part of the Hindukush/Karakorum chain until two centuries ago, when it gradually started to convert to Islam." Cacopardo, Augusto (2016) "Introduction." In *Pagan Christmas, winter feasts of the Kalasha of the Hindukush*, 1-2. Gingko Library. Edelberg, Lennart (1984). *Nuristani Buildings*. Jutland Archaeological Society Publications XVIII.

2. Edelberg, Lennart (1984) *Nuristani Buildings*. Jutland Archaeological Society Publications XVIII, Moesgaard, Aarhus: Universitets Forlag.

3. When Khosh Nawaz was young, he went to the elders who knew the myths, the gene-alogies and history and singing poetry. He educated himself by asking these elders to give their knowledge to him and he stayed with them till he had learned and demon-strated what he had learned. In return, he gave the elders traditional presents – bread, honor bands or goats. Khosh Nawaz was illiterate. When anthropologists began their research Saifullah Jan, the only English speaking Kalasha at the time, referred them to Khosh Nawaz, as he was poor. Gradually Khosh Nawaz became the most important cultural expert. His head contains what corresponds to the Kalasha national library and the national register of all Kalasha men fifteen generations back. The Kalasha needed his expertise in case of disputes on land and regarding whom to marry follow-ing the strict rules of incest. It was a tremendous loss when he passed away on May 4th 2015. His age was not known.

4. Robertson,G.S. (1896). *The Kafirs of the Hindu-Kush*. Reprinted Oxford; Karachi *Oxford University Press, Karachi, 1985.*

5. Both quotes are from Robertson 1896, 393.

6. Parkes, Peter 1991: "Temple of Imra, Temple of Mahandeu: A Kafir sanctuary in Kala-sha cosmology." In: *Bulletin of the School of Oriental and African Studies, University of London*, 54, Part 1: 75-103.

7. Castenfeldt, Svend 1996. A Pre-Muslim Temple in "Kafiristan." In Bashir and Israr-ud-Din (1996*), 109-16.*

8. Original text: Det er også ejendommeligt at tænke på, at engang i vinter vil i en af deres afsides bygder en mand løbe omkring udklædt som buk – ens tanker *kan* jo ikke lade være med at strejfe den nordiske julebuk. Og gang på gang må man spørge sig selv: Står vi her overfor ikke blot oldindiske kulturtræk, men overfor selve det fælles indoeuropæiske kulturgods? (Edelberg 1961, 27).

9. Personal communication, Gautam Sumit Bhattacharyya, who makes parallels between Indra and Thor.

10. Shishikú Valley is one of the side valleys of Chitral Valley. Shishikú is south of the Kalasha valleys and east of the Kunar River before it turns west into Afghanistan.

11. All the myths in this chapter were published in Danish in Birgitte Glavind Sperber (2017). *Balanguru – mennesker og myter I en kalashalandsby i Hindukus*h. Forlaget Mellemgaard.

12. Editor's note: This illustration is from G.S. Robertson's book The Kafirs of the Hindu-Kush. See p. 15 in that volume. Robertson's caption for the illustration is "Sacrificing Goats: Firing off the blood-stained Arrow".

13. According to Wazir Ali Shah (pers. comm.), the Kalasha were dominant during the sixteenth century.

List of references and relevant literature (including the author's publications)

Cacopardo, Alberto M. and Augusto S. Cacopardo (2001) *Gates of Peristan. History, Reli-gion and Society in the Hindukush*. Istituto Italiano per l'Africa e l'Oriente: Roma.

Castenfeldt, Svend (1996) "A Pre-Muslim Temple in Kafiristan." In: *Proceedings of the Second International Hindukush Cultural Conference*. Hindukush and Karakuram Studies, edited by E. Bashir & I. ud-Din. Oxford University Press: London & Karachi: pp. 109-16.

Edelberg, Lennart (1961) *Furer i Asiens ældgamle ansigt*. Gyldendal: København.

Edelberg, Lennart (1984) *Nuristani Buildings*. Jutland Archaeological Society: Højbjerg.

Parkes, Peter (1991) "Temple of Imra, Temple of Mahandeu: A Kafir sanctuary in Kalasha cosmology." In: *Bulletin of the School of Oriental and African Studies, University of London*, 54, Part 1: pp. 75-103.

Parkes, Peter (2004) "Fosterage, Kinship, and Legend: When Milk Was Thicker than Blood?" In: *Comparative studies in society and history*, 2004-46: pp. 587-615.

Parkes, Peter (2005) "Milk kinship in Islam." In: *Social Anthropology* 13: pp. 307-329.

Robertson, George Scott (1896) *The Kafirs of the Hindu-Kush*. Reprinted, 1985. Oxford University Press: Oxford & Karachi.

Sperber, Birgitte Glavind (1984) "Six broadcasts on Radio Denmark about the Kalasha Tribe in the Hindukush." In: *Proceedings of The Second International Hindukush Cultural Conference (1990)*, edited by E. Bashir and Prof. Israr-Ud-Din. Oxford University Press: Oxford.

Sperber, Birgitte Glavind (1990) "Kalashfolkets Verden." In: *Geografisk Orientering* 6: pp. 499-506.

Sperber, Birgitte Glavind (1992) "Nature in the Kalasha Perception of Life and Ecological Problems." In: *Nordic Proceedings in Asian Studies* No 3, NIAS (Nordic Institute of Asian Studies): pp. 110-130.University of Copenhagen: Copenhagen.

Sperber, Birgitte Glavind (1993) "Kalasha Development Problems." Paper from the *Conference of European Kalasha Researchers*, arr. by the Dept. of Ethnography and Social Anthropology, Aarhus University, Aarhus.

Sperber, Birgitte Glavind (1995) "Nature in the Kalasha Perception of Life." In: *Asian Perceptions of Nature, A Critical Approach, edited by Bruun & Kalland*: pp. 126-14. Curzon Press: Richmond, Surrey.

Sperber, Birgitte Glavind (1995-2006). All entries (except for Vol 1) on the Geography of Bangladesh and Pakistan. I: *Den Store danske Encyclopædi* (The Danish National Encyclopedia). Gyldendal: Copenhagen.

Sperber, Birgitte Glavind (1996) "Kalash Valleys." In: *Pakistan Handbook, edited by Mannheim & Winter*, UK: Trade and Travel.

Sperber, Birgitte Glavind (1996) "Kalasha Dresses, Body Decorations and Textile Techniques." In: *Proceedings of The Second International Hindukush Cultural Conference*," edited by E. Bashir and Prof. Israr-Ud-Din. Oxford University Press: Oxford.

Sperber, Birgitte Glavind (1999) "Kalash Valleys." In: *Pakistan Handbook*, edited by Mannheim & Winter: pp. 406-410.

Sperber, Birgitte Glavind (2000) "Water in the Kalasha way of Life." Unpublished paper for the Hindukush conference at the Linnean Society, London.

Sperber, Birgitte Glavind (2008) "No People is an Island." In: *Proceedings of the Third International Hindukush Cultural Conference (1995)*, edited by Dr. Israr-ud-Din: pp. 135-143 Oxford University Press: Oxford.

Sperber, Birgitte Glavind (2008) "Hos Kalashfolket i Hindukush, dragtstudier gennem 25 år". In: *Håndarbejde i skolen, May 2008*.

Sperber, Birgitte Glavind (2017) *Balanguru – mennesker og myter i en kalashalandsby i Hindukush*. Forlaget mellemgaard: Odense.

Lennart and the author celebrating the making of the publication of Nuristan. Kildehuset, Denmark. October 14, 1979.

174

9. Lennart Edelberg and Nuristan

By Schuyler Jones

As we go through life, we frequently meet all kinds of people. Some of them we never see again, some we meet occasionally in shops and offices as we go about our daily errands and business. Only a very few become friends. On rare occasions, we meet someone by chance who changes the course of our lives. We are unlikely to know in advance when such meetings are on the horizon – or even recognize them when they happen.

For me, one such meeting occurred in the early 1960s in Afghanistan on the Dar-ul-Aman Road halfway between Demazan and the Kabul Museum. By chance I fell into conversation with a European on a bicycle. We conversed in Danish briefly, which promptly revealed not only the limitations of my Danish but also my English-speaking background, so we switched to English. The man was Klaus Ferdinand. Although I had been in Afghanistan off and on since 1958, I was unacquainted with the Danish field research projects that not only had been ongoing for more than ten years, but dated back to the 1890s with Ole Olufsen's two Danish Pamir Expeditions. I learned about these gradually over subsequent weeks as I managed to see Klaus on several occasions. Although he had travelled in Nuristan in 1953, his primary interest as an anthropologist was in Afghan nomads. Since my own research interests were focused on Nuristan, Klaus urged me to get in touch with Lennart Edelberg.

Thus, the future course of my research and an abiding friendship with both Klaus and Lennart was set. It was through them that I met Professor Halfdan Siiger in Aarhus, Professor Wolfgang Lentz in Hamburg, Professor Georg Morgenstierne in Oslo, and gradually others in Aarhus and Copenhagen; P.V. Glob and Johannes Nicolaisen among them. I also came to know Dr. Carl Krebs when we sailed on the same steamship from Karachi to Djakarta, and I heard at first hand some of the experiences he had shared with Henning Haslund-Christiansen in Mongolia. Earlier I had come to know Werner Jacobsen, when I spent the winter of 1958-1959 in Nepal. To say that these Scandinavian associations widened and enriched my knowledge, bringing as they did a great many important publications to my attention – in addition to establishing enduring friendships – is an understatement. In the true spirit of scientific endeavour not one of these eminent scholars seemed to regard me as an interloper. Instead, I think many of them thought of me as a student who was eager to learn, and they generously did what they could to assist my research.

When I was next in Denmark, I followed Klaus' advice and I lost no time in getting in touch with Lennart who kindly invited me for a visit at his home in Ribe. I am not certain just when that meeting took place. I believe I had made at least two field trips into Nuristan when I first met Lennart. I recall that we spent some hours looking at both his and my photographs as well as discussing routes and villages and pouring over inadequate maps. Almost from the first hour, Lennart and I discovered that we were very much on the same wave length, as it were, even though he was the established scholar and I was very much a novice with a great deal to learn.

Lennart was a true scientist. He was interested in everything, and nothing escaped his notice. Although a botanist by both training and in his field research, he was also keenly interested in the problems that concern anthropologists. My training was in anthropology. But, as my fieldwork in Nuristan progressed, I found that again and again Lennart had noticed features of Nuristani culture that I had failed to observe, and he asked questions it had never occurred to me to ask. I learned a great deal about anthropological fieldwork from Lennart. Our meetings in both England and Denmark combined the features of a friendly get-together and anthropological tutorials. Between meetings, we corresponded frequently, I from my base at Oxford and Lennart from his home in Ribe. As time permitted, we were back in Afghanistan, though, unfortunately, usually not at the same time.

My training had been in Social Anthropology at Edinburgh. British social anthropology differs considerably from that which is taught in Europe under the heading of anthropology. I can do no better in describing the subject as taught in Britain than to quote my old Oxford professor, Sir Edward Evans-Pritchard who wrote:

> It studies … social behaviour, generally in institutionalized forms, such as the family, kinship systems, political organization, legal procedures, religious cults, and the like, and the relations between such institutions …

I mention this as it guided my field studies in Afghanistan. It will be noted that Evans-Pritchard's description does not include, for example, such aspects of a society as material culture. But gradually, and in no small measure due to Lennart's influence, my fieldwork in Nuristan began to include material culture. In studying my photographs Lennart frequently drew my attention to architectural features of village buildings I had admired and photographed, but had failed to investigate.

"What's this?" he would ask, pointing in a photograph to a construction problem the *bari* builder had encountered and solved. "Is that horizontal beam simply resting on top of that mullion or does the top of the mullion slot into the beam?"

Of course, I had no answer to such questions because I had not paid sufficient attention to details of house construction in the villages. Lennart's persistent questioning added an entire dimension to my fieldwork. I began to ask different questions and I began to take different photographs. Lennart was both friend and colleague and it was a learning experience to be associated with him.

In the decades between the end of World War II and the Soviet invasion of Afghanistan, it did not seem that there were any British anthropologists who had an interest in engaging in field work in Afghanistan. In those years, most British anthropologists went off to Africa to carry out fieldwork. This was due in large part to the influence of Evans-Pritchard's essential and widely read books, especially those on the Nuer and the Azande. So influential were these books in British anthropology that when a lecturer in the Department of Anthropology at Edinburgh University asked me about my fieldwork plans and I mentioned Afghanistan his startled response was: "That's a recondite subject!" Apparently, he failed to realize that the Nuer and the Azande were also recondite subjects before Evans-Pritchard made them famous, anthropologically speaking. In other words, the scientists I found most congenial as regards my interest in Afghanistan in general and Nuristan in particular, all seemed to be in Denmark, with important outliers in Norway and Germany. We were interested in the same cultural regions, and we were interested in the same problems; our research was complementary, our relations congenial.

It was during this post WWII period that Danish scientific field research again flourished in Central Asia, as it had done in the nineteenth and early twentieth centuries. This time, the focus was mainly in Afghanistan. Starting in 1947, the teams sent out from Denmark on the Third Danish Expedition called to mind those sent from Copenhagen in 1761 to Asia to carry out scientific research in Arabia. In both cases, the various team members had been chosen for their expertise in different fields. The scientists chosen for Afghanistan in 1947 were led by Henning Haslund-Christensen, the man whom Dr. Carl Krebs had taken to Mongolia many years before. Lennart was the botanist; Klaus Ferdinand, the anthropologist; Knud Paludan, the ornithologist; Halfdan Siiger, the religious historian; Johannes Humlum, the geographer. In all, between February 1948 and July 1970, Lennart spent a total of approximately seventeen months in Nuristan. Eagerly investigating everything he encountered; he restlessly recorded music with a tape recorder and everything else with camera and pen.

I have sometimes thought that Lennart went to Afghanistan as a botanist and emerged from that country as an anthropologist. Certainly when most of his botanical field research was behind him, he began to concentrate more and more on anthropological studies in Nuristan. His research, not counting the published results of his botanical studies, produced more than two dozen articles, reports, and books on that region of Afghanistan that was known in the nineteenth century as Kafiristan and is known today as Nuristan. One of the things that had frequently hindered our work, not to mention the work of others, was the totally inadequate maps of the region. With characteristic energy in his determination to leave no stone unturned, Lennart set out to map the whole of Nuristan. Quite aside from the practical difficulties involved in achieving accuracy on the ground, there was the problem of place names. Sometimes it seemed that no two informants would give the same name for a valley or village. This is only partly due to the fact that half a dozen languages are spoken in Nuristan. As Lennart explains in the short essay that accompanies his map of Nuristan, part of the problem is also the difficulty of distinguishing "between the name of the physical locality and the term used to designate the people who live there."

The linguistic complexities of the region are well illustrated by a comment that Professor Morgenstierne once made to me. We were sitting in a tea house in Ningalam at the confluence of the Pech and Waigal Rivers in southern Nuristan when Morgenstierne turned and said, "Do you realize that within a twenty-five-kilometer radius of where we are sitting no less than nine languages are spoken?" I had not realized it, but I have never forgotten his remark.

The idea for a volume of photographs and text on Nuristan came gradually, as again and again Lennart and I found ourselves resorting to examining the many hundreds of photographs we had taken in the field in order to clarify some new problem or to discuss further work that needed to be done. Early on we decided that an emphasis in the book should be on the photographs, conscious that it would eventually serve as an historical record of the region. Just how soon it would become 'historical,' we could not have imagined. The book was published in 1979. That same year, the Soviets invaded Afghanistan, thereby tipping the whole of that country into the abyss of war. That war has now been raging off and on for nearly forty years, even though the Soviets, completely defeated, retreated from the country after ten years.

Lennart had become interested in the arts and crafts of Nuristan – particularly domestic architecture. So, I became interested in calendar systems, finding that each village had its own calendar and various methods for keeping track of the days and the seasons. As I went from village to village, it was soon evident that a calendar is much more complicated than merely counting and keeping track of days. Having an economic system that relied both on arable irrigated terraces and livestock herding in a high mountainous region as far north as the 35th parallel, it was necessary to carefully observe the solstices and to reckon the equinoxes. This assured that agricultural activities – particularly the movement of livestock among the various the summer pastures – would be carried out when needed. I soon found that asking an informant to tell me the name of the current month would invariably start a heated argument among those present. This revealed the local methods employed to observe the solstices, as different men produced evidence to support their argument. Invariably, such discussions were settled by one or two elders who actually kept track of the passing days in a time-honored fashion, knew how the calendar worked, and observed the solstices. Each village had its own calendar because the required observations depended on the mountainous skyline surrounding each village. No two were the same. It was by observing from each village just where the sun set behind a mountain peak or ridge that revealed both the summer and the winter solstices. Once that was determined, then the vernal equinox or the autumnal equinox could be calculated. My investigation of these local calendar systems was greatly aided by my conversations with Wolfgang Lentz and a study of his pioneering publications on that subject.

Often when I was returning to Nuristan for further fieldwork Lennart would write and suggest that, while there, I might look into some particular problem that interested us both, or he would say: "While you are in Zhönchigal please have another look at the enclosed verandah of the *Kantar kōt*. We need some more photos of the interior." Lennart's remarkable publications on the architecture and the work of the bari in constructing houses and other structures in Nuristan was initially inspired by Hans Henrik Engqvist, who urged him to look into this aspect of Nuristani culture (i.e., the work of the bari).

The social standing of the bari in Nuristani society is at odds with the contribution they make to the very people who hold them in such low esteem. The largest social and political group in Nuristani society is that of the land-owning and livestock-herding atrožan. The bari occupy a separate class, and the main rules they must follow are: they may not marry outside their class, they may not own livestock, and they may not eat with *atrožan*. There are other restrictive rules, of course. And yet, the bari make all the houses and other buildings, they make all the furniture, they make the shoes, the blacksmiths among them make the tools, they do the carving, and do the weaving. In short, the bari produce all the material culture that is so characteristic of Nuristan and essential to the lives of the atrožan.

It was Lennart's interest in the work of the bari, primarily their skillful house construction, and my interest in social organization that brought our research most closely together. At the same time, both of us were keenly interested in publications by earlier writers. Most of them were British, though a German team whose interests were political as well as anthropological had been in Nuristan in the 1930s. Outstanding among the British writers with an interest in Kafiristan was Sir George Scott Robertson, author of *The Kafirs of the Hindukush*. This book was famous among those few scholars who had an interest in the nineteenth century history of Afghanistan. In 1889-1891, Robertson, a medical doctor who was working in the interests of British intelligence, spent a year in Kafiristan. His book was one to which we returned again and again for information about the people and the area, concerning the period before they were invaded by Amir Abdur Rahman and converted to Islam.

My interest in Afghanistan soon developed into a collection and compilation of all the published materials on that subject I could find, and it eventually resulted in two published bibliographies: one of books and papers on Nuristan and the other a bibliography of works on Afghanistan. Included in these volumes were dozens of papers I had received as offprints from colleagues. This large collection of offprints has since been donated to Moesgaard, as have the letters I received over the years from Lennart. The two bibliographies, like Lennart's map, were intended to be of use to future scholars interested in Afghanistan and Nuristan. The idea behind it was that if you are going to study or write about something, then you need to know what previous writers and scholars have published on that subject.

Lennart shared my interest in those nineteenth-century reports, articles, and books that had been written mostly by British officers and explorers. One of these men was known as Charles Masson from the books he wrote, but his real name was James Lewis. He was of particular interest because of the long periods he spent in Afghanistan. During my research in the India Office Library in London, I was able to examine the remarkable volumes of Charles Masson's diaries, notes, and drawings made during those years. When Lennart was next in England, I told him about the Masson papers. He took the first opportunity to spend several days in London going through those volumes and reading hundreds of pages of manuscripts in Masson's own hand. One day, needing a break from hours spent in the reading room, he stepped out to stretch his legs and get a cup of coffee. Passing a secondhand bookstore, he went in to ask if they had anything on Afghanistan. After showing him a few books, the man handed over a sheaf of papers and said, "Oh yes. There's this manuscript. It seems to be about Afghanistan." Having spent the best part of a week reading Charles Masson's manuscripts, Lennart recognized the handwriting immediately. He feigned no more than casual interest, and left the shop. Once out of sight, he broke into a run and went back to the India Office Library where he went to the office of Martin Moir, the Archivist, and said, "There's an original manuscript by Charles Masson for sale in a book shop near here!" Wasting no time, Martin put on his coat, went to the shop and purchased the manuscript for the India Office Library. As Lennart later remarked, it was a very satisfying day.

Throughout the twenty years of our collaboration, Lennart was for the most part in Denmark fulfilling his responsibilities as a lecturer in the Ribe Katedralskole, while I was in England fulfilling similar responsibilities at Oxford University. This meant frequent telephone calls between us and more than a few letters by way of discussing the problems we were working on for a book or research paper. With hindsight, I deeply regret that, in those days we did not have the speed and ease of communicating by e-mail. It would have been a precious boon and of inestimable value to our work.

Schuyler Jones in conversation with Hans Henrik Engqvist. Kildehuset, October 14, 1979. Courtesy of Pitt Rivers Museum, Oxford.

Here, I must confess to an abiding regret regarding a decision that was made between us: Lennart's pioneering research into the arts and crafts of the bari was, in research terms, of the utmost importance to him and his work. I shared this interest. But I feel now, as I did when I learned of his death by a telephone call from Torkil Funder, that he had been distracted by our joint work on the *Nuristan* volume when he would rather have been at work on *Nuristani Buildings.* In the course of our last telephone conversation, Lennart was excited by the fact that he had been given a year's leave from his lecturership at Ribe in order to continue work on the volume that was of primary importance to him. What I remember most from that conversation was his remark: "I should have taken *last* year off instead of this year." He did not say it, but I was left with the feeling that the *Nuristan* volume had been a diversion; it had taken him away from more important work.

Looking back, Afghanistan and Denmark loom large in my life. I shall always have a deep affection and respect for the friends and colleagues I was fortunate to make in those two countries. I welcome this opportunity to pay tribute to Lennart, who was in my estimation, a Renaissance man: a scientist, teacher, investigator, explorer; always enquiring, always seeking to learn.

Neither botany nor anthropology marked the boundaries of his interests. To me, he was an unfailing source of inspiration, and knowing him and having the privilege of working with him has been one of the most influential and rewarding events of my life.

List of references

Edelberg, Lennart & Schuyler Jones (1979) *Nuristan*. Akademische Druck- u. Verlagsanstalt: Graz.

Evans-Pritchard, E.E. (1951) *Social Anthropology*. Cohen and West: London.

Ferdinand, Klaus (2005) *Afghan Nomads: Caravans, Conflict, and Trade in Afghanistan and British India, 1800-1980*. Rhodos: Copenhagen.

Hansen, Thorkild (1965) *Arabia Felix*. Readers Union Collins: London.

Jones, Schuyler (1967) *An Annotated Bibliography of Nuristan (Kafiristan) and the Kalash Kafirs of Chitral*. Det Kongelige Danske Videnskabernes Selskab, Historisk-filosofiske Meddelelser: København.

Jones, Schuyler (1984) *On the Function of KK32: an ethnographic specimen from Nuristan*. In *Folk* 26: pp. 179-189.

Jones, Schuyler (1992) *Afghanistan*, World Bibliographical Series, volume 135. Clio Press, Oxford.

Lentz, Wolfgang 1978 [1938] *Zeitrechnung in Nuristan und am Pamir*. Berlin and Graz,

Scheibe, A. (1935*) Deutsche im Hindukusch: Bericht der deutschen Hindukusch Expedition, 1935*. Berlin, 1937.

Figure 1. Koresand. Photo: Claus Christensen, 2014.

10. How the drawings of Nuristani buildings were made in Denmark and some anecdotes about my friend Lennart Edelberg

By Erik Hansen

Let me start my story long before Lennart Edelberg and I ever met in 1961. Lennart started to work in the marshland close to Ribe soon after his exam as a biologist. He had married Margot in 1944. She has described their honeymoon in a tiny house on poles on the island of Jordsand in the tidal flats south of Ribe where Lennart had a summer job as supervisor of the bird life on Jordsand. This tiny island has since been washed away, but the view from the house is probably similar to the view seen in figure 1 of Koresand, which is nearby close to Mandø. The difference between this completely flat area and Lennart's later field of work in Nuristan's mountains is extreme.

The biggest problem for Lennart and Margot during their time on Jordsand turned out to be the German Gestapo. Because the Gestapo suspected them to be freedom fighters or spies, the couple had to leave Jordsand before the job was finished.

After the war ended, a new world opened up with trust and co-operation among nations through the United Nations and for us – especially through UNESCO, the United Nations Educational, Scientific and Cultural Organization.

In 1947, the Danish researcher Haslund-Christensen led an expedition for the scientific study of the old culture in Nuristan on the southern slopes of the Hindukush mountain range. The expedition consisted of anthropologists, botanists, geographers, and zoologists. The work was planned as one of a series of several campaigns. Unfortunately, it had to be stopped after the first year, because Haslund-Christensen fell ill and died in Kabul in September 1948. The project was later continued with the Haslund-Christensen Memorial Expedition of 1953-54. During this expedition, the ethnographical studies were taken over by the botanist Lennart.

After his first journey to Nuristan, Lennart returned to Ribe. In 1950, he became a teacher of natural history at Ribe Katedralskole. Here, he introduced a new approach to the subject – before it had been treated as an assembly of singular observations. Now the subject was considered more as a whole. It was said that when the Edelberg family came to Ribe, many activities started to happen, among others the revival of the museum in Ribe.

During a family gathering in Ribe, we met and understood our shared interests for art and for nature.

Lennart returned to Nuristan in 1964, this time together with his wife Margot and their daughter Susanne. Susanne became very ill during the stay, and probably her life was only saved because of the Nuristani women who treated her with their herbs (but the assistance of a Norwegian doctor also helped). During her illness, Lennart continued his studies. Later, when asked how he could concentrate his thoughts on work in such a situation, he replied that it would not have been of any help if he had stopped work.

Lennart had discovered that many Nuristani families had some beautiful old silver cups. They had been used for drinking wine before Nuristan became converted to Islam in 1896. Lennart managed to buy one of the cups.

It so happened that I was also in Afghanistan in 1964 together with my wife Kickan. I was working for UNESCO on a project with Kabul Museum. On their way home from Nuristan the Edelberg family visited us in our Kabul home. We had a single bottle of wine, and we used the silver goblet for a toast before it would take its final place in the collections of Moesgaard Museum.

During his work in Nuristan Lennart had collected many other ethnographic and architectural objects, and he had photographed and taken notes of the interesting buildings on the mountain slopes. Then Lennart took on the big task: How to translate all his observations of the complex timber constructions into meaningful architectural drawings. Certainly, Lennart had many

*Figure 2. From the left: Margot, Lennart and Susanne Edelberg, Erik Hansen.
Photo: Kickan Hansen, 1964.*

excellent photos, but he would also need diagrams and reconstructions that could explain details and principles as only drawings can do.

In Afghanistan among other tasks, I was occupied with the restoration of the Ghurid portal in The Friday Mosque in Herat.

The portal was built in the year 1200 by the Ghurid sultan Ghyath-ul-din Mohammad bin Sam. The Timurids restored the portal and the rest of the mosque in the fifteenth century. However, while the rest of the mosque had been restored and repaired several times since then, the Ghurid portal still stood with the crumbling remains of the Timurid façade decorations. My task was to restore this monument with respect to both the original Ghurid architecture as well as the works of the Timurids.

To do this work I had assistance from five young Afghan technicians. In figure 4 they are photographed on the roof of the Friday mosque together with me. The sitting person is Baba Morad Faraghi. The five young men did the job largely unsupervised and finished it with very good results.

After my work in Afghanistan I became busy with other tasks, so I did not manage to publish anything about the restoration of the Ghurid portal until 2015. Better late than never. I have published a book, *The Ghurid Portal of the Friday Mosque of Herat, Afghanistan*, together with an Afghan architect, Dr. Abdul Wasay Najimi, who was also my student from 1980 to 1982, and with Claus Christensen.

Figure 3. The Ghurid portal before restoration.
Photo: Kickan Hansen, 1964.

Figure 4. Erik Hansen together with the technicians.
Photo: Kickan Hansen, 1964.

Figure 5. The Ghurid Portal after restoration. Photo: Kickan Hansen 1970.

Now back to Lennart's drawings: The five Afghan technicians later came to Denmark for further education at the academy in Copenhagen. One of them was Baba Morad. Of the five, he made the best drawings. So we took him from his studies for some months and installed him with the Edelberg family in Ribe. I guess that was a tough time for him to be – among five young girls and asked to perform demanding work.

Perhaps he did not fully understand our need for the drawings, and Lennart was probably a demanding employer, who expected precision work. The results, however, were good, as can be seen in figure 6. In collaboration with Schuyler Jones, Lennart continued and accomplished the publication *Nuristan*.

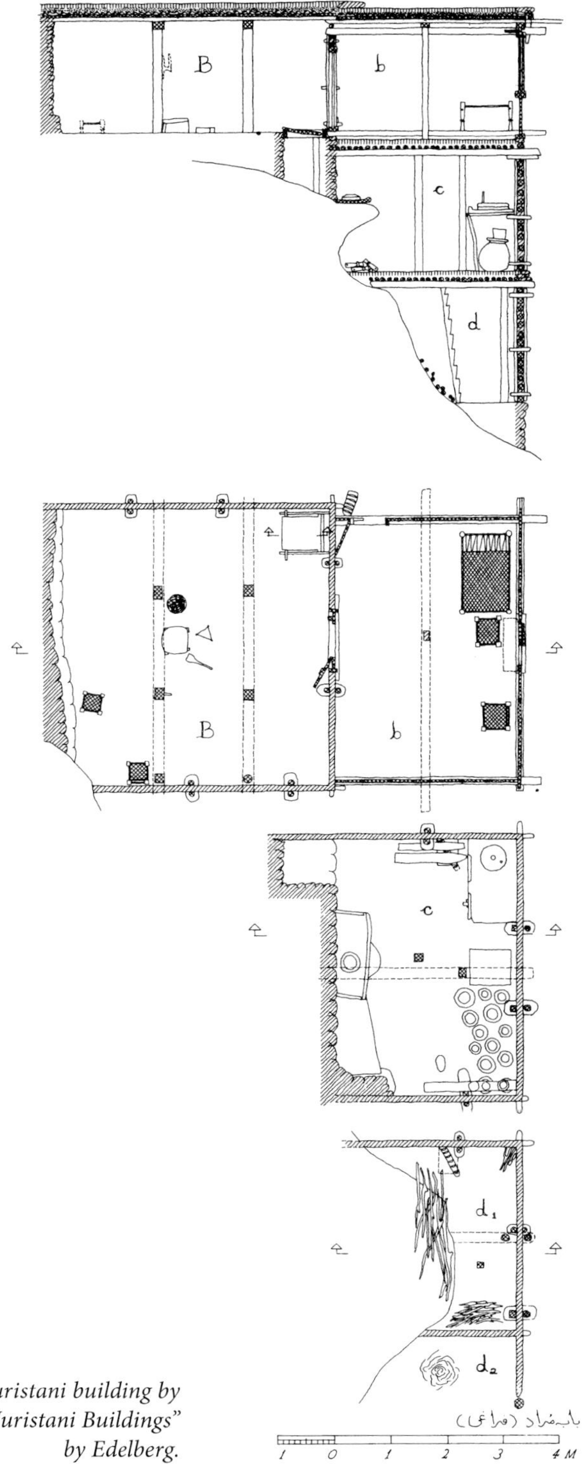

Figure 6. Drawing of a Nuristani building by
Baba Morad Faraghi. From "Nuristani Buildings"
by Edelberg.

Lennart was so far along in his work with preparations for *Nuristani Buildings* that it was possible to publish this book after Lennart's all too early death. The book include many drawings made by Baba Morad based on Lennart's sketches but also has drawings made entirely by Baba from artifacts brought to Moesgaard by Lennart.

Figure 7. Drawing of wooden columns from a Nuristani building measured and drawn by Baba Morad Faraghi. From "Nuristani Buildings" by Edelberg/Jones.

Figure 8. Reconstructed Nuristani building. Photo: Claus Christensen, 1970.

In 1970, Lennart and Klaus Ferdinand arranged a special exhibition and a seminar about Afghanistan at the new Prehistoric Museum at Moesgaard.

A Nuristani building was reconstructed using some of the building components and other artefacts that Lennart had brought to Moesgaard. The characteristic Nuristani wall construction was recreated. On figure 9, showing the interior, we can recognize the wooden column that Baba had measured and drawn in the far-right corner.

During the seminar, I, a young inexperienced scientist, expressed the wish to preserve the unique buildings of Nuristan. In response, the experienced scientist Morgenstierne from Norway replied that this is a development that cannot be stopped.

In 1970, Lennart was once more in Nuristan. Claus Christensen happened to meet him in the Kabul home of the Danish architect Gilbert Jespersen, who worked for Danida.

Figure 9. Interior of the reconstructed Nuristani building. Photo: Claus Christensen, 1970.

Figure 10. Gilbert Jespersen, his wife, and Lennart. Photo: C. Christensen, 1970.

Figure 11. Baba Morad and Erik Hansen. Photo: Kickan Hansen, 1970.

I was also in Afghanistan once again in the autumn of 1970 to register buildings to be preserved in Herat province. Baba Morad became my valuable assistant in this work. Figure 11 and 12 shows us doing some measurements at the Hussein Bay Musallah in Herat city.

When our task was done, Lennart arranged that Baba and I would travel to Nuristan, so that together we could experience the building tradition that Baba had documented so carefully with his drawings. Lennart had arranged that an UN-jeep with driver was at our disposal. The fasting month of Ramadan had just started. During daytime, out of respect for our driver, we did not eat any of the food that we had brought along. The last section of the journey to the village of Keshtagrom was on foot, and darkness fell before we arrived. We had considered eating on the way, but thought it more important to reach the village. So, we were very hungry when we finally arrived at Abdullah's house, after he and his family had finished eating. They immediately slaughtered a chicken for us, but it took of course a long time before the meal was ready. It was unthinkable that we would eat our own food, so Baba was not happy that our host let us wait so long.

Figure 12. Baba Morad and Erik Hansen. Photo: Kickan Hansen, 1970.

Before our return two days later, we were advised to leave early so that driving in the mountains could take place in daylight. Not only would it be dangerous to drive on the winding mountain roads in the dark, but the risk of robbery would also be higher. We had agreed that one of the villagers could join us in the jeep back to Kabul, but he had so many tasks to perform that we had to wait until long after lunch before he was ready. When darkness came, we were stopped by a group of robbers who had blocked the road with a tree trunk. It was not possible to pass, but Baba convinced them to allow us to pass by emphasizing that one of the passengers was a distinguished foreigner, who had his own UN-vehicle.

Baba Morad continued his work first at Kabul Museum and then in the Department of Monuments until he retired around 2005. Figure 13 shows him at the drafting board in 2002, when Dr. Najimi met him in Kabul. Baba Morad died October 23, 2016.

Allow me to conclude with some anecdotes about Lennart in Denmark: from 1966 to 1973 Lennart was a member of the Council for Technical Co-Operation with Developing Countries In that capacity, he travelled regularly from Ribe via Esbjerg on the night train to Copenhagen. Then he would come to our home in Wildersgade to get breakfast before the meetings in the ministry close by. He appreciated that very much although he usually declared: "I have not come to Copenhagen to eat but to work."

Figure 13. Baba Morad.
Photo: A.W. Najimi 2002.

From an uncle, Lennart had inherited a small country house, *Kildehuset* close to Vordingborg. It was frequently used by the family and their five daughters – not least because of a large growth of dock leaves, which were perfect for playing hide-and-seek and other games for which I do not know the proper English names.

Here Lennart had also built a hut in Nuristani style. In the small lake close by, it was possible to sail in their homemade dingy. At midsummer, the traditional bonfire would be made, and, at one time, it even provided a reason for the fire brigade to turn up.

In 1979, Lennart invited guests to Kildehuset, and we saw the Nuristan book for the first time. My wife Kickan and I, Najimi and Masoum, who was another Afghan student, were also invited. Najimi met Schuyler Jones, and it seems that they have remained friends since.

Lennart's house in Ribe, which he had designed himself was boldly built close to a small river. During the floods in 1953, Lennart drove to the sea wall along the North Sea to observe the flood danger – natural scientist as he was. However, he had to return quickly. The sea was only a few centimeters below the top of the sea wall. Fortunately, the wall withstood the pressure, and his house was left undamaged.

Other dangers were threatening along the road where NATO had a drill. Lennart stood in the darkness with a large sign showing "Denmark out of NATO." Lennart was also an active opponent against Denmark's association with the EU in 1972. He had a sign with the word *NEJ*, (NO) posted at the road. The farmer on the opposite side of the road had painted *JA*, (YES) on his barn wall. They were good friends all the same.

Lennart's way to tend his garden was interesting: He let all plants and weeds grow as they liked. When he saw what came up, he would use his scythe to remove the unwanted plants and leave the rest.

One time as Kickan and I arrived for a visit, we found Lennart in the garden swinging his scythe in a threatening manner and yelling: "You have arrived in the midst of an ant nest." At first, we thought that he might have hit an ant nest with the scythe, but no. He had just received the information that a German car filled with artifacts from Nuristan had left Afghanistan. He wanted to find a way to purchase all the items for the exhibition in Denmark, but he did not succeed.

Lennart felt responsible, as he has described in the foreword of the book *Nuristani Buildings,* that by writing books and articles about Nuristan he had created considerable interest for such items outside scientific circles, and it had resulted in these greedy purchases.

Najimi visited Kamdesh and the villages in the valley in 2000. He was disappointed to notice how many of the houses were reconstructed by new and plain timbers, rooms with modern fittings – doors and windows just as Morgenstjerne had predicted. Much of the historic woodwork was gone – sold across the border to an antiquity market in Swat valley in Pakistan to international buyers. Wars in the valleys with the presence of insurgents and foreign forces have also damaged the villages further. Lennart's documentation is of scientific value for conservators should the opportunity arise to work in Nuristan again.

List of references

Edelberg, Lennart & Schuyler Jones (1979) *Nuristan*. Akademische Druck- u. Verlagsanstalt: Graz.

Edelberg, Lennart (1984) *Nuristani Buildings*. Jutland Archaeological Society: Højbjerg.

11. Working with Lennart Edelberg in Ribe and Luristan

By Henrik Thrane

Ribe

I returned from Syria and Persia in mid-December 1960 as a fresh magister of Prehistoric Archaeology without a job. A few days later, however, Olfert Voss at the National Museum, who had been digging in Southwest Jutland for years, asked me if I was interested in a three months' curatorship at the museum in Ribe. Although I had never been there and knew nothing of the place, I accepted immediately.

So it was that Lennart Edelberg on Twelfth Night 1961 picked me up at the railway station in his old car and took me to his house on Holmevej with its view of the wide western horizon. He had just acquired the car and, typically for him, it was a 1930 model. Later, his consciousness about the environment would not have let him buy such a petrol eater, but those were still innocent days.

I was immediately accepted as an old friend by the family, Margot, and their five daughters, plundering the Christmas tree as the old tradition went. Margot was the pivot of this happy family – calm, caring, and loving. She must be a central person in any account of Lennart's work. She was the solid pillar round which the family functioned. After school, she was the stable center of the family, providing the logistics for their five daughters, Lennart, and the many guests – no easy matter. She was mild but firm and effective, gently monitoring the activities. Her infallible good humor, boisterous laughter, and common sense were indispensable in this family of individualists – Lennart, of course, being the most diversely active and frequently away from home. That she also managed to accompany him to Nuristan twice was no mean feat and showed her courage.

It was a completely novel experience for me, as an only child, to live in close proximity with this family. It was an intense and marvellous one, on which I thrived for the next years. Lennart had found a nice room for me on top of the local office of the newspaper *Vestkysten*, overlooking the Cathedral Square and *Hans Tausens Hus*. He was chairman of the Antiquarian Collection, the oldest provincial museum in present Denmark, and I was to be the first professional at the museum. It had just received a status that allowed state subsidies, and this meant an academic could be paid.

The museum had acquired the old merchant house *Quedens Gård*; now, the immediate task was to move all the artefacts from the tiny and very crowded Hans Tausens Hus. There was no money for professional assistance. To complete this menial job there was me, members of the board –of which only a couple were active participants, and the Edelberg family. This group of artefact movers were known in Ribe as the 'canaries', because of the yellow raincoats they all wore. (I have not been able to find a photograph of them.) At the time, I did not realize that the effort was part of Lennart's preparations for a nuclear attack – as was the storage of food at home. Every day after school, the family turned up with their bicycles and carts, and we all moved furniture and all sorts of objects the few hundred meters to Quedens Gård. Once that was done, the old house had to be fitted for its new life as a home for the Prehistoric collections. Old boards were made into shelves and had to be treated so that worm attacks could be prevented – the chemicals stank.

The museum soon developed from a very modest beginning into a flourishing city museum as the books on the Settlement of the Marshlands (Jensen 1998) and the series *Ribe Excavations 1970-76* published 1981-90 demonstrate – and as my successor and editor of the series, Mogens Bencard, could tell you at length. Without Lennart's initiative and continuous drive the museum would no doubt have continued its Tornerose sleep for years.

From these primitive beginnings that I was a part of, the Antiquarian Collection grew into a thriving research institution that has changed our knowledge of the earliest town in Denmark several times and continues to do so. All this may have little to do with Nuristan, but in Ribe everybody had heard Lennart's name and knew that the eccentric lecturer from the Cathedral School had a second life in *Langtbortistan* (far away land) as we say. There was enough energy left over from our menial work to make use of the shop windows at Quedens Gård for small displays of fresh acquisitions. Everything seethed with energy and busy goodwill. There was a great sense of purpose and nobody was spared, except for the two smaller daughters, and Margot; her time of course was limited, as she had to take care of the family apart from her job at the school. It was an inspiring experience rewarded with Sunday lunches for the whole family at *Landmandshotellet* and other restaurants that relieved Margot of some housework. It was a completely relaxed and lively company. I remember skiing in moonlight with the family. The Edelbergs will no doubt agree with me, remembering, for example how New Year was celebrated and how we skated in the castle moat. They were a musical family, playing various instruments and singing. It was a pleasure to join them when we sang in the evenings at their summerhouse *Kildehuset* on South Zealand. Lennart knew some rather special songs; the repertoire was good, sometimes rather quaint. The Ribe milieu was certainly a different experience from what I had expected and knew from the National Museum.

Lennart was a botanist, but his interests covered a much wider field and made him a fierce humanist. His background was important for his appreciation of the landscape, as he showed in his Luristan study in Iran. He had many other occupations and interests beyond school and the museum, however. He was much in demand as a lecturer in the small towns where he would lecture in schools or community houses on nuclear power, the marsh landscape, environmental issues, and local Ribe history, etc. I sometimes accompanied him on these evening excursions and, when we returned late to where we were staying, we would have a night snack (*natmad*) with beer, snaps, sucked fresh eggs (as you could then without risk of poisoning), *fedtemad*, etc. – and talk. He did most of the talking, needless to say, and it was a good education for a nerd like me. I can still hear in my inner ear his long drawn *Jaavel,* when he had heard something that needed a bit of thinking over. Needless to say, Lennart was among the group that had advocated the establishment of a fourth Danish university at Ribe. That would no doubt have become a different one from the resulting semi-university at Esbjerg. Because of Lennart's enthusiasm, I joined the family on one of the Easter marches from Roskilde to Copenhagen against nuclear power.

In June, we ran the first long-awaited excavation for the museum in *Storehøj* at Tobøl. At this site, a local farmer had uncovered a unique Middle Bronze Age burial years before. This was one of the fortunately rare clandestine excavations in a scheduled monument and was a bit of a scandal. The farmer had mishandled a unique context with a miniature wheel and other remarkable rarities; fortunately, he had left enough in a mess in the ground so that a reconstruction was somehow possible (Thrane 1963). It was important to interpret its contents and describe what the farmer had overlooked. I borrowed Lennart's car and he and few others would come to assist me after school whenever possible – which wasn't that often (Thrane 1998). The Bronze Age mounds at Tobøl have now acquired prominent status due to the complete multi-disciplined excavation of *Skelhøj*, one of Storehøj's neighbors (Holst & Rasmussen 2013 & 2015). I particularly remember one happy day (among many), sitting with Lennart at the edge of the yellow grain field in the sun eating our sandwiches, looking over the old border river *Kongeåen*, watching birds, and listening to the song of the larks.

When my term was over, he asked me to stay. I was sorely tempted, but decided to return to Copenhagen where the research opportunities lay. Ribe was a good place, but remote from the academic centers at that time. The following years proved how difficult it was to maintain close connections from the sixties. We kept in touch, however, and I visited the family whenever possible, enjoying its hospitality. The end of the sitting room at Holmevej was covered by Afghan rugs with Nuristani stools by the hearth. It was a sort of trial whether a guest could sit on the floor with the family. Many were tried, i.e. visiting museum colleagues and lecturers for the Antiquarian Society, where Lennart of course was indispensable too.

Luristan

Now I will turn to something completely different. Why Luristan after Nuristan? A brief introduction seems necessary.

While constructing a main road down through the inaccessible and virtually unknown Central Zagros mountains in Western Iran – South of Kurdistan, the Danish engineering firm Kampsax was struck by the number of prehistoric cemeteries that flanked the road. All had been thoroughly rifled by the Lurs. So, the National Museum of Denmark was invited to go and excavate there, and Kampsax provided local logistic support. The Carlsberg Foundation, once again, paid for the project. Knowledge of the archaeology of this region had been a desideratum ever since a unique Bronze Age culture had been tentatively reconstructed from artefacts reaching the international antiques market over decades. The only ones to benefit were the local landlords and the dealers supplying the international antiquities market with these illicit finds. Contrary to rules for excavation in Denmark, illicit commercial digging was the rule rather than the exception in Luristan and among the other isolated mountain tribes. It was our challenge to find undisturbed contexts for scientific excavations. The so-called Luristan bronzes have a primitive yet highly artistic style that is completely their own, but there was no information available about provenance or context except the vague label *Luristan*. The Luristan bronzes are now dated c. 1200-700 BC.

The total absence of documentation for all these bronzes was the reason why Kampsax took this step. The National Museum formed a small expedition that concentrated its efforts on the small mound called Tepe Guran on the Hulailan plain in the Pish-i Kuh. We worked on two projects: the Bronze Age and the Early Neolithic, which turned out to reach back to c. 6800 BC. Hoping to find undisturbed graves so that contexts and dates could be analyzed, we were able to combine the search for Luristan Bronze graves with a trench down into the thick Neolithic deposits. Peder Mortensen's excavation of eight meters of settlement deposits was a major step in the search for the beginning of agriculture. It proved to be fundamental for the understanding of the transition from hunting to agriculture in the Zagros mountains, which was one of the crucial areas in what Robert Braidwood called "the Fertile Crescent" (Mortensen 2015).

I was in charge of the excavations of the Bronze and Iron age levels of Tepe Guran. We did not produce a coveted intact Luristan Bronze burial, but we did manage to document a settlement sequence and several earlier and later burials – all completely new knowledge (Thrane 2001). Although we had only two and a half months for our field work, we managed to reach virgin soil in both trenches just in time – the day before we had to leave Luristan. What we managed to do was but a drop in the ocean, but at least that drop was well documented (Thrane 2015). Now an Irano-Danish project involving Copenhagen and Kermanshah universities is tracing the local culture in Luristan even further back beyond the Neolithic.

For us, the greatest fascination was the Lur culture that literally surrounded us. The black tent was something we had read about in Freya Stark's and the Danish ethnographer C.G. Feilberg's reports (1935 & 1944). To me, it was a great surprise and adventure when our workmen from Guran village suddenly went through a metamorphosis and became nomads again. They struck camp at the foot of our tepe so that we could see not only our own workmen

Figure 1 & 2. The black tents of the Guran villagers on their first stop of the annual migration. At the foot of Tepe Guran. Photo: Henrik Thrane, June 1963.

but their whole tribe at close range. Here we were surrounded by the local villagers; in May, they had begun their annual move to the summer pastures in the famous black tents right there at our feet. Our workmen invited us for tea, and it was pleasant to sit there *siah chador* and relax. The permanent village of modern mud-brick houses was only a few 100 meters from this first stage of their tour of the country, closer to the river and the fields for grazing livestock. The whole landscape was fascinating, but we had neither the means nor the time to explore the subject. Meldgaard had observed the winter houses in contrast to the black tents; he had seen them as being similar to Danish Iron Age houses – that was all. This was an exotic experience for us Danes and pure adventure; I wanted to know more about these nomads.

Figure 3. Lennart in his usual stride through the landscape – behind the Tarhan Valley, Luristan. Photo: Henrik Thrane, 1964.

Figure 4.

That is why Lennart came out to Luristan on his way home from Nuristan. When I got the opportunity to return to Luristan in 1964 for a second campaign, I asked him to come and do an ethno-archaeological study. That approach had just become a trend by then, with Patty Jo Watson's work in Kurdistan as a good example (1979). Lennart, Margot and Susanne dropped by Teheran on August 29 on their way back from Nuristan. From there, he accompanied the expedition to Luristan. He was the obvious choice with his experience from Nuristan, with his knowledge of Farsi that was far beyond mine, his being available, and his good old-fashioned common sense – as well as being a good friend.

We stayed at the small village of Sar Cham by the river Saimarreh that waters the Hulailan plain (figure 4). Lennart usually went his own way with his informant Ali Askari using his Farsi from years in Afghanistan to make do without an interpreter. The authorities would have liked to control his movements with a gendarme and interpreter, but he managed to get along without the interpreter. Lennart followed the villagers on their migration to the leaf huts, the *kula*, which were the midsummer dwellings on higher ground. His observations of the annual cycle were done just in time and formed the basis for his model. That alone was justification enough for his participation (1967). The annual cycle that Lennart was able to (re)construct was thus to some extent witnessed by us in May and June. Anyhow the winter houses stood there for us to see, so only the third stage was missing. Lennart's model (figure 5) shows how natural environmental conditions determined the main stages.

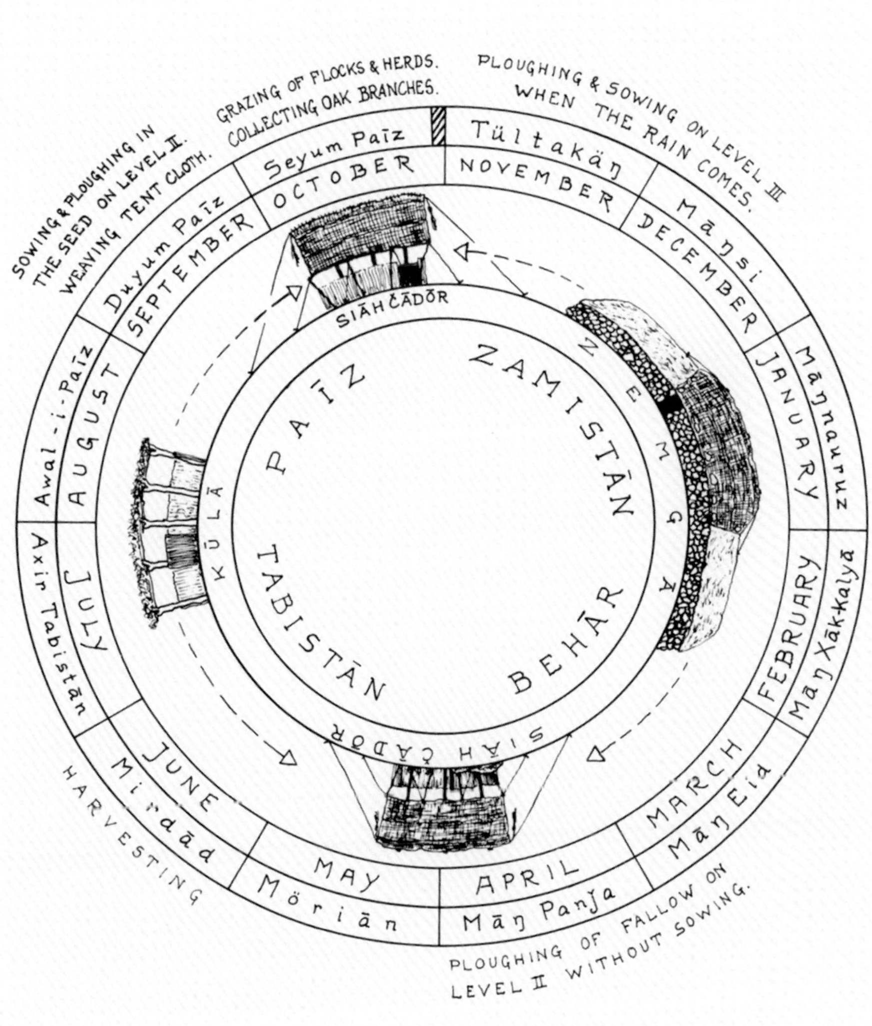

Figure 5. The annual migration calendar as reconstructed by Edelberg in the Danish ethnographical yearbook "Folk" 1967.

The branch and leaf kula may be considered the least necessary, but it was probably a pleasant way of spending the hottest season – and the roof served as fodder for the animals when the kula were pulled down. These structures presupposed a natural-oak-forest vegetation, which had already in the 1960s been seriously depleted because of the demand for fuel and the extensive charcoal trade – and for the kulas. Even if they were still needed, it will no longer be possible to find sufficient wood and leaves for the kula nowadays. Yet, I am told that some groups still follow the traditional seasonal migration rhythm, albeit mechanized (see Hojjat Darabi 2017). So, in more than one sense, it was a sort of salvage ethnoarchaeology that Lennart practiced during his brief sojourn in Luristan.

Figure 6.

Figure 7.

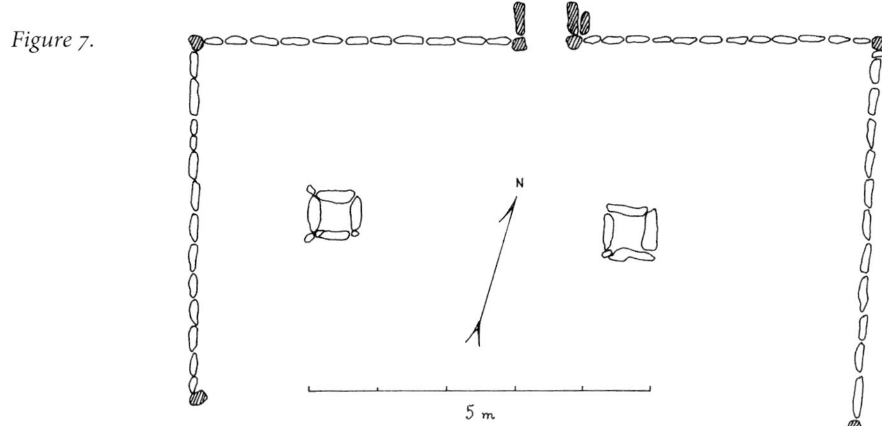

The archaeological evidence left of the annual cycle was extremely scarce, even if the old tent sites were still to be seen when we were there (figure 6). One disadvantage of short field work such as we did in Luristan is that you are only just a guest; no matter how good your insight and intentions may be, there is no way of ensuring any long-term effect of what you may suggest or want to happen. Lennart felt this and managed to return so often to Afghanistan that he was able to remedy some of the deplorable results of his having drawn attention to the qualities of the local cultures (1986). I think that a main reason for his successful fieldwork was his empathy for the people he studied. The negative effects of his publications, bringing Nuristan antiquities to the attention of 'the market', worried his conscience and certainly did nothing to alleviate his attitude toward capitalism. They illustrate a sad aspect of modern internationalization (Edelberg 1984, XIV). He was able to communicate with the people of Nuristan and the Lurs in a way that made them feel he respected them. On his last two expeditions to Nuristan, Lennart was accompanied by Margot, Susanne, and Miriam – not without risks – which just illustrates how close he felt toward the people of Nuristan.

Lennart was above all a great observer! He saw and described what he saw in text and drawings. Always an experienced draughtsman – from childhood – his drawings are to the point, recording the essentials of what he saw without unnecessary fuss. Nowadays when everyone photographs everything all the time without any perception of essential details, the advantages of drawing are in danger of being lost. When you draw you are forced to notice the qualities of the recorded object. That is apparent from his drawing of the tent sites, etc. (figure 7).

Figure 8. Lennart making notes, Ali Askar informing him, in the Hulailan valley on the left bank of the Saimarreh by Kuran Buzan, Sept. 1964, author's photo.

Neither he nor I were keen on theory. Back in Luristan, we worked before the breakthrough of theory in archaeology. So, there was no reason for subscribing to any particular school of thought. Lennart freely admitted what he did not know – honesty being a basic element of his character. His training as a botanist served him well, stressing the importance of precision of the observations and their documentation. In Luristan he picked an informant who was reliable, even if not the brightest of Lurs, but of course he did not restrict his information gathering to Ali Askar.

His observations of the annual settlement pattern fitted well with his basic interest in settlements in their natural environments. This was something that he practiced in his teaching and his fieldwork in the Ribe landscape. In that respect he was close to what we as archaeologists tried to achieve. Both of us moved on virgin soil. He managed a complete model better than we were able to do for the life in the Zagros 3000 years ago. His accomplishment shows the difference between mute archaeology and living anthropology. He promised a second paper on Luristan, but it never materialized, alas.

Lennart's work with the black tent is typical, combining precise practical observations and common sense. He did not just buy a tent; rather, he had the Lurs erect it, so that he would know how they did it. Of course, Lennart being the practical man had to re-erect the black tent on the meadow next to his house in Ribe in 1965. That was documented in a way he could not manage out there in Luristan – and was repeated at Moesgaard years later. Of course a sheep had to be provided to celebrate the acquisition. As we were busy at our excavations, I did not see how they got on, we only heard about the result and tasted the food when we returned from digging. It was of course Lennart who took charge of loading the lorry when we had finished and returned to Teheran on October 26. Once again, he was the practical man (figure 9).

Figure 9. Loading the lorry with the expedition's equipment and finds at Sar-i Tarhan. Oct. 1964. Photo: Henrik Thrane.

Figure 10. Lennart relaxing in local dress on a "yom al jomah," typically writing up his field notes in the expedition house in Sar Cham, author's photo Oct. d. 1964.

When the *kadkhoda* of Sar Cham presented us with the grave stele that served as a stepping stone over the drainage canal outside the loo, an endless series of troubles was the result. Not only were Lennart's activities questioned time and again by the gendarmerie, no doubt influenced by local discontent, his permits were also discussed and complaints launched. The stele became a serious thorn in the eye and the subject of many discussions right up until it finally reached Moesgaard. Many talks with a representative of the Antiquities Service, the kind Mr. Sarfaraz, were needed to calm down the excitement. When he realized Lennart's interest, the katkhoda gave him the stele.

There was an ingrained suspicion of foreigners' work in Luristan anyhow, but such an unorthodox approach as ethno-archaeology and an interest in the "primitive folk culture" was extremely suspicious for the Iranian authorities. Their misgivings were fueled by some of the locals who preferred to see our backs – and the sooner the better – so that they could go back to their business of looting the countryside of its antiquities. Lennart needed all his tact and stubbornness to make his way with the bureaucrats.

Of course, Nuristan was his top priority once he was back in Ribe, so Luristan had to wait, much to my regret. Lennart wrote well, but working on his publications was hard going. He had trouble finding the time for writing up his notes, what with all his manifold other activities that continued to consume his time. Even leaves of absence from the school did not benefit his writing quite as much as intended. Still, the results are both abundant and praiseworthy (Edelberg & al. 1984, 222 ff). His collections and his observations together with C.G. Feilberg's from 1935 on the Papis formed a solid basis for Inge Mortensen's handsome volume on Luristan that fully documents Feilberg's and Lennart's ethnographic collections (1993). She had worked in the Hulailan valley with her husband, Peder, mentioned above, so she had a personal knowledge of Luri culture. It was a happy result when the great Danish Nomad project managed to recruit her so that she could continue her work on the grave stele of the Pish-i Kuh (2010) and write this monumental volume in the Carlsberg Nomad Research Project series, which now stands as a lasting memorial to my friend and companion in the field, Lennart Edelberg.

When he sent me his small but seminal paper published in the Danish ethnographical periodical *Folk* (1967), Lennart wrote: "Thanks because you took me with you and enriched my world." I can only echo his words here.

Vibeke and Miriam helped me in various ways during the writing of this chapter.

List of references

Edelberg, Lennart (1967) "Seasonal Dwellings of Farmers in North-Western Luristan." In: *Folk* 8-9, pp. 373-401.

Edelberg, Lennart (1984) *Nuristani Buildings*. Jutland Archaeological Society: Højbjerg.

Feilberg, C.G. (1935) *Les Papis*. Copenhagen.

Feilberg, C.G. (1944) *La Tente Noire*. Copenhagen.

Felbo, J. (1965) En halv-nomade i Ribe. In: *Berlingske Tidende,* May 16, Copenhagen.

Jensen, S. (ed.) (1998) *Marsk, land og bebyggelse Ribeegnen gennem 10.0000 år*. Jutland Archaeological Society: Højbjerg.

Meldgaard, J. (1964) En landsby i Luristan. In: *Skalk* (1964): pp. 22-25.

Mortensen, I. Demant (1993) *Nomads of Luristan*. London.

Mortensen, I. Demant (2010) Luristani Pictorial Tombstones. In: *Acta Iranica 47*.

Mortensen, P. 2014, "Excavations at Tepe Guran. The Neolithic Period". In: *Acta Iranica*.

Stark, F. (1932) The Bronzes of Luristan. In: *The Geographical Journal* LXXX: pp. 498-505.

Stark, F. (1947) [1934], *The Valleys of the Assassins: and other Persian Travels*. London.

Thrane, H. (1963) Hjulgraven fra Storehøj ved Tobøl. In: *Kuml* 1962: pp. 5-37.

Thrane, H. (1995) Forord. In: *Marsk, land og bebyggelse. Ribeegnen gennem 10.000 år, edited by* S. Jensen: pp. 9-12. Jutland Archaeological Society: Højbjerg.

Thrane, H. (2001) *Excavations at Tepe Guran in Luristan. The Bronze Age and Iron Age Periods*. Jutland Archaeological Society: Højbjerg.

Thrane, H. (2015) "A Valley in the Zagros Mountains – the Danish Expedition to Luristan." In: *The Past in the Present, edited by* B. Bundgaard Rasmussen: pp. 95-112. Aarhus University Press: Aarhus.

Watson, P.J. (1979) *Archaeological Ethnography in Western Iran*. Tucson.

12.
Lennart and Edelberg

By Torkil Funder

In Berlingske Tidende, May 16, 1965. Jørgen Felbo: "En halvnomade i Ribe" ("A semi-nomad in Ribe.") Photo: Berlingske/Ritzau.

The black tent in Ribe

In the spring of 1965, my final examination at the University of Copenhagen was approaching. After that, I planned to carry out training as a teacher at an upper secondary school. I would be learning to teach from a teacher of my subjects: natural history, which had not yet been renamed biology and geography. So, in May '65, at the end of the term, I was going home on the Grenå-Hundested ferry, expecting to have four or five quiet hours at sea.

In the ferry's lounge I found a newspaper, *Berlingske Tidende*, that someone had left behind on a table. The US had ceased bombing North Vietnam, China had set off another nuclear bomb, and Japan was going to complain to Peking. The Conservatives had enjoyed a 5% increase in voter support since October, the Social Democrats an 8% decrease. The court case over the returning of the Icelandic Manuscripts continued. Outside the sea was calm all around.

It was Sunday, May 16. In the third section of the newspaper, there was a picture of a man in a Faroese sweater with a grey pattern. Kneeling in the grass in a meadow in front of his white house, he was struggling to tighten a corner guy rope attached to a large black tent in the background. You could tell from his hair that it was a windy day.

"The semi-nomad tightens the guy ropes of the tent in front of his house in Ribe," the caption jokingly states. I figure that it takes sixteen guy ropes to keep a tent cloth of this size stretched over the inner frame, which proves to be four meters high. The tent itself does not reach to the ground; rather, it ends roughly at face level and appears to have loose walls made of mats tied together.

The article is about the man tightening the guy ropes. His name is Lennart Edelberg. His concentration, the Faroese sweater, and the weather swirling around him makes him look like a Faroese bird catcher. In fact, he is a teacher of geography and natural history at the upper secondary school in Ribe. In September-October 1964, he had spent six weeks among the nomadic Lurs in the Zagros Mountains in northwestern Iran. During this leave of absence from school, he had been charged by the National Museum in Copenhagen with studying the pattern of the Lurs' yearly migrations.

Due to their mobile lifestyle, ethnographers considered the Lurs to be nomads; yet, their housing and their agriculture during the year marked them as sedentary. While in Luristan, Edelberg had primarily investigated the phases of the year of these semi-nomads. Using the information he had collected, he had made a circular Lur calendar. For each month, he gave a brief description of the associated dwelling and their work with the land and animals at the same time.*

While in Luristan, Edelberg had collected objects pertaining to many aspects of Lur daily life. The biggest and most important object being the tent, which plays a major role in the moves to different locations over the course of a year. The tent itself consists of two halves, each eight meters long, woven from black goat's wool. It is heavy and worn after many years of use. Then there is the naturally formed wood used for the roof ridge and the tent poles, also well worn, and the guy ropes and smaller staffs and the rolled-up mats and the sharpened, tough wooden pegs used to stitch together the two halves of the tent. All of these items were indispensable and carefully carried from place to place by the many equally indispensable pack animals.

In Jørgen Felbo's interview with Edelberg in *Berlingske Tidende,* one learns that, "The tent with all its contents has been bought in Luristan in Persia. It belonged to a semi-nomadic tribe. I bought it for the museum in Aarhus on my last trip there."

Approximately one year after the tent had been dismantled for the last time in Luristan, it was pitched in the thick grass in Ribe in Western Jutland, supported by all of Edelberg's knowledge.

The local museum in Ribe, the Antiquarian Collection, of which Edelberg was chairman, announced that the tent was open to the public.

For a modest entrance fee, the townspeople could see and hear some of the stories that surround all objects, if one observes and listens. Visitors were encouraged to experience the light in the tent as well as the old smells of smoke and animals along with the dust itself that still clung to the black tent cloth; and maybe in the end to sit in the tent on one of the woven rugs on the ground at just the right height – just like in Luristan. "It is good to use one's own eyes and not be served with everything already processed," Edelberg said in the interview.

Later that evening, having read about the black tent in Ribe on the ferry, I wrote a letter in which I immediately set out my goal: "Master L. Edelberg, Ribe. With this unsolicited request, I wish to ask whether it might be possible to undergo teacher training with you in the autumn of 1965."

Soon after, I received an enthusiastic reply. And on one of the first days of August 1965, I entered the school yard of Ribe Katedralskole, where I met Lennart Edelberg under one of the old pollarded linden trees on the north side of the yard. He wore a dark, checkered shirt and corduroy trousers and carried his narrow glasses on a cord around his neck.

Two weeks later, we went on a week's school camp to Løvenholm Manor in Djursland in Denmark with a class of younger students. At the end of September, we went on another camp with two older classes to the island of Hooge in the German Wadden Sea. A close professional relationship and a far-reaching friendship had begun.

*   Edelberg, Lennart, "Seasonal Dwellings of Farmers in North-Western Luristan." In **FOLK** 8-9 (1966/67): 373-401.

The check list

When Lennart Edelberg gave away books, offprints, and articles as gifts to colleagues, friends, and family, he would often inscribe them well-worded messages, thus placing the gift in a particular temporal, geographical, and situational context – a link between the giver and the receiver of the gift, so that it would be more than merely an isolated item in the eyes of posterity.

Margot Edelberg once related that one evening in the years following World War II, marine biologist Erik Smidt – a relative and close friend of Lennart's – attended a dinner party with the explorer Henning Haslund-Christensen. During dinner, Haslund told about his plans for an expedition to Afghanistan, a reflection of a greater plan he had had in the 1930s before the World War had rendered it impossible. Haslund now had revived his idea of exploring certain large areas of Afghanistan, which for a long time had been a little-known buffer zone between the Russian bear to the north and the British lion to the south.

The expedition would be concerned with natural science, cultural history and, in particular, ethnographic studies. Now his plan was to explore various parts of Afghanistan beyond the northwestern border provinces of British India, later Pakistan, from the desert regions and the town of Herat in the west to the Hindukush mountains and the Nuristan area in the northeast. Haslund's intention in '47 was to bring ethnographers, botanists, zoologists, and geographers along. However, this expedition, which could well last several years, was short of a botanist.

Erik Smidt answered that a highly educated relative of his, Lennart Edelberg, was in truth made for such a journey and also had the appropriate skills. He was at present working for the public institute for weed control in Denmark, and Erik Smidt would get in touch with him the very next day.

One day, while carrying out his Herculean task of collecting, sorting, registering, and establishing the Edelberg Archive in the Moesgaard Museum, ethnographer Svend Castenfeldt picked out yet another scrap of paper from the great pile of material before him. As he read it, he immediately understood that this was one of those finds that can sweeten the work of an archivist for years to come.

The piece of paper was 21.1 × 14.7 cm. It was a concise check list concerning only two items, written in Lennart Edelberg's characteristic hand. "Stereoscopic images," it says, and below that "Eye drops." As it was a large piece of paper, it had been reused at a later date. A message had been drafted upon the recycled scrap of paper to go with an unknown present from Lennart Edelberg to Erik Smidt. We do not know the nature of the present, but the scribbled message together with

Til min kære fætter Erik,
som med sin telefonopringning hin
torsdag i 1947 udløste den
afghanske lavine, som rev mig
med siden.

fra din hengivne
Lennart

Archives of Moesgaard Museum, "EA 375 – Lennart Edelberg Archive".

Margot Edelberg's anecdote about the dinner party, is yet another example of the accidental game of coincidence. The reused check list ended up in the museum and became the final PowerPoint slide at the May 2016 Edelberg seminar at Moes-gaard.

The dike around Pellworm. Photo: Torkil Funder, September 9, 1965.

Man on dike

His attire is correct and discreet, appropriate for late September. His years as a student of natural history have left their mark: yellow raincoat, visible in the landscape, grass-grey trousers and fisherman's sweater. Green wellingtons with soft legs so that they do not take up much space in the backpack. He works his sextant with an intense effort as a musician. In fact, the man used to play the cello.

His feet balance on the steep slope of the great dike that tells its grave story of how much it takes to resist a flood like the one in 1634, which broke through the dike of those days and swept away three quarters of Nordstrand, the big and prosperous island, and took the same share of its farms and people in thirteen parishes. When the weather calmed down, there was nothing but waves, where there had been fertile fields. Part of the land that was subsequently recovered, became the island of Pellworm, where we stand now, and the new Nordstrand further east.

The man knows this. He is busy with his gear, but he is also the unifying centre of a school class from the upper secondary school in the town of Ribe. It is late September 1965, and it is the seventh year that the school holds a one week school camp here: one week in the Halligen islands in the German Wadden Sea. Scattered across the island, there are few houses; a few families live here on the artificially built "warfts", or mounds of earth in the sea. Roman travelers mention these structures around the beginning of the Christian era. During a regular high tide, from a distance it looks as if the houses are floating on the water.

The man has charged himself with a message in life: to show his students – and actually everybody – the big pattern: the grand design consisting of humans and their surroundings and their ever-present responsibility to these. Here in the Wadden Sea, where the rise and fall of the waters never ceases, the pattern is evident. In the midst of it – on the islands and sailing the seas – people have found ways to thrive here for 2000 years. young students now have the opportunity to try to interpret, to depict, or to enquire about the original circumstances.

With his students following in a procession, he crosses the tidal flat when the tide is out. Some carry tubs; one has a big plastic container; another carries a spade; some carry glass jars with lids; one has a stainless-steel knife; another has a net. "Now this shared piece of equipment is your responsibility," he tells them. An expedition! They study life in the puddles, some of it they take with them; where they see traces on the surface, they dig, and put the creatures from the depths into the tubs for later scrutiny. Standing still and listening to the gurgling and sighing of the tidal flat's surface, they see how the streams of water merge with foam along the edges. They cross a water-carrying trench and see that the tide has turned.

They see the straight, linear marks where saline peat was cut centuries ago and removed to be burned and seethed to make the valuable Frisian salt. Walking with heavy steps, they reach the low-lying coast where old peat sticks out underneath the younger marsh sediments.

Finally, as if they were carried by the eager rising streams around them, they reach firm Hooge island that stretches before them in unchanging green till they reach the Ockelützwarft. It is here that they are staying – as 'cathedral school students' have every year since 1958. The houses in the warft form a small cluster of human habitation under a vast and bright blue sky. Behind them and the low summer dike, the sea spreads soundlessly and eager over the tidal flat and erases all trace of the expedition.

They carry their tubs home full of live creatures; alongside a container of salt water, there are glass jars and the day's collection of snail shells and other findings. They eat together, finishing with Frau Binge's pudding that they know well from older students' stories. Today it consists of a slice of sponge cake containing diced pork and pink fruit sauce. After dinner, they will discuss the events of the day. To do so, they push tables and chairs together that the Binge family has collected – particularly for the benefit of Master Edelberg from Ribe and his colleagues and students. After eight years, they have good working conditions, matching the simple furniture of the locals.

The expedition members start writing and sketching the experiences of the day. Some have glued-together sheets of graph paper, on which they draw the long cross section they have measured from the surface of the sea to the summer dike and beyond that to the base of the warf and all the way to the house where they are now sitting. The big haystacks on the mound are also included. Sailing away on those could provide a last means of escape; indeed, they have served as such not too long ago.

The air pump in the tubs with salt water and sea animals serves as the sound of the living tidal flat. Some students are reading various reference books and are writing about "The sea in a tub." The texts are illustrated with drawings of the fanworm Pectinaria's tube made of grains of sand cemented together and pictures of the worm itself next to it. Others draw Pellworm's ruined church tower, its masonry, patterns, and reparations in the weathered brickwork. From the church itself, they draw various sketches and tell us about the font, the pulpit, and the altarpiece with images and contents; all of these are often better understood through the act of drawing.

As the man, Lennart Edelberg, stands there on the dike, he is again on an expedition; he is participating in an exploration – just as in Afghanistan and Iran. But actually, he is always travelling, observing, asking, responding, taking notes, and publishing, sometimes sharply. To him, the school camps are expeditions – journeys away from the base that will

end with a return with new insights. On
the big blackboards at his lectures, where
he made drawings with chalk to explain
both the yearly pattern of the nomads
and the chemical-biological cycles of life,
his stories had an underlying invitation:
seek out the world, investigate it, and act
accordingly.

What Lennart measures with his
sextant from the dike on the island of
Pellworm is an angle on the tower of the
Alte Kirche church. The ruins of this
structure have been preserved since the
1634 flood. He wonders whether the
same master builder may be behind not
only this tower but also the great tower of
the cathedral in Ribe. Finding out about
this could be another good school camp
assignment.

Arrival

On page 210 of *Ripenserbladet,* the journal of the students' association of Ribe Katedralskole, one can read Lennart Edelberg's speech to the new students at the yearly celebration in *Ripensersamfundet,* the alumni association, on November 23, 1968. Edelberg's speech bore the title "The so-called harmless", an account of his arrival in Ribe and at the school described in the first part of his speech.

> I was immensely pleased when, eighteen years ago, Principal Jørgensen came down to the basement of the National Museum in Copenhagen, where I was engaged in some casual work, and asked how I would like to come to Ribe Katedralskole. At that point, I had struggled in vain for seven years to gain employment at an upper secondary school; the last year after I had returned from Asia had been particularly frustrating.
>
> I very much wanted to go to Ribe. What an unexpected surprise! Suddenly, out of the blue, you get just what you wished for – like when you turn the corner and unexpectedly see your girlfriend before you.
>
> When I reached the top of the Kalvslund hill and saw Ribe there on the horizon – the windbreaks were not so tall then – I knew that I would want to stay in this place. And indeed, Ribe turned out to be right up my street.

Photo: June 20, 1969. Archives of Ribe Katedralskole.

The teaching staff at Ribe Katedralskole
in 1969. Lennart Edelberg sits in front at
the far right. Thomas Alvad, the school's
music teacher sits third from the right in
the front row. Alvad worked on the music
recordings from Nuristan together with
Lennart and Margot Edelberg and the
composer and ethnomusicologist Poul
Rovsing Olsen.

Photo: Torkil Funder. October, 1965.

Geography class

The geography classroom is at the end of the long corridor in the main building. Walking down the hall in 1966, one passes all the photographs of each year's graduating students from 1880s onwards. The classroom has three large, south-facing windows. The back wall is painted deep blue. Across this expanse, the Milky Way has been painted as a delicate, white trail – more sensed than actually seen. There are various projectors in the room, including a big epidiascope that can project both books and slides of different sizes.

On the wall to the left of the back wall, but not visible in the photograph, there is an embroidered prayer rug from Bukhara, the famous oasis, bought in Afghanistan by Edelberg. Protected by a pane of glass and hung on the wall. A strange fate for a prayer rug. Usually, when in use, they lie on the ground.

There is much more in the room: framed colour prints of Mecca and Medina; small, pressed plants from Greenland in black frames; a plaster model of the geography of Northern Jutland, and a wooden pillar in front of the window displaying black-and-white stereo photos, 6 × 6 of the world around 1910 in an endless loop lit by the changing daylight of western Jutland.

The wall behind the teacher's desk is oxblood red; it carries a big blackboard and a crowd of large, pull-down maps from the ceiling. There is a handsome carved wooden peg from Afghanistan, also from Edelberg, of course. In the corner by the blackboard stands a very large, white cupboard, full of objects from all over the world.

The long wall in the classroom has a door to the adjoining room. This is the geography library, with its new pinewood shelves that reach almost to the ceiling. There are maps in many different scales and from many different periods of time under the black worktables. Placed against the wall, there is a large cabinet with fifty-four large drawers full of stones that are from different geological periods and feature different processes of formation as well as a collection of minerals. A dark samurai suit of armour from Japan stands next to this cabinet. Such is part of this part of Edelberg's geography kingdom.

The stones used in today's lesson come from two cabinets containing smaller samples in old cigar boxes. They are labelled according to a system developed by the geologist S.A. Andersen for use in schools. A book describing the system is found in each drawer; a cardboard placard that Edelberg has hung on the door shows how to maintain the order of the cigar boxes.

Safely back from a one week school camp on the island of Hooge in the German Wadden Sea, here we are – eleven students out of sixteen in class 2. math – working with the stones this morning in October 1965. Edelberg is sitting with Christiane to the very far right. Two other girls are absent today.

There are two students for each drawer. This is appropriate as they sit at old double school desks. "The last upper-high-school class in Denmark with such desks" according to Edelberg. As you sat there all students scrutinizing the same stone, discussing it, reading about it in S.A. Andersen's book or the textbook, the stone was a thing in common. And you could continue the studies together, maybe focusing on the stones labeled with a capital A and a number. They are all from the island of Bornholm according to Andersen's book. Some examples were the Rønne granodiorite, or E 28, which turns out to be travertine. Travertine was a rock formed by deposition, a sedimentary rock. You could hold the stones in your hands. Feel their weight. Take a closer look or test their hardness with a nail or a knife.

The reason why the teacher participates with his back to the students is that this lesson is being taught by Torkil Funder. Edelberg is supervising his teacher trainee. Torkil seems to be a little shaky, as the photo seems to attest. The real teacher has taken the place of a student, and one may remember that in the 1960s, even a liberal, open-minded teacher like Edelberg would be addressed *De*, which is the formal 'you' in Danish. You would write "Mr. Edelberg" next to the photos in the school camp report. But there was warmth and respect behind the laughter in this unusual situation.

Edelberg's students never forgot his lessons. His voice, his manner, his knowledge, his engaging warmth and inclusive smile. Lennart looked right at you and listened to you. You were *there*. Present.

Ethnographic cupboards

In 1950, when Lennart Edelberg arrived at Ribe Cathedral School to teach geography and natural history, he discovered that the school housed a great collection of preserved animal specimens stuffed, stored in alcohol, and placed behind glass in many big cupboards painted dark green.

But the school also housed an ethnographic collection. Like the animals, these objects originated from around the world. Unlike the animals, the ethnographic objects had no real connection to the subjects being taught. These objects included strange instruments, weapons and religious items. In many cases, they were presented to the school around 1860 by J. F. Møller, a sea captain native to Ribe.

Edelberg must have been mightily excited by the sight that met him in those rooms. Yet, strangely enough, he never mentioned the existence of all those objects at the time, nor where they were being stored. The many animals and parts of animals, which Captain Møller had collected during his years of sailing and presented to the school, were all registered in the school yearbook as they arrived and were listed under their Latin or Danish name. Yet only once – in 1860 – is there any mention of "Captain Møller having presented to the school many ethnographic objects."

Not only had Edelberg travelled in Afghanistan, he had also undertaken long journeys through the rooms containing the ethnographic collections of the National Museum in Copenhagen. So he was not a stranger to objects from such faraway places as those in Captain Møller's collection: the Pacific Ocean, China, the islands of Southern Asia, the Pacific Northwest. However, Edelberg may well have been surprised to see so many items from around the world here in Western Jutland. He was probably pleased at the prospect of spending his days not just with the large collection of animals but also among objects from countries and places that in 1950 still were very far away from the old cathedral town.

As early as 1950, Edelberg must have sent a selection of the school's ethnographic objects to the National Museum in Copenhagen, inquiring about their place of origin, age, use, name and other relevant information. Thanks to his taking part in the 1947-52 Afghanistan expedition, Edelberg was well-known at the National Museum. In May 1951, the objects were returned to him, "packed in two wooden crates."

In 1950, schoolmaster Edelberg is thirty-five years old. That year, for a weekly total of twenty-eight hours, he teaches geography and natural history. He will be very pleased with the course's widespread scientific content.

When the crates of ethnographica are returned from the National Museum, he considers the very slim information provided by the professionals on labels

Photo: Torkil Funder. November 1992.

that are still preserved today. Once it has all been appropriately placed around the school, he decides to create his own index of the school's ethnographica.

The school is full of cupboards. They became a necessity around 1850, as new regulations stipulated that natural history and the new subject physics besides books should be taught by means of objects, instruments, and exercises. Since then, more and more equipment has entered the teaching of those subjects.

Edelberg places various objects in a tall, brown, somewhat rustic, pinewood cupboard. It includes part of Møller's old collection. Its boards are broad and solid, and there is a thin layer of blue paint on the inside. At the very top of the cupboard is still painted from an earlier use "The Paleolithic Age."

In 1862, Captain Møller died at the age of fifty-two in Batavia in Java. At that time, his collection included more than a hundred items. Edelberg revived the collection in the early 1950s. At that time, he reinstated the double-seated kayak – originally registered as number one in Captain Møller's collection – as number one also in his own newly established index and went on from there to include the rest of the original objects, although not without considerable difficulties.

Edelberg searches Captain Møller's other objects for the original numbers, but only finds a few. Almost too conspicuously, the highest number he finds is 100. This is written inside a fez, a red felt cap with a black tassel. In Møller's time, such caps were much used by men in the Middle East and North Africa. Hence,

Edelberg writes on the index card: "Fez, Oriental, J.F.M. Orig. No. 100 (top of fez, on the inside)." On the back of the card he adds: "The loosened sweatband reattached in Ribe (with a sewing machine!)."

If he encountered difficulties determining the name, use, and place of origin of any object, Edelberg would often turn to the pictures and texts of ethnographic works. Particularly, *Etnografien* (Ethnography) by Danish ethnographer Kristian Bahnson (Copenhagen: Det Nordiske Forlag, 1900), and *Kulturens Veje* (The Paths of Culture) by Kaj Birket-Smith (Copenhagen: Jespersen og Pio, 1941), and then of course the exhibited ethnographic collections of the National Museum in Copenhagen.

While the tall, brown cupboard holds many objects connected to Captain Møller, the great white cupboard contains mostly Edelberg's objects. It has sixteen small glass panes. It is an old school cupboard, but has no known history. The red and golden wallpaper with which Edelberg himself covered the back wall gives it a remarkable background. He put the many individual objects into some order by having loose crates specially made of pale, lacquered wood. Each had a painted symbol, so that one could choose the Arabian, the Chinese, the South American, or the Native American crate for use in teaching. There is no Western European crate, as the collection holds very few objects from this area.

In the close-up photograph of a shelf in the white cupboard; in the upper part, one can see a pair of men's shoes from India and a baking pan with bread typical of northern Afghanistan, bought by Torkil Funder in Mazar-e-Sharif in 1970. And to the left, there is part of a meal-time hand-wash kit, a jug with a long spout and a water bowl with a sieve-like lid, the whole set made of tinned copper. Often the host will pour the water for the guest to wash hands. In time, the long neck of the jug will be so worn that the copper shows through. This one was bought in Kabul by Lennart Edelberg in 1954.

To the right, there is a Danish preserv-ing glass jar from the 1940s. It contains pine cones that have opened and lie on a thick layer of dark seeds. A white label reads: "*Pinus gerardiana*, cones and seeds. Kafiristan/Nuristan. The seeds are eatable." Botanical matters continue: the next shelf holds a box of slim, sturdy glass bottles containing dried plums and mulberries. There is also a box of dried leaves from the small-leaved, prickly ever-green oak, *Quercus balout*, the holly oak. The entire botanical collection is dated December 17, 1947. These items must stem from the 1947-52 Haslund Expe-dition. Edelberg has kept these dried-up botanical remnants for 15-17 years. Each time he passed them round a class and told about them, they would come alive again.

To the left of the glass bottles lies a *katara,* a dagger in a metal sheath. An important weapon and sign of dignity in Nuristan. Edelberg placed a sketch of the katara in the middle of the small, dark-blue, oval labels carrying his name and town. He used these as ex-libris identifiers in his books.

At the back of the top shelf lies the collec-tion's no. 103: a muzzle loader with its ramrod and flintlock. It is made of dark and well-worn wood, with inlaid moth-er-of-pearl and polished metal. It was purchased in 1953 by Edelberg from a man in the mountains of Panjshir north of Kabul. The man was on his way to the bazar to sell the weapon.

Photo: Torkil Funder. March 11, 1968.

*In the mountains of Panjshir north of Kabul. Photo: Lennart Edelberg or Peter Rasmussen,
December 25, 1953.*

The collector

Edelberg brought home objects for the National Museum in Copenhagen and for the Aarhus Museum from his travels in 1947-49, 1953-54, 1964, and 1970. Using the yearly sum allocated to the Department of Geography, he also bought objects for the school in Ribe. During his travels he bought from the bazaars, in the villages, and wherever else one could acquire objects with a story useful for teaching.

On December 25, 1953 in the Panjshir region north of Kabul, Edelberg met a man, who was on his way down from the snow-covered mountains. He was carrying a muzzle loader that he intended to sell. The old weapon may be from the mid-1800s. Nevertheless, with both flintlock and ramrod well preserved, it might still be in working order. Edelberg bought it "On Christmas Day 1953, for approx. 90 Danish kroner." There is a photograph of a man in the mountains carrying such a gun. His family may have used it in the time of the Afghan Wars. The photograph may well have been taken by Peter Rasmussen, the expedition photographer.

Many of the objects that Edelberg bought for the Ribe school are religious images and related items. Tools for working the land are also collected: numbers 97 and 101 in the card index are both keraus, bought in Nuristan in 1953-54. A *kerau* is a naturally grown wooden tool shaped like a spade or a fork. While one person steers it, another pulls it – in Nuristan generally this means two women – using a rope tied to the bottom part of the tool. It is very important for cultivating the soil in the narrow terraces and small fields on the steep mountain slopes of Nuristan.

Edelberg writes on index card no. 106: "Prayer rug. Kabul. The Shahr-i-Nau bazaar. Jan 54". Used during the five daily prayers, the niche pointing towards Mecca. The rug has probably been embroidered in the Bukhara area. Islam only allows depictions of plants, 'arabesques'. The text has four lines with end rhymes and reads from right to left. It has been unstitched – maybe because the rug initially belonged to a woman and was later passed on to a man, maybe because of spelling mistakes and, finally, maybe because it is not a quote from the Quran. A translation of the text: 1) Oh God, grant me prosperity and good fortune in this world! 2) Oh King, remember me, a humble woman! 3) Would that my mother and father be united in (with?) their souls! 4) Let them (?) experience not the slightest misfortune in this world!" Most index-texts are short. This one covers two cards.

Edelberg would also buy things in Copenhagen if he found that they held a story he could use in his geography or religion lessons, or if he came across a particularly good deal. The conditions for buying such material were good at the school in Ribe in the 1960s and 70s.

During this period, quite a large collection of religious prints and objects was gradually established in the geography library. This fitted in well with the contemporary fascination with the great Eastern religions, not least among young people. Until 1985, it seems to have been the general situation that religion was taught in one lecture a week for two years, the teaching at this time being carried out by qualified but not examined members of the school's teaching staff. In 1965, Edelberg thus taught religion in two classes, religious aspects since youth being an important interest of his life.

In the archives of the department, there is a receipt from Sunde's shop, "Etnografica", in Copenhagen, dated December 7, 1962. It lists: "Six divine representations from India, made of alabaster of Brahma, Vishnu-Varaha, Durga, Shiva-Parvati, Ganeca, and Hanuman; furthermore, a 'Japanese thunderbolt (*vajra*)', and a 'Tibetan tantric drum (*damaru*)'; and 1,375 Danish kroner in total. There is also a note that Edelberg has bought a 'knotted curtain' for a tent entrance, at Quedens Gård in Ribe, DKK 275." In total, the items come to 1,650 Danish kroner – a sizeable withdrawal from the department's miscellaneous expense account for 1962. The "curtain," which is from Afghanistan, was placed above the door between the geography classroom proper and its library.

Later, Edelberg bought a number of objects, primarily of a religious nature, in the unique Indian shop *Maharani* located in the posh street of Bredgade in Copen-

hagen. Here, in 1967, he bought a thangka (Tibetan?) decorated with a Buddhist motif (painted on silk and approximately 5 m long) and a painted narrator's canvas from the Bhil people in India with an accompanying gramophone record, *Musique Indienne de Rajahstan.*

The artefacts bought for the school do not take up much physical space, but nevertheless more space in the imagination. Index card No. 227, a censer, must have been bought by Edelberg during a short visit ashore on the outward journey of the Haslund-Christensen Memorial Expedition in 1953-54: "Censer, the village of Uthman, outside Aden. May 53. Used for myrrh, which is spread on top of embers placed at the bottom of the cup. The censer may at times be carried under the shirt so the fragrant smoke rises from the neckline." A very precise description of a small but important local artefact and its use.

Index card No. 226 is a "Carved peg. Wama, Nuristan. Nov. 53. L. Edelberg. The hanger was attached to one of the four carved pillars around the fireplace in a Kafir house using leather straps. Note also the half-finished carvings. The bifurcation may be a stylized representation of the horns of the wild goat."

In December 1964, Lennart Edelberg wrote a piece for *Ripenserbladet*. In his piece, he describes "the ethnographic collection at Ribe Katedralskole" and points out how alumni have in the past supported the school with non-monetary gifts for use in the classroom. He encourages the continuation of this tradition:

…It would be *extraordinarily valuable and welcome* if, in the future, alumni abroad or with connections abroad would also remember their old school with items that can offer an impression of daily life, etc. in the various corners of the world. It *does not in any way have to be valuable objects* – often cheap trinkets from bazaars, market stalls and villages tell a much more multifaceted story than showpieces.

A collection of items from one particular tribe, which sheds light on the daily life of that tribe, would of course be particularly welcome. The same goes for objects that offer insights into religious beliefs.

Through gifts of this nature, alumni can partake in connecting the classroom to distant lands to a very great degree.

At the time of Lennart Edelberg's death in 1981, the index contained more than 500 numbers. One of the last items he registers is No. 509, "Nuristan, Parun Valley, L.E. leg. 1953, vessel made of poplar, used in the mountain pastures, note repair. The Parun tribe produces such vessels for the entire Nuristan region."

No. 515 is an Islamic colour print on paper. It shows "The names of Allah and Muhammad written in roses. L.E. bought in Kabul 1970."

Photos: Miriam Edelberg. April 2016.

STUDIO means enthusiasm

In October 1965, the 75th anniversary of the Danish National Union of Upper Secondary School Teachers was celebrated. On October 18, at a ceremony in the big hall of the University of Copenhagen on the day of the anniversary, Lennart Edelberg was presented with the Union's gold medal and an honorary award of 10,000 Danish kroner.

The medal is awarded "an upper secondary school teacher whose work has been characterized by professional excellence." This is expressed in the inscription on the medal: 'STUDIO INVESTIGATIONIS ET EXPLICATIONIS' – 'For eagerness in research and interpretation.'

The award was presented by Professor Axel Schou, a member of the Union's Anniversary Foundation. In his introductory speech, Schou stated the reasons for awarding Lennart Edelberg: "The upper secondary school teacher must arouse the kind of excitement in the best students that leads to a desire to carry out research and do science." He also emphasized Edelberg's great contribution to the Antiquarian Collection, that is the museum in Ribe, and its importance for Danish city history as well as to his efforts to make Ribe a university town.

And Axel Schou continued: "But beyond that, Lennart Edelberg has studied the old nomadic cultures on well-planned and successfully executed expeditions to countries in the Near East such as Afghanistan and Iran. In particular, he has studied the connections between commercial, geographic, and ethnographic characteristics as well as climate variations in the surrounding environment. In this way, he has unearthed some of the deepest roots of our culture. He has broadened our understanding with a wealth of new knowledge and called attention to a range of connections not previously known.

Thanks to Master Lennart Edelberg's skill in pedagogic production, he has managed to popularize, in the most positive sense of the word, his material through presentations and radio programs. His contribution to the Sunday university presentations on the public broadcasting service deserves a particular mention: Titled 'Furrows in the ancient face of Asia,' these presentations are also available in book form.

Master Lennart Edelberg has, through his efforts in research and in communicating his results to a broad selection of the Danish population, continued one of the most beautiful traditions of this teaching profession in a most noble manner."

Lennart Edelberg, the award winner, expressed his thanks that "this award has fallen into my turban – my Afghan turban." In his acceptance speech, he expressed three wishes – just like in traditional fairytales:

My first wish is that we, in the mother country of Niels Steensen and Niels Finsen, continually honour the simple, independent observation – not least in biology. The challenge is to keep our balance in this modern age, so that our wonderful subject does not lose its identity. Our task, then, must be to make biochemistry *immediate*, alongside the study of classic natural history… Classic natural history has so many fine qualities that it ought to enjoy a renaissance now when so many schools have got better collections and better equipment.

Those aspects of biochemistry that cannot be made directly accessible to students because they require electron microscopes and equipment so complicated that it distracts from the thing at hand, must wait. And 'wait' means wait until our students enter the institutions of higher education, where such equipment and the time to use it are available. However, biology cannot become a subject one must learn from a book, in school or later on. Once this happens, it will have lost its identity.

Could the universities, etc. ask for anything better than upper secondary school graduates who have the skills to observe independently, with the naked eye or a simple microscope, and objectively describe what they have seen and experienced? Moreover, if students are able to draw well-considered, decent conclusions, I would suggest that we would be in a much better situation than would be the case if they had been only taught the latest there is to know from books.

My second wish is that music will permeate the upper secondary schools much more than is the case today – not merely that it will be a subject in its own right, but that all the other subjects will be saturated with its juice.

My third wish pertains to my second mother country. I wish that there may be sufficient Danish will and ability to establish the "Danish Institute for Scientific and Pedagogical Cooperation with Afghanistan" that I have at times advocated for.

Holberg was the first Dane to mention Afghanistan. I hope his spirit will help me today in this hall. The problem is that there is no direct diplomatic link between Afghanistan and Denmark. Thus, I feel that I have a duty to express this wish, which is shared by the Afghan Education Secretary and a circle of ministers and prominent government officers around him. Already Haslund-Christensen has been preoccupied with such plans.

Lennart Edelberg ended his speech by saying:

Without Haslund's confidence in me and the magnificent hospitality I met among the Afghans in Kabul and out in the villages, I would not be standing here today.

And in all this and behind all this, a happy thank you to the Anniversary Foundation for this grand award. [*]

The 10,000 DKK that Lennart Edelberg received along with the medal was a significant sum in 1965; the amount would need to be multiplied more than ten times to come close to its value today. The award allowed the family to build an extension on their house in the western-most part of Ribe; the new construction included an annex that also had room for a large study.

On January 15, 1967, Lennart wrote in a
letter: "I now have the best study here at
home that any private or public person
has ever been granted."

* For iver ved forskning og tolkning. In: Gymnasieskolen 19 (29 okt. 1965): 1059-62.

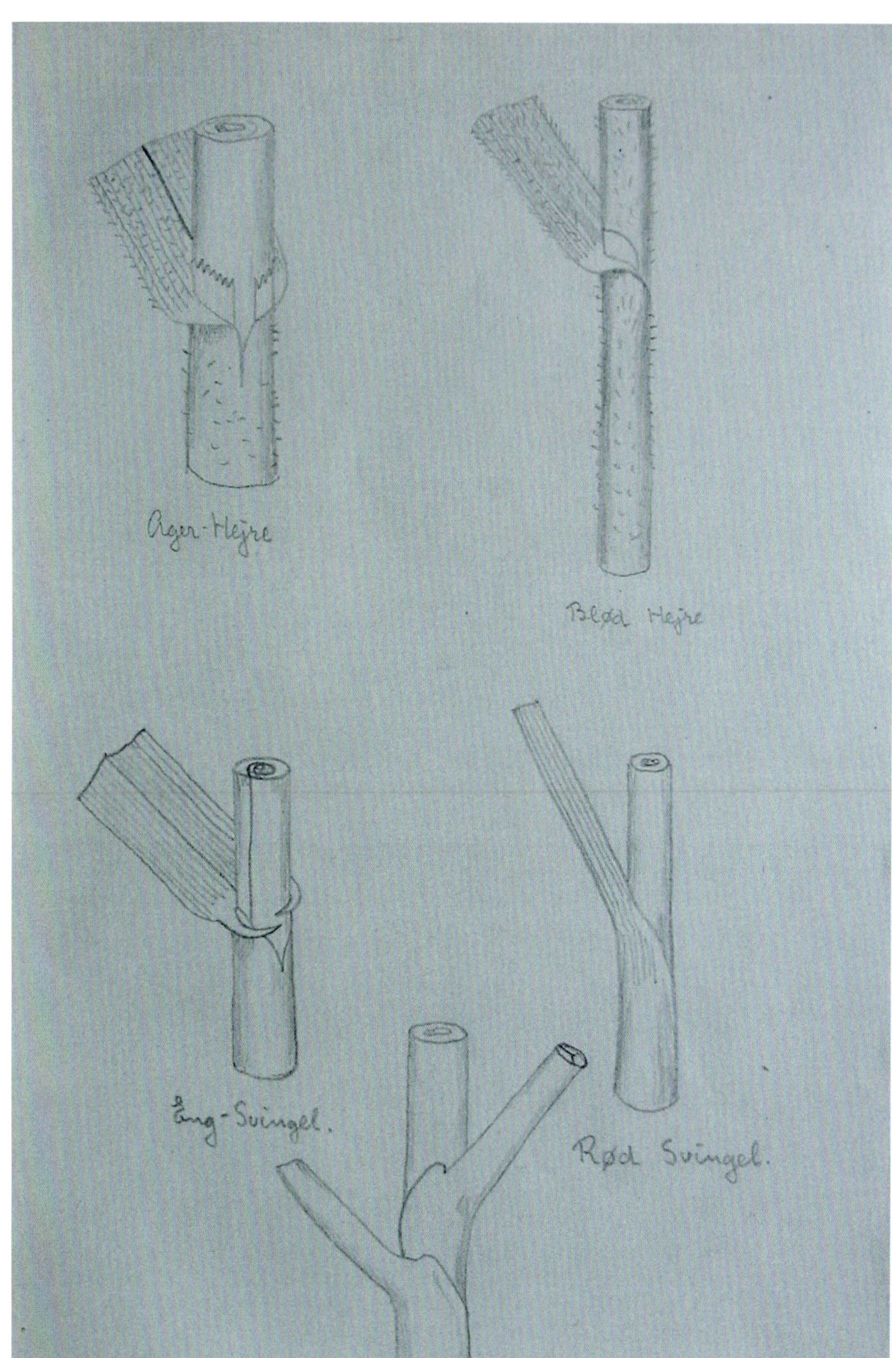

Pencil drawing: Lennart Edelberg. Photo: Torkil Funder.

To draw a grass

Among the many books on natural history in Lennart Edelberg's library, there were several that clearly originated from his university days. Among them was a small book about grasses, suitable for fieldwork and written by the botanist August Mentz (1867-1944): *Danske Græsser og andre græsagtige Planter. Med 111 Figurer i Teksten*. København 1902 [Danish Grasses and other grass-like plants. With 111 Figures in the Text. Copenhagen 1902]. In the front of the book, the following is written in ink: "Mr. V. Balslev, MA, with kind regards, A.M."[*]

When you turn over the pages, you find that the book contains several original pencil drawings on loose sheets, seventeen in all. The drawings show the form and development of the ligule membrane of the grass plant, an anatomical detail that can assist in determining the name of a species of grass at a stage when it has neither flowers nor seeds.

It seems that, once Edelberg learned this method for identifying grasses, he became so fascinated with the variety found in nature that he himself collected different species of grass and created detailed drawings that showed how the ligules were formed. The drawings depict how the ligules of the grass soft brome (*blød hejre*) is curved and has a smooth edge; in contrast, that of the field brome (*ager hejre*) is obtuse with a serrated edge.

An initial observation, a pencil, a piece of paper and the grass itself is all it takes for some of the grasses to be transferred to paper. Larger insight emerges from having drawn something out of its contained reality.

I can see how those little drawings from his student years supported the many drawings I saw Lennart sketch with chalk on the blackboard, or on spirit duplicator sheets and later sheets to be photocopied also as well as on meter after meter of big paper rolls that were an integral part of his communications. Often such drawings provided a starting point for students to draw and write their own way through particular tasks he had given them to lead them towards a greater understanding.

* Vilhelm Balslev, another naturalist in the Edelberg family.

A hayloft in Nuristan

In the summer of 1964, Lennart Edelberg went to Nuristan for the third time, as he had been granted a paid leave of absence in continuation of the school holiday. His wife Margot and their daughter Susanne went with him. He had prepared some subjects of inquiry beforehand; among them a registration of the types of houses in the area.

In 1958, Edelberg had become chairman of the committee for the Antiquarian Collection in Ribe, the original name of the museum of local history. In this capacity, Edelberg met the preservation architect Hans Henrik Engqvist on several occasions and showed him sketches and photos of houses and buildings in Nuristan from his previous journeys. Engqvist enthusiastically encouraged him to measure different types of houses, and this became one of the main objectives of the 1964 journey.

In July 1964, Lennart and Margot Edelberg were travelling south on a mountain path between the villages of Zhönchigal and Muldesh. Some days previously, as they had followed the same path in the opposite direction, they had noticed a building with a pitched roof. Most roofs in Nuristan are flat, but in this area, the Waigal region, many smaller buildings have pointed pitched roofs and the lower floor is built differently. Therefore, they had decided to return and measure the pitched roof house.

On the way there, they met two local men who were evidently very occupied with and interested in the project these strangers were undertaking. They assisted with the measurements, leaving their belongings in a tree in the meantime.

The pointed gables of such houses can be fully open or partly covered. The upper part of the building usually serves as a hayloft, especially during the winter. Hay collected during summer can be thoroughly aired in this upper area, due to the air passing the loose layer of laths separating the floors.

Three of the walls of the hayloft that were measured are made of horizontal logs with layers of stone and clay in between, as is typical for the Waigal-Ashkun area. One of the walls of the house has been reinforced with flagstones stacked against the outside of the wall. The wall with the door is made of flat, hewn panels, which are fitted into the sill and lintel by means of grooves cut in the wood.

The lower floor is often used as a stable for goats or some cattle. Like the pastures, these haylofts are located far from the villages. When there is much to do in the field in spring and winter, it is better to spend the night in the hayloft than to return the long way to the village. Hence, the lower floor is sometimes made habitable with sleeping quarters, a fireplace, and a low cellar. New villages can develop around such original haylofts and their surrounding fields, not least because still more land is being cultivated.**

Zhönchigal, Nuristan. Photo: Lennart Edelberg, 1964. Archives of Moesgaard Museum.

* See Schuyler Jones' comment in: Edelberg, Lennart 1984, *Nuristan Buildings* (Moesgård, Aarhus: Jysk Arkæologisk Selskab), p. 185.

* See Torkil Funder's comment in: Edelberg, Lennart 1984, *Nuristani Buildings*. Moesgaard, Aarhus: Jysk Arkæologisk Selskab, pp. 109-118.

From the left: Lennart Edelberg, Ulf Timmermann, Torkil Funder, Britta Edelberg. Photo: Greta Funder, August 5, 1969.

A hayloft in southern Zealand, Denmark

It is August 5, 1969, and the weather is fine. The dense foliage glistens in the sun, as it hangs thick and dark in the summer heat. We are working in a clearing where the grass is now dry and worn. A selection of trees have been felled and are waiting to play their part in the Nuristani building that is being constructed here on the basis of Lennart's and Margot's measurements from Zhönchigal in Nuristan in 1964.

Lennart and Ulf try to ensure that the pole on the left is vertical to hold the horizontal logs of one of the gables in place. At the same time, Torkil supports a pole on the right, making sure that the long beam for the vertical boards stays in place. Margot and Lennart's daughter Britta, who is actually a skilled carpenter, are quietly watching the proceedings, and Greta photographs it all.

This replica of a Nuristani barn or hayloft from the mountains at Zhönchigal is now situated standing as it was meant to be: on a hillside overlooking the Edelberg family estate in southern Zealand.

If one seeks a higher vantage point, pretending that the grounds are in the Nuristan mountains, one will at some point, between the trees and the sky, get a sudden view of the glittering sea, far away among the dark contours of the islands. One will then have found the perfect place to tell the story of Lennart's Nuristani friend, Abdulla Khan Wakil, who back in the 1940s was the only person in Nuristan ever to have seen the ocean.

Edelberg inherited all this from his mother's brother: the apple orchard, the spring, and the house in the valley, *Kildehuset*. The old orchard and its hilly landscape became a place for the growing family and their friends to come together. Side by side, they have kept the lush, green forest at bay and carried out projects, such as the building of a Nuristani hayloft that ethnographer Edelberg has brought home in sketchbooks, measurements, photos, and countless considerations.

Hearing the sound of the iron triangle ringing from the house, we walk down the narrow path, attracted by the meal, the company, and the shade of the old half-timbered house of wood, clay and reeds. In the working place in the clearing, we leave behind the first courses of three half walls – all timbered and sealed with clay-filled mortar. We have yet to address the plan for the pointed pitched roof with open gables, and a fourth wall, the front, with vertical panels between a sill and a beam, and a door.

Edelberg studies the Nuristan hayloft by building it. The ethnographer thus carries out his task by combining handicraft, observation, contemplation, and actual use.

The traditional door lock is a mobile, wooden bolt on the inside of the door; this bolt can be moved across the door and door frame with a bent stick adapted to the purpose and stuck through a hole in the door from the outside. Using the stick, you can move the wooden bolt horizontally across the door, enter, and sleep on one of the charpoys, the woven beds downstairs. Or, you can climb *kråken*, the ladder, which consists of a tree trunk with roughly carved steps, leading up to the hay in the actual hayloft. Here, one may easily misplace even very important belongings, as Lennart wrote to the 9-year-old Mikkel Funder on July 27th 1978: "And Mikkel, I've found your long-barreled, white-handled revolver in connection with a nap in the hayloft. It was lying on the top 'nakura' on the back wall opposite the door."

Charpoy

In July 1978, in the Edelberg family's country house, Kildehuset, Lennart, his daughters Britta and Miriam, and Cousin Jens made a charpoy for use on the lower floor of the hayloft. In Nuristan, this part of the house is often fitted out for overnight stays.

Cousin Jens made the frame and the nicely carved legs. The cord was probably bought in Afghanistan in 1970, along with the turned legs of the other charpoy; the weave of the netting of this charpoy is now being used as a model. The cord was probably made of jute, but may also be cotton or silk, or, some tell, sisal hemp and coconut fiber. The weave of the netting can have many different patterns. Lennart was the experienced one in this art.

The bed is called *charpoy, chaarpaai,* or *charpoi*: "four-legs"; its name varies slightly across the wide area where it is in use. Seen from the side, the bed appears evidently regal: it stands straight on tall legs, calm and ancient. Made of hardwood with inlaid gold and such, it would be suitable for a burial chamber with the necessities of an Egyptian pharaoh. Its modern reality is somewhat different. This is the bed that millions of people wake up on across a vast territory encompassing Bangladesh, India, Afghanistan, Iraq, Pakistan, the Arab area and its surroundings, on city roofs, in the tea houses, in the caravan serai, on the steppes, and in the pale clay houses of the villages.

In the central room, the *ámá*, the "hearth room" in the mountain villages of Nuristan, you will traditionally find two or three charpoys around the four heavy, square pillars that surround the central hearth.

In the morning when Cousin Jens and Lennart first discussed how to proceed, there was only the naked wooden frame and the bundle of cord lying on the ground. At midday, when shadows are short, the weaving was well on its way. In the evening, the weaving had been finished, and all of the cord had been tightened up. The new charpoy was ready for sleep.

Photos: Torkil Funder. July, 1978.

Hallig Hooge at ebb tide. Visible in the distance from the left: Ockelützwarf, Kirchwarf, Backenswarf, Hanswarf. Photo: Torkil Funder, September 11, 1965.

Meditation

When Lennart Edelberg decided to donate his body
to science when he died, his family encouraged him to
think of a farewell gathering for family and friends and
write down the programme for future use.

When Lennart died unexpectedly in November
1981, the family searched in vain for his parting paper,
until the tab "Look here when everything fails" was
found in one of his filing systems. And there it was, the
programme for the gathering, perhaps left there with
a smile.

The first item on the programme was for everyone
to meet in the family's house in Holmevej, the place
of many shared memories. The distinctive, low house
with the split-level, sloped roof and red wood on white
concrete had been a center of the Edelberg family life
through the years.

Despite the sudden and short notice, close to a hundred people congregated in the house, and the mood was intimate, almost cheerful, in the low November light from the grey-green marsh land. Many of those gathered once spent much time together; now they met more rarely. The thoughts of Lennart's many serious and merry projects called for smiles of reminiscence and respect rather than for tears.

It was just outside of here, at Shrovetide, that the children in their fancy dresses were tilting at the rings along the brook on their bicycles instead of horses, the brook where Lennart kept his white dinghy. And it was here on the green meadow by the house that the long nomad tent made of black goat hair was pitched and displayed after Lennart in 1964 had bought it in Iran.

And it was here in the meadow, facing the main road that Margot and Lennart put up a great big banner made of stitched-together sheets during the 1972 EC election, saying: "NO EC." After which the farmer on the *Inder Bjerrum* farm on the other side of the main road painted an enormous "YES" on his tall barn door. And it was here, on the outskirts of Ribe – where the sky, the marsh, and the west begin – that the family time and time again, at weddings and birthdays, pitched a party tent and filled it with songs, performances, playing children, speeches, music, and dancing under the high canvas roof.

And it was here, in the house itself, that the small, green cupboard in the corner was opened at Christmas so you could have a peek and take out the contents. Little old things, just right for the small, dark green shelves. Lennart was given the cupboard as a child, and everything in it was from his childhood: a small paper house, cut out and glued together; a top that hums when it spins; a Russian icon made of metal; a picture of Christian IV. These were old toys telling stories that must be kept, like the ethnographic object, like the biological specimen, like the extraordinary stone you once found. Lennart became the collector, the conserver, the one who understood things. Did it all start with that cupboard from early 1800s in the corner?

And it was here that the lights would sometimes be on till late. Because the rugs had been rolled up and they were dancing in there to the singing. "I saw a wolf, a fox, a hare. I saw them dancing – all three of them, in the cold of winter's snow. I saw them dancing – all three of them." How they would dance and sing the music under that sloping ceiling?

And it was here, on the inner brick wall, that they had hung pictures of the Edelberg family. Among them, in oval, dark frames, there were also those old photos of Black Elk and Red Cloud and one more – Sitting Bull.

Thus, there were many different items on the programme during the gathering

in Holmevej. He had chosen two texts
to be read aloud for this last occasion,
which he had probably envisioned with
his customary vivid interest. Together
they cover a wide field – in terms of tone,
gravity, and social intention. They were to
mark both an ending and a way forward.
Poul Sørensen's poem from 1946 and
John Donne's Meditation 17 from 1623.
Everyone has his individual destiny, yet
remains part of the community. That may
be Lennart's message.

Hence, Lennart's own choices become
once again the last stories told about him.

"Life is a misery," says one man.
"Life is a laugh!" says another
It makes me think of the 15 tram
Especially of the conductor.

He follows that same route, come what may
The very ideal of persistence.
He rings all the bells and he asks you to pay.
And why? For the sake of existence!

And life, to which he thus earns his right
By ringing and charging and whistling.
How is it all spent? You can tell at first sight.
On board the tram number 15.

*Poul Sørensen 1946**

No man is an island,
Entire of itself,
Every man is a piece of the continent,
A part of the main.
If a clod be washed away by the sea,
Europe is the less.
As well as if a promontory were.
As well as if a manor of thy friend's
Or of thine own were:
Any man's death diminishes me,
Because I am involved in mankind,
And therefore never send to know for whom the bell tolls;
It tolls for thee.

*John Donne, 1623**

---

* Poul Sørensen ('Poeten'). 1946: "Filosofi" [Philosophy]. In: *Collection of poems Løgn og Lyrik* [Lies and Lyrics], 1946.

* From: John Donne. 1623. "Meditation XVII." In: *Devotions upon Emergent Occasions*, 1623.

Photo: School camp report from Hallig Hooge, 2.gs, September 1961. Text: "Master Edelberg on the roof of the fishing cutter, which sailed us to Hooge."

Lennart Edelberg
A bibliography I

Per E. Børdahl

The published works by Lennart Edelberg (1915-1981) – from scientific articles and books to reader's letters in newspapers – comprises almost 190 entries, and there are good reasons to believe that the list I have compiled is not complete. I have not had access to all the Danish newspapers and journals I wanted to see. The bibliography presented here, includes scientific articles, books, feature articles, and larger newspaper commentaries. About 70 readers' letters have been omitted from the list for the sake of balance and clarity. Nevertheless, these letters also illustrate Edelberg's attitudes, his sense of responsibility, and his activities as a citizen of Ribe and Denmark. I shall try to provide a summary of their contents in my conclusion. In addition to his published articles, he was a frequent lecturer on the radio and at national and local scientific and public meetings. His first radio lecture, on a botanical theme, was in 1947. One of his books was based on radio lectures he had given about Asia [72].[1]

Although I have read the great majority of the items, there are a few instances where I know only the title, but not the contents. I might therefore have mistakenly classified a feature article as a reader's letter and omitted it from the present bibliography. And vice versa; two or three of the entries in the bibliography might be reader's letters, not features. I am, however, convinced that none of Edelberg's major works have been overlooked. A few years after his death in 1981, I compiled a preliminary list of his publications, major and minor, to provide his widow, Margot Edelberg (1921-2014), with a survey of his written works. That list was mainly based on the incomplete archives in his study. Stimulated by the invitation to participate in the Moesgaard symposium in 2016 and hence the invitation to contribute to this book, I expanded my search considerably. I have examined many bibliographies on

Central Asia and spent days in The Royal Danish Library in Copenhagen, The University of Oslo Library, and the National Library of Norway in Oslo. I have searched *worldcat.org*, the portal for all Danish libraries (*bibliotek. dk*) and the *Rex database on Danish newspapers* (The Royal Danish Library) in addition to the Norwegian searching system for resources in Norwegian scientific and educational libraries (*oria.no*).

Throughout his life, Lennart maintained a wide field of interest, and this is reflected in his bibliography – even if we omit the corpus of reader's letters. In his preface to the work on the locality of Ribe, *Marsk, land og bebyggelse* (1998), Professor Henrik Thrane has given a poignant characterization of Edelberg's achievements as a scientist and as a citizen: "Lennart Edelberg was not that kind of a scientist who concentrated on a special topic for months. There was too much that interested and engaged him. He was the type of a man who never stopped. New themes came continually and took his interest. Therefore, it was difficult for him to finish old tasks, even if it gnawed at him that they were not done"[2]

His publications from 1946 to 1981 and those issued posthumously, demonstrate an intellectual development in orientation and scientific work, from natural science to ethnography, nature conservation, the old history of Ribe, as well as local, national and international politics. It is not difficult to see coherence in his interests. After his graduation as cand. mag. (M.Sc.) in geography and botany at the University of Copenhagen in 1943, his first four articles were classical scientific studies with an ecological edge that were published in Danish scientific journals in 1946 and 1947 [1-4]. His last article in a Danish journal reflected his abiding interest in Nuristan. He wrote about the Russian invasion of Afghanistan in December 1979, and the ecological edge was still there [120]. His last reader's letter, published posthumously in *Afghanistan Journal* in 1982 was about the Stockholm verdict on the Soviet intervention in Afghanistan.[3]

The Third Danish Expedition to Central Asia

It is useful to classify Edelberg's writings [1-122] into periods. His first four papers on natural history were followed by thirty-seven travel articles from Asia in three major Danish regional newspapers [6-42]. In 1947 he left Denmark as a member of the Third Danish Expedition to Central Asia (1947-52), led by Henning Haslund-Christensen (1896-1948). Two other members of the first team who arrived in Afghanistan in December 1948, the zoologist and doctor Knud Paludan (1908-88) and the theologian and religious historian Halfdan Siiger (1911-99), also wrote for Danish newspapers about the expedition. Probably there was an agreement in the group to provide information about the expedition to the general public, and this endeavor was certainly successful. The press coverage was frequent and prominent throughout the two years of the expedition. The readers of *Aarhus Stiftstidende* were told that the paper "in the next couple of years will bring a series of articles from the great journey into Asia's unexplored world, written by the young scientist, the botanist Lennart Edelberg.[4] In *Fyens Stiftstidende* one could read that: "Dr. Henning Haslund-Christensen's Central Asian Expedition… will explore territories in inner Asia where no white man has ever set foot. About this remarkable expedition's adventures and results Lennart Edelberg (M.Sc.) will write a series of articles, to which *Fyens Stiftstidende* has secured the sole and exclusive rights, and we promise that it will be astounding reading".[5]

Edelberg's first newspaper articles give accounts of his experiences on the journey up to the time they left India [6-13]. He provides vivid descriptions of the adventurous atmosphere in which the members of the expedition set out to explore these remote parts of the world. Some of his observations may seem strange, even a bit comical, in retrospect. One may wonder why such a prominent place was given to descriptions of the markets in Bombay, the crowded Indian trams and cows in the streets in the newspapers of those days, and how the expedition could obtain such amazing coverage. The newspapers dramatized the expedition, "Letters to *Fyens Stiftstidende* arrive by caravan," and "With jeep into deep mountain valleys, where no motor vehicle has ever been seen." This was another world – half a century before the concept of the global village and the "event travels" of present-day society. Television in Denmark belonged to the future.

When I grew up in the Norwegian countryside in the early 1950s, neighbors who had been in *both* Sweden and Denmark were considered well-travelled. Denmark was a long way from Asia. Although the scientists arrived in Afghanistan in December, articles appearing in Danish newspapers nine months later would have told of the expedition's departure from India, "We are past our dreams, the adventure begins." [11, 12]

Botanist and ethnographer

Edelberg had been accepted as a member of the expedition because of his qualifications as a botanist. His participation was decisive for so much of his later life. Haslund-Christensen encouraged him to work not only in the field of botany, but also to engage in ethnographic research.[6] It was this latter field that increasingly attracted his scientific interest. During his time in Afghanistan Edelberg collected some 2,500 botanical specimens,[7] described in Køie's and Rechinger's *Symbolae Afghanicae*,[8] many of them not previously recorded at all, and a still larger number not previously described in Nuristan. Many were classified as isotypes or paratypes. Upon his return to Denmark, Edelberg was, however, modest about his achievements as a botanist and the efforts associated with his plant collections. In an interview with the Danish newspaper *Politiken* in October 1949, he said that "There are of course from a botanist's point of view several interesting plants from these arid regions, but probably only expert botanists will find them interesting".[9] Thorough botanical knowledge was necessary to find and preserve the plants, and his efforts were recognized. Today there are types and subtypes of plants with such names as *Agropyron edelbergii Melderis, Couisinia edelbergii Rech., Scrophularia edelbergii Rech., Eremostachys edelbergii Rech.,* etc.[10] *Carduus edelbergii,* a cotton thistle of the sunflower family with dark red flowers, is an especially conspicuous plant.[11]

Edelberg's and Køie's work on the Third Danish Expedition to Central Asia is thus the core foundation of the first standard monograph on the flora of Afghanistan. Edelberg did not subsequently write about Afghan plants, and to the best of my knowledge he did not collect plants in Afghanistan again. From this time onwards he concentrated on studying the people and their culture. "New themes came continually and took his interest". But his training as a botanist and as a meticulous observer (Fig. 1) was reflected in much of his work in other fields. In his grammar school teaching of natural history at Ribe Katedralskole he emphasized close observation and detailed description of whatever was studied. This aspect was especially prominent in his camp school teaching [69, 80].

Afghanistan, and first and foremost Nuristan, the mountainous area to the far north-east, became his main object of research. Edelberg returned to Nuristan in 1953 as a member of the Henning Haslund-Christensen Memorial Expedition (20, 22, 119), in 1964 as leader of the Danish Scientific Mission to

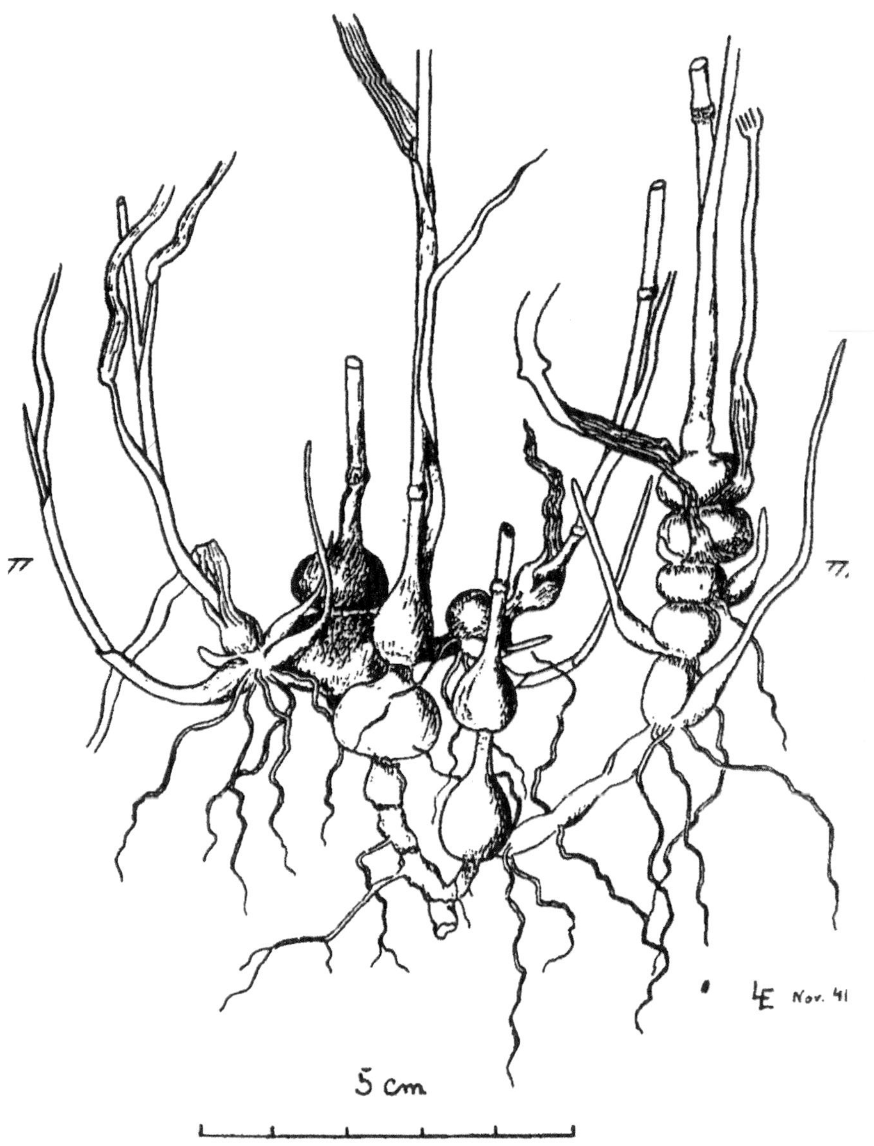

Figure 1. Onion couch. Drawing by Edelberg 1941 [4].

Nuristan, and again in 1970. During all these expeditions, he continued his ethnographic studies and made collections of ethnographica. Throughout the 1950s, he was engaged in his scientific projects in Afghanistan and Nuristan and wrote about his Asian experiences in scientific publications [43-44, 47, 59-61] and newspapers [52-55, 57-58]. During this period he also developed his ideas regarding the importance of and prospects for Danish research in Central Asia [48, 64 (figure 2)].

Figure 2. "Danish scholars About Afghanistan" [100].

After his second visit to Nuristan in 1953, he took the initiative to embark on a documentary film project: *They were Kafirs* [56, 62].[12] The educational aspect of this was as important as was his writing. The film was aimed at public lectures and for classroom teaching [62].

From the late 1950s and through the 1960s and 1970s Edelberg published results from his expeditions in English and French scientific journals as well as in Danish journals with extensive English summaries. He published on pre-Islamic art [63, 66, 68, 71, 86, 97 (figure 3)], physical anthropology in the Hindukush and in the Punjab [83, 90], Nuristani silver cups [85], agricultural tools in Nuristan [99 (figure 4)], and Paruni myths and hymns from the Parun Valley in Nuristan [107].

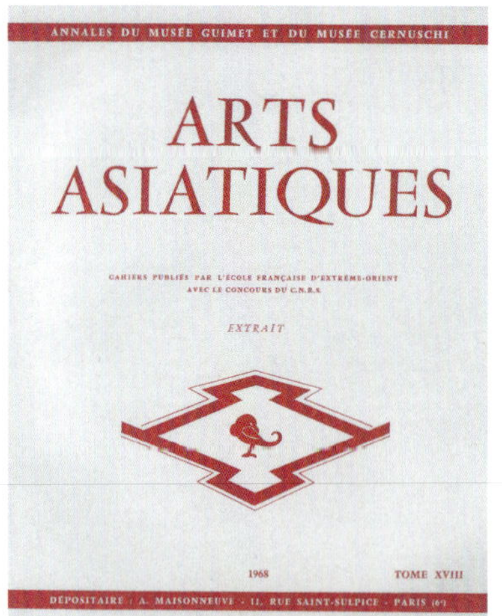

Figure 3. *"A Kafir Goddess" [97].*

Figure 4. *"Ard and Yoke in Nuristan" [99].*

Figure 5. *"Danish research in Central Asia" [64].*

He also published in an Afghan scientific journal a survey of Danish scholars who were carrying out research in Afghanistan with an annotated bibliography [100 (figure 5)]. In the autumn of 1964, he worked one month with the first Danish Archaeological Luristan Expedition in Western Iran. He wrote an article on his observations [93] and collected ethnographica, which today are in the National Museum in Copenhagen and at Moesgaard Museum, Aarhus. He did not describe the ethnographic items in detail; they have later been systematized and described in Inge Demant Mortensen's Nomads of Luristan.[13]

Edelberg also, in collaboration with the ethnographer Klaus Ferdinand (1926-2005) collected music recordings from Afghanistan (84), later studied by the musicologist Christer Irgens-Møller and published in his book Music in Nuristan.[14] In 1970 he co-arranged the Hindukush Cultural Conference at Moesgaard, which resulted in later publications [108-10].

He also wrote on more local themes such as Appenholt, in the Southern Jutland tidal area [49], and the Antiquarian Society in Ribe [65, 70], which was another major field of activity throughout his life. In 1973, he was appointed an honorary member of the society.[15] During the 1960s and early 1970s, he wrote several articles about the town of Ribe [73-75, 77 (figure 6), 101-02, 105].

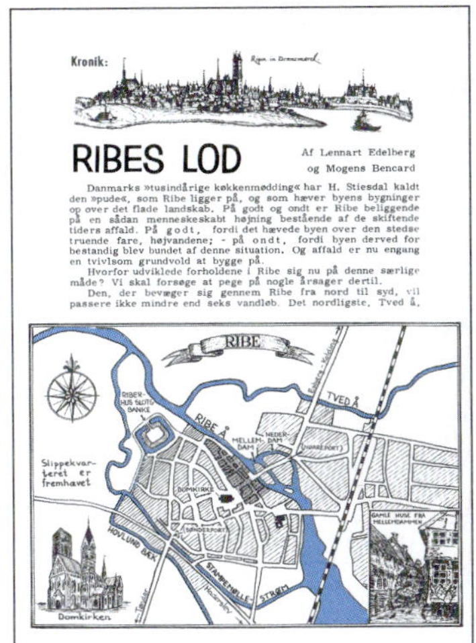

Figure 6. *"Ribe"* [77].

Figure 7. *"Nuristan"* [117].

Figure 8. *"Nuristani buildings"* [122].

In 1979 came the profusely illustrated book on Nuristan [117 (figure 7)] written together with the anthropologist, Dr. Schuyler Jones, director of the Pitt Rivers Museum, Oxford. Edelberg considered the book to be his *major opus*, and he was extremely pleased to see this work completed. He was, to the very end, intensely occupied with publishing the scientific results of research he had carried out years before. He was interested in the traditional and special buildings in Nuristan, and his training as an observer did not fail him [116]. He worked on a book on this tradition, but died suddenly and unexpectedly in 1981, when it was only partly finished. In 1984 *Nuristani Buildings* [122 (figure 8)], was published posthumously, based on the efforts of Birthe Stubsgaard, Torkil Funder, and Schuyler Jones, who edited his manuscripts and illustrations for the book. In 1981, his last international scientific article, "Notes on the 'Horn Chairs' of Nuristan," [121] was published in *Momentum Georg Morgenstierne,* a tribute to a friend and pioneer in Central Asian research.

All four of his books [72, 103, 117, 122] are about Asia, in particular about Afghanistan. In 1961, *Furer i Asiens* ældgamle *ansigt* [72], based on a series of his radio lectures, was published. Ten years later, with Lis Gramstrup, he published, *INDEX to Sir George Scott Robertson The Kafirs of the Hindukush, London 1896 and 1900* [103]. This was an index to a seventy-five-year-old classic on the peoples of the Hindukush. Lennart's participation in the Third Danish Expedition to Central Asia 1947-52 was in fact a turning point in his life.

Reader's letters

In the 1950s, Edelberg wrote a handful of reader's letters, but this activity increased considerably in the 1960s and 1970s. His letters were printed in different newspapers chosen in light of their various subjects: letters on national themes most often appeared in the newspaper *Information*. Apart from their specific aims, these letters also reveal his deeply felt philosophy of life. The majority are about his views of the future prospects for Ribe and for Denmark. He participated eagerly in the big demonstrations and marches against nuclear weapons in the 1960s and wrote reader's letters, which were commented on by both the editors and other newspapers. He was firmly against Denmark being a part of the Common market (EF) and wrote against it in 1964 and 72. He wrote about assistance to "underdeveloped countries," as poor countries were called at that time [76, 78-79, 88, 104]. He worked hard to have a university in the Ribe-Esbjerg region [88, 92]. In the local newspapers, he wrote about traffic, roads, and the need to have green areas in cities. After the flood in January 1976, he participated energetically in discussions concerning constructing better protective dikes [114].

Over the years, he became more dedicated to radical political activism. Although one might tend to agree with him regarding many of the views he expressed in his reader's letters, the way he styled his letters was not necessarily suitable to convince opponents or to win new friends.

Concluding remarks

In his scientific articles, books and reader's letters there was always a pedagogical edge to Edelberg's writing. His employment as a teacher in Ribe from 1950 was very important for him. In 1965, the Danish Association of Grammar School Teachers celebrated their seventy-fifth-year jubilee by giving a prize to a grammar school teacher who had given "outstanding contributions in science and in teaching." That prize was given to Lennart (figure 9). In the local newspapers his contributions to the Antiquarian Collection in Ribe were especially emphasized. At the same time, he demonstrated his range of interests with a feature article about Holberg and Afghanistan [87].

Figure 9. Lennart Edelberg receives the Danish Association of Grammar School Teachers' 75 year's jubilee prize from Professor Axel Schou in 1965. Photograph by Erik Gleie, Politiken. Courtesy Ritzaus Bureau.

In his obituary for Lennart, Professor Wolfgang Lentz of Marburg (1900-86) depicted him as a scientist of "ungewöhnlichen Forschergaben" (remarkable gifts for research). He also drew attention to an aspect of the book *Nuristan* that I think is relevant for many of his amply illustrated articles: "…hier wird nicht nur illustriert, was man weiss, sondern auch, was man noch nicht weiss und warum das so ist" (What is illustrated here is not only what is already known, but indeed also what is not known and why it is so).[16]

The Danish anthropologist Jan Ovesen (1945 2016) in his review of *Nuristan* (1981) also emphasized Edelberg's talent for observing details and presenting them in drawings or photographs: "The pictures of the book provide considerable information and are worth studying in their own right on a par with the text".[17]

Lennart's sense of a scientific attitude to life was consistent: Observation – observation – observation. That was what characterized his best writing and teaching.

Notes

1. The numbers in square brackets [ ] refer to the entries in the bibliographic list.
2. Thrane, Henrik (1998): "Forord." In: Stig Jensen (ed.). *Marsk, land og bebyggelse. Ribeegnen gennem 10.000 år,* two volumes. Jysk Arkæologisk Selskabs Skrifter XXXV, Aarhus Universitetsforlag, Aarhus.
3. Edelberg, Lennart and Ulf Timmermann (1982). "The Soviet intervention in Afghanistan is put to trial." In: *Afghanistan Journal* (Graz), 9, no 1: 20.
4. *Aarhus Stiftstidende* (1947), October 12.
5. *Fyens Stiftstidende* (1947), November 6.
6. Ferdinand, Klaus (1981). "Dansk etnografisk forskning i Afghanistan." In: *Jordens folk* 16, no 3: 94.
7. Halam, Mohammed (2009). "Plant Collectors in Afghanistan." In: *Bull. Soc. Vaud. Sc. nat.* (Schweitz) 91, no 3: 301-40.
8. Køie Mogens, Rechinger Karl Heinz (1954-65): *Symbolae afghanicae I-VI. Enumeration and Description of the Plants Collected by L. Edelberg and M. Køie on «The 3rd Danish Expedition to Central Asia» and by W.Koelz, HF Neubauer, OH Volk and others in Afghanistan.* Biologiske Skrifter, Det Kongelige Danske Videnskabernes Selskab (The Royal Danish Academy of Sciences and Letters), København.
9. I had no access to any Politiken database, and can therefore not give the exact date, The interview is from mid October 1949, shortly after Edelberg had returned to Denmark.
10. http://plants.jstor.org/search?si=26&filter=name&so=ps_group_by_genus_species+asc&Query=edelbergii, May 6, 2017.
11. http://www.flowersofindia.net/catalog/slides/Edelberg's%20Cotton%20Thistle.html., May 6, 2017.
12. Ferdinand Klaus (1980): "Lennart Edelberg." In: Dansk Biografisk leksikon, https://biografiskleksikon.lex.dk/ Lennart_Edelberg, April 25 2021.
13. Mortensen, Inge Demant (1993). *Nomads of Luristan.* Rhodos, Copenhagen (413 pages).
14. Irgens-Møller, Christer (2009): *Music in Nuristan.* Jutland Archaeological Society, Aarhus University Press, Aarhus (221 pages).
15. *Vestkysten* (1973), September 13.
16. Lenz, Wolfgang (1982): "Lennart Edelberg 1915-1981. In memoriam." In: *Afghanistan Journal (Graz),* 9, no 2: 53-54.
17. Ovesen, Jan (1981): "Hedningenes land blev til Lysets land." In: *Forskningen og samfundet,* 7, no 3: 3-7.

Lennart Edelberg

A bibliography II

1. Edelberg, Lennart (1946) "Jordsands Vegetation." In: *Botanisk Tidsskrift*, 48, no 1: pp. 91-96.

2. Edelberg, Lennart (1946) "Hvorledes virker Indsamlingen af Maaseæg? Erfaringer fra Jordsand. Uheldig bivirkning ved ugræsbekempelsen." In: *Naturhistorisk Tidende*, 10, no 3: pp. 41-42.

3. Edelberg, Lennart og Søren Thorup (1947) "Vækststoffernes Skadevirkning paa Korn." In: *Ugeskrift for Landmænd*, 92, no 5: pp. 1-4.

4. Edelberg, Lennart (1947) "Knoldet Draphavre – et sjældent, men besværligt Ukrudt." In: *Tidsskrift for landøkonomi*, 133: pp. 294-302.

5. Edelberg, Lennart (1948-49, 1953-54, and 1964) *Dagbøker (Diaries)*. Moesgård Museum, Højbjerg.

6. Edelberg, Lennart (1948) "Gennem Taarernes Port til Indiens solskinsfyldte Idyl." In: *Fyens Stiftstidende*, March 3.

7. Edelberg, Lennart (1948) "Sørejsen." In: *Aalborg Stiftstidende*, April 11.

8. Edelberg, Lennart (1948) "Shandu – min indiske Tjener og Hjælper." In: *Aalborg Stiftstidende*, September 16.

9. Edelberg, Lennart (1948) "I Indiens Drømmeland på Vej til Centralasien." In: *Aarhus Stiftstidende*, September 16.

10. Edelberg, Lennart (1948) "Europæerne gaar sjeldent til Bunds i Bombays Heksekedel." In: *Fyens Stiftstidende*, September 16.

11. Edelberg, Lennart (1948) "Hvilket stakkels Land og hvilket herligt Land." In: *Aarhus Stiftstidende*, September 27.

12. Edelberg, Lennart (1948) "Farvel til Indiens Drømmeverden, Eventyret tager sin Begyndelse." In: *Fyens Stiftstidende*, September 29.

13. Edelberg, Lennart (1948) "Velsignet af Saduen." In: *Aalborg Stiftstidende*, October 10.

14. Edelberg, Lennart (1948) "Nurerne – det blonde folk fra vilde bjergdale i Hindukush." In: *Fyens Stiftstidende*, November 8.

15. Edelberg, Lennart (1948) "Blandt Bjergfolk i Hindukuch." In: *Aalborg Stiftstidende*, November 9.

16. Edelberg, Lennart (1948) "For Vamas skønne kvinder er livet slid og slæb fra de tidlige pigeaar." In: *Fyens Stiftstidende*, November 9.

17. Edelberg, Lennart (1948) "INDRA, Vamas glemte gud, og de sønderbrudte vinkar." In: *Fyens Stiftstidende*, November 10.

18. Edelberg, Lennart (1948) "I Guden Indras By." In: *Aarhus Stiftstidende*, November 11.

19. Edelberg, Lennart (1948) "Den 3. danske centralasiatiske Ekspedition." In: *Aalborg Stiftstidende*, November 28.

20. Edelberg, Lennart (1948) "Den sidste ekspedition." In: *Fyens Stiftstidende*, November 30.

21. Edelberg, Lennart (1948) "Nurerfest med mandsdanse i landsby-øverstens bolig." In: *Fyens Stiftstidende*, December 18.

22. Edelberg, Lennart (1948) "Den sidste Ekspedition med Haslund." In: *Aarhus Stiftstidende.*" December 19.

23. Edelberg, Lennart (1948) "Danse i Nuristan." In: *Aalborg Stiftstidende*, December 19.

24. Edelberg, Lennart (1948) "Opfordret til dans med en dolk blinkende for øjnene." In: *Fyens Stiftstidende*, December 19.

25. Edelberg, Lennart (1949) "Dansens Kunst i Nuristan." In: *Aarhus Stiftstidende*, January 8.

26. Edelberg, Lennart (1949) "Hvor teglstensrøde klipper spejler sig i bjergsøernes blaagrønne vand." In: *Fyens Stiftstidende*, February 6.

27. Edelberg, Lennart (1949) "Hingst-kampen." In: *Aalborg Stiftstidende*, February 6.

28. Edelberg, Lennart (1949) "Til drabelig hingstekamp langs Afghanistans ældgamle silkevej." In: *Fyens Stiftstidende*, February 7.

29. Edelberg, Lennart (1949) "Hingste-Kampen i Hindukush." In: *Aarhus Stiftstidende*, February 10.

30. Edelberg, Lennart (1949) "Broderskab besegles med Kushtos-stammen." In: *Aarhus Stiftstidende*, June 11.

31. Edelberg, Lennart (1949) "Indviet til Broder af Kushtos-stammen." In: *Aalborg Stiftstidende*, June 12.

32. Edelberg, Lennart (1949) "Abdullah fra Nuristan fik en Odense-Dolk som Gave." In: *Fyens Stiftstidende*, June 14.

33. Edelberg, Lennart (1949) "Møde med Sumri." In: *Aalborg Stiftstidende*, June 17.

34. Edelberg, Lennart (1949) "Hos den blinde Sumri i Kamdesh." In: *Aarhus Stiftstidende*, June 18.

35. Edelberg, Lennart (1949) "Feltmarskalk Robertsons Sumri er endnu blandt de levendes Tal." In: *Fyens Stiftstidende*, June 29.

36. Edelberg, Lennart (1949) "Op til Dammene med de hellige Fisk." In: *Aarhus Stiftstidende*, November 24.

37. Edelberg, Lennart (1949) "På vej ind i Hezaradjats Bjergland." In: *Aalborg Stiftstidende*, November 27.

38. Edelberg, Lennart (1949) "Store opgaver venter i Afghanistan." In: *Aalborg Stiftstidende*, December 2.

39. Edelberg, Lennart (1949) "Med Jeep ind i dybe Bjergdale, hvor intet Motorkøretøj før har vist sig." In: *Fyens Stiftstidende*, December 4.

40. Edelberg, Lennart (1949) "Mellem Afghanistans Nomader." In: *Aarhus Stiftstidende*, December 13.

41. Edelberg, Lennart (1949) "Det uudforskede og ikke kartlagte Land." In: *Aarhus Stiftstidende*, December 16.

42. Edelberg, Lennart (1950) "I Afghanistans indre." In: *Aalborg Stiftstidende*, January 22.

43. Edelberg, Lennart (1950) *Afghanistan, nomadernes land*. Ledetråd ved Folkelig Universitetsundervisning, no 263, Munksgaard, København (4 pages).

44. Edelberg, Lennart (1950) *Det centrale Hindukush og dets særprægede befolkning (Kafiristan)*. Ledetråd ved Folkelig Universitetsundervisning, no 278, Munksgaard, København (4 pages).

45. Edelberg, Lennart (1950) "Asiens fortid er vor fortid." In: *Hjemmet*, no 20, May 16.

46. Edelberg, Lennart (1951) "En ukendt dansk opdagelsesrejsende." In: *Information*, May 30.

47. Edelberg, Lennart (1952) "Træk af Landbrug og Livsform hos Bjergstammer i Hindukush." In: *Næsgaardsbogen*: pp. 14-35.

48. Edelberg, Lennart (1952) "Afghanistan som område for fremtidige etnografiske undersøgelser. (Erfaringer fra 3. danske centralasiatiske expedition)." In: *Naturens Verden*, 36: pp. 97-128.

49. Edelberg, Lennart (1953) "Appenholt, en fortidsskov i det sønderjydske vadehav." In: *Sønderjysk månedsskrift*, 29, no 5: pp. 65-68.

50. Edelberg, Lennart (1953) "Hvad tilkommer der kulturgeografien?" In: *Gymnasieskolen*, 34: pp. 112-114.

51. Alvad, Thomas in collaboration with Lennart Edelberg (1953) "The Nuristân harp". *Afghanistan* (Kabul), 8, no 3: pp. 34-44.

52. Edelberg, Lennart (1954) "Over alle bjerge til "lysets land"." In: *Politiken*, March 7.

53. Edelberg, Lennart (1954) "Afghanske folkelivsbilder." In: *Aftenposten aftennummer* (Oslo), December 8.

54. Edelberg, Lennart (1954) "Templer, tanker og sang fjernt i Afghanistan." In: *Aftenposten aftennummer* (Oslo), December 9.

55. Edelberg, Lennart (1954) "Kæmpe uden had. Ekspeditionen til de saakaldt "vilde" og "primitive" og "underudviklede" bjergstammer i Afghanistan." In: *Politiken*, December 19.

56. Edelberg, Lennart og Klaus Ferdinand (1954) *"Kafiristan- Hedningernes land (They were Kafirs)*. Film. Instruktion: Børge Høst. Statens Filmcentral 1953-54.

57. Edelberg, Lennart (1955) "Bjergfolket og bulldozeren." In: *Politiken*, January 4.

58. Edelberg, Lennart (1955) "Det grønnes langs Helmand, Afghanistans største elv." In: *Aftenposten aftennummer* (Oslo), October 6.

59. Edelberg, Lennart (1956) "Fra Kafirhytte til Ildtempel." In: *Næsgaardsbogen*: pp. 25-44.

60. Edelberg, Lennart and Klaus Ferdinand (1956) "Henning Haslund-Christensens minde-ekspedition 1953-55 til Afghanistan." In: *Statens almindelige Videnskabsfond. Årsberetning 1955-56*: pp. 10-19.

61. Edelberg, Lennart (1957) "Pakthunistan." In: *Salmonsen Leksikon 15 – Tidsskrift*: pp. 43-46. J.H. Schultz Forlag: København.

62. Edelberg, Lennart (1957) "Film fra Kafiristan." In: *SFC film* (Statens Filmcentral), no 1: pp. 16-17.

63. Edelberg, Lennart (1957) "Fragments d'un Stûpa dans la vallée du Kunar en Afghanistan." In: *Arts Asiatiques* (Paris), 4, no 3: pp. 199-207.

64. Edelberg, Lennart i samarbejde med Klaus Ferdinand (1958) "Arselan – Et udblik over dansk forskning i Centralasien." In: *Naturens Verden*, 41 (September): pp. 257-89.

65. Edelberg, Lennart (1958) "Det antikvariske Selskab I Ribe." In: *Vestkysten*, June 4.

66. Edelberg, Lennart, Albert Schäfer and Wolfgang Lenz (1959) "Imra, The Creator-God of the Kafirs and His Main Temple in the Parun Valley (Nuristan, South Hindu-Kush)." In: H. Franke (ed). *Akten des vierundzwanzigsten Internationalen Orientalisten-Kongresses, München 1957*. Franz Steiner Verlag: Wiesbaden.

67. Edelberg, Lennart (1960) "På sporet af skvatmøllerne." In: *Skalk*, 4, no 4: pp. 19-27.

68. Edelberg, Lennart (1960) "An Ancient Hindu Temple in Kunar." In: *Afghanistan* (Kabul), 15, no 3: pp. 11-12.

69. Edelberg, Lennart og Jørgen Raasted i samarbejde med II G mn 1958, Ribe Katedralskole (1960) "Værf og fedding." In: *Naturens Verden*, 43, no 5: pp. 136-44.

70. Edelberg, Lennart (1960) "Quedens gård i Ribe og Den Antikvariske Samling." In: *Vestkysten*, December 13.

71. Edelberg, Lennart (1960) "Statues de bois rapportées du Kafiristan à Kabul après la conquête de cette province par l'Emir Abdul Rahman en 1895-96." In: *Arts Asiatiques* (Paris), 7, no 4: pp. 243-86.

72. Edelberg, Lennart (1961) *Furer i Asiens ældgamle ansigt*. Gyldendal: København (99 pages).

73. Edelberg, Lennart (1961) "Ribes tilblivelse – set ud fra et geologisk-arkæologisk synspunkt." In: *Vestkysten*, December 30.

74. Edelberg, Lennart (1961) "Den etnografiske samling på Ribe Katedralskole." In: *Ripenser-bladet*, 4, no 33: p. 228.

75. Edelberg, Lennart (1962) *Ribes tilblivelse set ud fra et geologisk-arkæologisk synspunkt*. Den antikvariske samling: Ribe (12 pages).

76. Edelberg, Lennart (1962) "Etnografer – mellemmænd i u-landsarbejdet." In: *Folkevirke*, 17, no 2: pp. 21-26.

77. Edelberg, Lennart og Mogens Bencard (1962) "Ribes lod." In: *Skalk*, 6, no 3: pp. 20-29.

78. Edelberg, Lennart (1962) "Etnograferne og u-landene." In: *Aktuelt*, February 16.

79. Edelberg, Lennart (1962) "Sikring af fremtiden." In: *Jyllands-Posten*, June 28.

80. Edelberg, Lennart (1962) "Ferskvandsbiologi på lejrskolen." In: *Den Nordsjællandske lejrskole*, Årsskrift, 24: pp. 3-9.

81. Edelberg, Lennart (1962) "Det Maaltid glemmer jeg aldrig." In: *Jyllands-Posten*, November 25.

82. Edelberg, Lennart (1964) "En reception." In: *Mercurius*, 3, no 1: pp. 15-20.

83. Balslev Jørgensen, Jørgen, Lennart Edelberg, Carl Krebs and Halfdan Siiger (1964) "Anthropological Studies in the Hindu Kush and the Punjab." In: *Folk*, 6, no 2: pp. 37-51.

84. Edelberg, Lennart (1964) *Tape-recordings from Nuristan*. Danish Folklore Archives, Copenhagen.

85. Edelberg, Lennart (1965) "Nuristanske sølvpokaler / Silver Cups of Nuristan." In: *Kuml*, 15, no 15: pp. 153-201.

86. Edelberg, Lennart (1965) "Hedninger i Hindukush." In: *Jordens Folk,* 1, no 3: pp. 102-103.

87. Edelberg, Lennart (1965) "Ludvig Holberg og Afghanistan". In: *Aarhus Stiftstidende*, October 19.

88. Edelberg, Lennart (1965) "U-landsinstituttet i Ribe." In: *Politiken*, November 19.

89. Peter, H.R.H. – Prince of Greece and Denmark, Lennart Edelberg, Jørgen Balslev Jørgensen, Knud Paludan and Halfdan Siiger (1966) "Anthropological Researches from the 3rd Danish Expedition to Central Asia." In: *Historisk-filosofiske Skrifter udgivet af Det Kongelige Videnskabernes Selskab,* 4, no 4, Munksgaard, København (76 pages).

90. Edelberg, Lennart, Jørgen Balslev Jørgensen, Knud Paludan and Halfdan Siiger (1966) "Physical Anthropological Investigations from Afghanistan. From the 3rd Danish Expedition to Central Asia." In: *Peter, H.R.H. Prince of Greece and Denmark et al.*, op. cit.: pp. 47-76.

91. Edelberg, Lennart (1966) "Map of Nuristan." In: *Schuyler Jones. An Annotated Bibliography of Nuristan (Kafiristan) and the Kalash Kafirs of Chitral, Part I*. Hist.Filos. Medd. Dan.Vid.Selsk. Copenhagen, 41, no 3: pp. 109-10 + map.

92. Edelberg, Lennart (1966) "Institut for sammenlignende kulturforskning." In: *Ribe Amts Regionsutvalg: Universitetet i Ribe-Esbjerg området III*: pp. 52-56.

93. Edelberg, Lennart (1967) "Seasonal Dwellings of Farmers in North-Western Luristan." In: *FOLK*, 8-9: pp. 373-401.

94. Edelberg, Lennart (1967) "Automatik og familieliv." In: *Aalborg Stiftstidende,* September 10.

95. Edelberg, Lennart (1968) "Det nye landskab." In: *Politiken*, March 1.

96. Edelberg, Lennart (1968) "Det såkaldte harmløse." In: *Ripenser-Bladet*, 5, no 24: pp. 210-12.

97. Motamedi, Ahmend Ali and Lennart Edelberg (1968) "A Kafir Goddess, The statue KK 11A and its circumstances." In. *Arts Asiatiques* (Paris), 18, no 1: pp. 3 21.

98. Edelberg, Lennart (1968) "Besættelse. En studie i baggrunden for amerikansk sindelag." In: *Frit Danmark*, 27, no 3: pp. 3-6.

99. Edelberg, Lennart (1968) "Ard og åg i Nuristan/ Ard and Yoke in Nuristan." In: *Kuml* 18, no 18: pp. 137-158.

100. Edelberg, Lennart (1969) "Danish Scholars About Afghanistan. With an Annotated Bibliography." In: *Afghanistan* (Kabul), 22, no 1: pp. 47-56.

101. Edelberg, Lennart (1970) "Otto Frederik Müller 1730-1784, del I." In: *Ripenser-Bladet,* 6, no 5: pp. 42-45.

102. Edelberg, Lennart (1970) "Otto Frederik Müller 1730-1784, del II." In: *Ripenser-Bladet,* 6, no 6: pp. 48-50.

103. Edelberg, Lennart and Lis Gramstrup (1971) *Index to Sir George Scott Robertson The Kafirs of the Hindu Kush. London 1896 and 1900. With a map by Lennart Edelberg.* Jutland Archeological Society: Højbjerg (59 pages).

104. Edelberg, Lennart (1971) "Bistand uden indsigt er blind." In: *Information*, March 31.

105. Edelberg, Lennart (1972) "Beslutningsprosessen i Ribe." In: *Ripenser-bladet*, 6, no 14: pp. 146-147.

106. Edelberg, Lennart (1972) "Almanakken før og nu." In: *Information*, December 22.

107. Edelberg, Lennart (1972) "Some Paruni Myths and Hymns." In: *Acta Orientalia*, 34: pp. 31-94.

108. Jettmar, Karl in collaboration with Lennart Edelberg (eds.) (1974) *Cultures of the Hindukush. Selected papers from the Hindu-Kush Cultural Conference held at Moesgård 1970.* Beiträge zur Südasienforschung, Südasien-Institut Universität Heidelberg, Franz Steiner Verlag: Wiesbaden (146 pages).

109. Edelberg, Lennart (1974) "The Nuristani House." In: *Jettmar, Karl and Lennart Edelberg,* op.cit.: pp. 120-123.

110. Edelberg, Lennart (1974) "The Traditional Architecture of Nuristan and its Preservation. Clan Houses and Temples." In: *Karl Jettmar and Lennart Edelberg,* op.cit.: pp. 124-126.

111. Edelberg, Lennart (1974) "Kalender og økologisk balance i Hindu-Kush." In: *Almanak Skriv- og Rejse-Kalender. Københavns Observatorium,* Nyt Nordisk Forlag, Arnold Busck: København: pp. 131-141.

112. Edelberg, Lennart (1974) "Ny mur – gamle fjender" In: *Frit Danmark,* 33, no 2: pp. 9-11.

113. Edelberg, Lennart (1975) "Lad fortiden tjene nutiden – og fremtiden." In: *Danmark-Kina,* no.16.

114. Edelberg, Lennart (1976) "Stormflod – springflod – almanak." In: *Vestkysten,* February 28.

115. Edelberg, Lennart (1977) "Værn det verdiløse i det kulturskabte land." In: *Natur og Miljø,* 4, no 2: pp. 4-6.

116. Edelberg, Lennart (1979) "Et skråbånd i Hindu Kush." In: *Arkitekturstudier tilegnede Hans Henrik Engquist,* edited by Niels Bech et al. Arkitektens Forlag: København.

117. Edelberg, Lennart and Schuyler Jones (1979) *Nuristan.* Akademische Druck- u. Verlagsanstalt: Graz (186 pages).

118. Edelberg, Lennart (1980) "Afghanistan – det svigtede land." In: *Jyllands-Posten,* February 1.

119. Edelberg, Lennart (1980) "Haslund-Christensen." In: *Dansk Biografisk Leksikon, https://biografiskleksikon.lex.dk/Henning_Haslund-Christensen,* April 25, 2021.

120. Edelberg, Lennart (1981) "Nuristan – Skov og Folk. Om den økologiske balanse i et senter for motstandsbevegelsen." In: *Jordens Folk,* 16, no 3: pp. 295-302.

121. Edelberg, Lennart, Schuyler Jones and Georg Budruss (1981) "Notes on the 'Horn Chairs' of Nuristan." In: *Monumentum Georg Morgenstierne,* (Hommage et Opera Minora, VII). E.J.Brill: Leiden.

122. Edelberg, Lennart (1984) *Nuristani Buildings.* Jutland Archaeological Society: Højbjerg (223 pages).

Epilogue

By Ulrik Høj Johnsen

1970 was a remarkable year for Lennart Edelberg. In early 1970, he was eagerly planning his next trip to Nuristan. Six years had passed since his last trip to the remote Afghan mountains, and twenty-two years since his first meeting with his 'second homeland', as he refers to Nuristan in his diary. Besides tending to his students in Ribe Cathedral School, he had published regularly on the cultural life, material culture and the history of Nuristan over the years. Moreover, he had taken up specific research questions – particularly on Nuristani architecture – which had secured him recognition in the enclosed circles of Hindukush scholars. The 1970 visit, or expedition, as Lennart liked to refer to his trips, was different from those in 1948, 1953-54 and 1964. Firstly, because it was going to be his last journey to Nuristan; secondly, because he was in the midst of preparing a major Nuristani exhibition in the soon-to-open Prehistoric Museum in the old Moesgaard Manor, south of central Aarhus. Lennart wanted to acquire additional artefacts for the exhibition as well as plan the reconstruction of a Nuristani house in the exhibition itself. The reconstructed house would become a spectacular installation in the ethnographic exhibition of 1970 and it remained on display until 2001. To accomplish these achievements, Abdullah, Lennart's sworn Nuristani brother, was crucial.

Sitting on Abdullah's veranda in Nuristan during the picturesque summer evenings in 1970, the two men had many plans to make and matters to discuss. Lennart had already purchased some discarded components from old houses in Nuristan, but additionally a couple of carved beams and a door needed to be acquired. According to plan, Abdullah would follow Lennart to Denmark later in the summer in order to build and prepare the house properly in the exhibition gallery. As Kakail Nuristani, Abdullah's grandson, recounts in this volume, his grandfather's journey to Denmark exceeded all expectations. He returned to Nuristan after the exhibition (and museum) opening having been knighted by the Danish king.

Indisputably, together with his old time friend and co-expedition member from the 1948 expedition, Halfdan Siiger, Lennart was a driving force of Danish Nuristan research. For various reasons, Halfdan never managed to publish his Kalasha material. Lennart, on the other hand, certainly did. Located in Aarhus, however, Halfdan was in close proximity to Klaus Ferdinand and the students of ethnography in Aarhus University. Lennart, though located in Ribe and fulfilling his duties as a teacher, was the decisive force driving Danish research in Nuristan and the Hindukush forward. Unlike Halfdan and Klaus, Lennart kept returning to Nuristan; he kept delving into his research questions, and he kept publishing his findings. And, importantly, he discussed these issues with people who worked in and with Nuristan. With dedication he expanded his network of scholars, many of whom he not only considered able colleagues, but also friends. His scholarly collaboration and personal friendship with Schuyler Jones was of particular importance to Lennart's work. The book *Nuristan*, which was published in 1979, was the result of several year's hard work, discussions and collaboration.

A key to an understanding of Danish Nuristan research and Lennart's accomplishments is his approach to research and colleagues. Through his own collaborations and engagements, Lennart seems to have encouraged inclusive and supporting dialogues with colleagues with whom he shared research interests. Such an approach was (and is) far from always a standard procedure; especially in German-speaking countries (which produced a number of Hindukush scholars), there was often a pervasive tendency to competition between researchers; such competition was not only inspired by funding and university positions, but indeed also academic prominence. As is evident from the present publication, Lennart's approach differed significantly; he wanted to strengthen research in Nuristan by *joining forces* with colleagues for a *common good*. This is an approach which is evident in many of the chapters in this publication written by colleagues and friends who worked with Lennart.

There is another reason why the year 1970 stands out – not only for Lennart personally, but also for the Danish Nuristan research tradition. From November 10 to November 18, 1970, more than twenty prominent scholars from around the world gathered in the then newly opened Moesgaard Museum. Their aim was to "discuss and throw light on scientific problems" of the Hindukush, as an ensuing letter to the General Secretary of UNESCO in Paris states. The one-week long Hindukush Cultural Conference, which was the first of three conferences of its kind to date, was a real achievement. The conference president was Georg Morgenstierne, the Norwegian linguist, who had carried out research in the Hindukush as early as the 1920s. The mainspring of the conference, however, was indisputably Lennart, who served as the conference secretary.

For him, the conference was a culmination of his own work in Nuristan, stretching over more than two decades. His vision was to gather scholars who had worked in the area and to join forces, inspire and support each other and pursue research questions in a collaborative spirit. These insights were not only intended to strengthen research and scholarly knowledge of Nuristan and its people, but also to safeguard the landscape and culture and improve the livelihood of Nuristanis. The previously mentioned letter to the secretary general of UNESCO in Paris presents seven specific actions to be taken by UNESCO for the protection and preservation of the "rich cultural inheritance" of the Hindukush mountain cultures – including landscape planning, preservation of traditional buildings and archaeological sites, ethnographical objects, as well as school materials for children in Nuristan and the Kalasha area. Moreover, the importance of further research to be carried out was stressed.

The conference lasted for a full week, and the gathering undoubtedly furthered personal ties between the participants as well as infused a shared sense of direction in the endeavors of the participants. Importantly, it also set the trajectory for further initiatives and paths to pursue. During the conference Lennart strengthened the idea of establishing an international center for research and publications regarding the mountain cultures of the Hindukush at Moesgaard. During and in the wake of the conference the time and location certainly seemed ripe. Moesgaard Museum had Lennart's as well as Halfdan's large collections from Nuristan and the Kalash area at its disposal, as well as their collections of sound and film recordings. Klaus was in charge of the ethnographic collections, and through his contacts in Aarhus University, he could support the efforts in various ways. On top of that, the museum had just opened its doors with the Nuristan exhibition.

During the conference, Wolfgang Lentz, Halfdan Siiger, as well as Lennart himself, pledged to donate relevant personal archival material to the museum in due time. This archival material today constitutes the backbone of the Hindukush Research Archive at Moesgaard Museum. All considered – the artefacts, sound and film recordings and archival material – constitute a remarkable collection of research material on the mountain cultures of the Hindukush. As the conference progressed in November 1970, the outline of something important in this research was getting clearer. This was most likely the intent which Lennart had shared with Klaus Ferdinand and Halfdan Siiger. Political developments in Afghanistan, however, were working against them.

In 1973, Mohammad Daoud Khan launched a *coup d'état* in Kabul, abolishing the Afghan monarchy and making himself president of the newly acclaimed Afghan republic. This event also marked the beginning of a dark era of modern Afghan history, which continues to rage well into the 21st century. Almost 50 years of invasions, civil war and strife have left Afghanistan and its peoples in an extremely vulnerable and unfortunate position. At the same time, any foreign presence in Afghanistan has become problematic. Especially after the Soviet invasion in 1979, it became dangerous for anthropologists to carry out fieldwork in Afghanistan. The rugged mountains of the Hindukush were no exception. These highly disastrous developments have therefore hindered further academic research in Nuristan.

The research agendas and questions discussed during the 1970 conference had to be put on hold as the 1970s progressed. Most of them, unfortunately, are still in abeyance due to the political situation. And time passes. At the time of publishing this book, fifty years have passed. Lennart's work in Nuristan, the artefacts he collected, the photographs he took, and the drawings, sketches and notes he made, have lived a rather quiet life since he passed away forty years ago. It is all there, though, in the museum, where it has been carefully organized in the hands of Svend Castenfeldt, and where it is safeguarded. As a part of the Hindukush collections in Moesgaard Museum, this material represents a formidable research resource for future work.

So far, further work in Nuristan has been impossible, and there seem to be few – if any – opportunities in the near future. This book has been written and edited with the strong hope that Afghanistan will emerge from decades in darkness and strife and return to the years of hope and peace she enjoyed between the end of World War II and 1970, where Lennart successfully managed to outline and describe the fascinating mountain cultures of Nuristan. The book is also written in the hope that the Danish tradition of scientific research in Asia – and Afghanistan in particular – will continue, as there remains enough to be studied to keep us busy for generations to come.

List of contributors

Bakker, Peter (chapter 3). Associate professor, Linguistics, School of Communication and Culture at Aarhus University.

Bau, Flemming (chapter 5). Retired exhibition designer and visual artist. Flemming worked in Moesgaard Museum in the period 1965-90.

Bøegh, Kristoffer Friis (chapter 3). PhD, Linguistics, School of Communication and Culture at Aarhus University.

Børdahl, Per E. (chapter 13 and 14). Retired chief senior consultant and professor of medicine, University of Bergen, Norway.

Castenfeldt, Svend (chapter 4). Retired ethnographer and research archivist, Aarhus University and Moesgaard Museum.

Funder, Torkil (chapter 12). Retired senior lecturer in Ribe Cathedral School.

Goldshtein, Yonatan Ungermann (chapter 3). PhD student, Nordic, School of Communication and Culture at Aarhus University.

Hansen, Erik (chapter 10). Erik was professor emeritus and architect with building preservation as a particular field of interest. Sadly, Erik passed away December 31, 2016. **Claus Christensen** has been instrumental in the making of the chapter.

Irgens-Møller, Christer (chapter 2). Independent musician, composer and music ethnologist.

Johnsen, Ulrik Høj (introduction and epilogue). Museum curator in the ethnographic department in Moesgaard Museum and lecturer in the Department of Anthropology, Aarhus University.

Jones, Schuyler (chapter 9). Anthropologist, CBE. Retired professor of anthropology at Linacre College, Oxford University and has served as head curator and director of the Pitt Rivers Museum, Oxford.

Kalash, Taj Khan (chapter 7). PhD student, Pateion University, Greece.

Nuristani, Kakail (chapter 1). Grandson of Lennart's sworn brother, Abdullah Nuristani.

Sperber, Birgitte Glavind (chapter 8). Retired senior lecturer Biology and Geography from UCS, Denmark.

Thrane, Henrik (chapter 11). Professor emiritus, Department of Archaeology, Aarhus University.

Vium, Christian (chapter 6). Associate professor in the Department of Anthropology, Aarhus University.

Toward the horizon
Lennart Edelberg and the Danish Hindukush research

Edited by: Ulrik Høj Johnsen, Schuyler Jones, Torkil Funder and Taj Khan Kalash

English translation and language revision: Schuyler Jones, Annie Thuesen and Cynthia Col

Proofreading: Schuyler Jones and Cynthia Col

Cover and layout: Louise Hilmar

Print: Narayana Press, Gylling

Cover: Nuristan, 1953. Photo: Peter Rasmussen

Published with financial support from

C.L. David Foundation

Research Project 'Precious Relics: Materiality and Value in the Practice of Ethnographic Collection', Aarhus University

The Anthropology Research Program, Dept. of Anthropology, Aarhus University

ISBN 978-87-93251-22-9